Cecil C. Humphreys

The Exciting Years

The Exciting Years

The Cecil C. Humphreys Presidency

of

Memphis State University

1960–1972

WILLIAM SORRELS

MEMPHIS STATE UNIVERSITY PRESS

MEMPHIS

Manufactured in the United States of America

International Standard Book Number 0-87870-212-1, trade
International Standard Book Number 0-87870-213-x, deluxe

Illustrations are courtesy of the following offices of Memphis State University:
    desoto (yearbook): pp. 34, 100, 211; Mississippi Valley Collection: pp. 6, 7, 17, 24, 52, 53, 73, 78, 87, 93, 106, 119, 129, 246; Photo Services: pp. ii, 143, 157, 177, 197, 199, 206, 234, 252, 255; University Community Relations: pp. 87, 137, 184, 221.

FOR

CECIL C. HUMPHREYS AND

HIS FAMILY

Our accomplishments were not unlike those of the rest of the nation's colleges and universities; but, we believe, with some pride and with the support of statistical evidence, that the accomplishments were greater and disruptions fewer at Memphis State University than at most other campuses in the country.

CECIL C. HUMPHREYS, 1972
"Closing Report"

Acknowledgements

This book in large measure reflects the dedicated work of others.

I am indebted most of all to Cecil Humphreys, who entrusted me with box after treasured cardboard box of notes, reports, newspaper clippings, pictures, letters, and other personal memorabilia that burnish his marvelous sense of history.

He shared more than the material side of his twelve-year presidency at Memphis State University.

Cecil Humphreys also sat down and patiently talked me through the 1960s, the most turbulent decade for higher education in this nation's history. The conversations added the necessary insight and truth to the rich materials grist which otherwise might have provided only the cold, bare skeleton of a remarkable story. His recollections mined the gold from the mountain of yellowing paper, and his gentle, but persistent, quest for accuracy provided the essential editorial direction.

It must be said, with the deepest of appreciation, that Cecil Humphreys took the time to help the author place the trace chains in the social and historical harness appropriate to evaluating the university in his presidential years.

There also were others whose aid and interest must be acknowledged: Dr. Thomas G. Carpenter, president of Memphis State University, and Dr. Eugene Smith, vice president of financial affairs, who made the university's resources available and lent encouragement; and Charles F. Holmes, director of community relations and my coauthor in an earlier book. Once again he proved to be a valuable writing and editing partner. J. Ralph Randolph, director of the Memphis State University Press, provided wise counsel and skillful editing.

These friends have my respect and gratitude for their dedicated assistance. They poured the coffee.

WILLIAM SORRELS

Contents

Chronology

1929 First West Tennessee Latin Tournament started by Dr. Nellie Angel Smith.

1930 Prof. Richmond Croom Beatty came to WTSTC from Vanderbilt and started small intellectual renaissance.

1931 First weekly student newspaper, *The Tiger Rag.*

1933 Great Depression nearly caused closing of WTSTC.

1935 Agricultural department discontinued.

1938 Coach Allyn McKeen's undefeated, untied football season.

1939 Richard C. Jones became president.

STATE COLLEGE, 1941–1957

1941 Name changed to Memphis State College.

1942 Military training on campus.

1943 Dr. Jennings B. Sanders, scholar-historian, became president.

1945 GI's to campus; peak number of 800 by 1948.

1946 J. Millard (Jack) Smith, first alumnus to be named president.

1947 MSC coed Barbara Walker crowned Miss America.

1950 Graduate studies initiated.

1951 Organization change: Schools of Arts and Sciences, Business Administration, Education and Graduate Studies.
First B.A. degrees awarded.
Building program: new Field House, Student Center and Cafeteria.
First ROTC unit (AFROTC).
Greater Memphis State support group founded.

1954 Memphis State Press started.
Changed from quarter to semester system.
Hillman Robbins won National Intercollegiate Golf Championship.

1956 Evening School Divisoin established.

1957 Basketball team reached NIT finals in New York.
First substantial gift from city of Memphis to MSC—$100,000 to complete gym.
Prof. R. W. Johnson gave $100,000 for Social Sciences building.

1957 Tennessee legislature designated full university status.

1958 First entrance examination.

1959 Successful integration; first black students admitted.
First large Federal government grant—$128,000 for special course for teachers of science and education.

1960 Dr. Cecil C. Humphreys became president.

1961 MSU Foundation board organized.
Goodwyn Institute lecture series moved to campus.

1962 Record growth of students began (20% gain over previous year).
Chucalissa Indian Village became part of MSU.
Computer Center established.
School of Law established.
Division of planning and development opened.

1963 Undefeated football season.

1964 Herff College of Engineering established.

1966 Doctoral programs began.

1967 Nursing program (associate degree program) started.
Speech and Hearing Center operated at MSU.

1968 Division of Continuing Studies for adults opened.
University College established as counseling center for all freshmen and sophomore students.
Distinguished Teaching Award program started.

1969 Hudson Health Center opened.

1970 Married student housing on South Campus.

1971 Institute for Criminal Justice opened.
Institute for Governmental Studies opened.

1972 Humphreys resigned presidency to become first chancellor of State University and Community College System; Dr. John Richardson became acting president.
Library volumes to 700,000 (up from 80,000 in 1960).
Full-time faculty to 700 (up from 200 in 1960).
Budget of $31.5 million (up from $3.5 million in 1960).
Financial aid to 2200 students for total of $1.5 million (up from

400 students and $100,000 in 1960).

Endowment to $25 million and annual contributions to scholarship support program of $150,000 per year from 3,000 donors.

176 buildings on campus (up from 20 in 1960); value of these buildings $60 million (up from $10 million in 1960).

1973   Dr. Billy M. Jones made president.

Basketball team finished second in nation to UCLA in NCAA finals in St. Louis.

Ed Hammonds won 1973 NCAA National Championship in 100 yard dash—MSU's First National Championship in Track.

1974   Bureau of City and Regional Planning started.

University honors program established.

Research grants from Federal and State governments to MSU—$3,309,000.

1976   C. C. Humphreys Presidential Scholarship program started.

1977   College of Communications and Fine Arts established.

1979   Revision of funding formula by Board of Regents to inject academic excellence into MSU's mission and comparing it to similar southern schools with like missions.

1980   Dr. Thomas G. Carpenter became president.

Annual Fund reaches $1 million.

1983   Early Scholars program established to attract high school graduates with outstanding academic records.

MSU becomes only public university in Tennessee with full accreditation. (All of MSU's 67 programs which are subject to accreditation by national professional organizations accredited.)

1984   MSU's overall appropriation reached $52.8 million.

Further revision of MSU's funding formula to gain comparable funding with ten peer universities such as University of Alabama, University of Louisville, and University of Mississippi.

First chair of excellence made possible through a $625,000 matching gift from Dr. W. Harry Feinstone, distinguished professor of research at MSU. The endowment provided for MSU chair of molecular biology.

1985   Basketball team to NCAA Final Four.

Six centers of excellence and two chairs of excellence.

1986   Fogelman Executive Center opened.

The Exciting Years

I

An Overview

CECIL HUMPHREYS SMILES AT THE IDEA that his half-century association with Memphis State University suggests an odyssey, the material for a Homer. As for himself, he admits only to a journey of the heart, something that cannot be reckoned by milestones alone.

The relationship between Memphis State and Humphreys, a cup and saucer, began in 1937, an exceedingly untimely year for a first jubilee at a small teachers college that opened its doors on September 10, 1912, as a normal school. Some older Memphians say in the 1930s they would have wagered more on the roll of the dice than on the chances of West Tennessee State Teachers College surviving the Great Depression and eventually blossoming into Memphis State University. It scaled the arduous peaks, however, and in 1987 the City of Memphis hoisted banners Blue and Gray, the union of colors chosen by students in 1912, to salute the university's seventy-fifth anniversary. Everyone felt that a flagship of higher learning had added immeasurably to the quality of life in Tennessee's largest city.

It took time to achieve this bonding. For almost half a century Memphis offered a cold hearth to the institution, which failed to bestir itself. Many public officials, if they thought of it at all, considered "the little teachers school" a poor relative of French ancestry—*école normale*. At best, they felt the school was the responsibility of the State of Tennessee and parents who could afford to pay the college expenses of their children.

Much of the intriguing story of how the relationship dramatically changed can be traced to Cecil Clarence Humphreys and his presidency, which began in 1960 and ended in 1972 with his promotion to chancellor of a new statewide university system.

Memphis State's acceptance in the community, and its tremendous improvements, have unmistakable ties to Humphreys and the 1960s, a decade when the United States struggled with its international power role, saw its President slain, and majestically mastered space and lifted men to the moon. During those ten years awesome social, political and scientific changes rocked the world, and all across America student unrest rattled the windows of academia. Each day seemed to put new challenges in the faces of college presidents, whose tenures averaged only three and a half years in those violent times. Promise wrestled peril throughout the decade. But it was precisely in that era of alienation that Memphis State University accommodated change and became a prestigious institution.

An uncommon amount of common sense seemed to guide Humphreys. His personal notes and official acts suggest that he had a keen ear to the changing winds when he became president of Memphis State University on January 1, 1960, at the age of forty-five. He knew he had to continue erasing an image of the school as an outsider, a lonely waif with its nose pressed at the window of Memphis, a growing city of a half million people.

Humphreys had initiated the process of bringing the college and town together in the 1950s—the years of the Eisenhower presidency, the "quite decade" on college campuses when some professors complained of student apathy. Humphreys was an eager educational John Alden, bidding for the city's hand on behalf of President J. M. (Jack) Smith. Smith was a strong-willed, old-school educator who preferred to look inward rather than outward. In Cecil Humphreys he found a marvelous public relations surrogate, an educator who defied rural logic and successfully drove three mules. He directed athletics and the graduate school while serving as Smith's presidential assistant without extra pay. In that unusually busy way Smith groomed a future president without so much as a single promise, something he could not have made legitimately in any case.

When he became president, Humphreys was prepared to abandon Smith's ivory tower. Humphreys felt the city and Memphis State, which had gained university status by state legislative action in 1957 after a campaign he quarterbacked, had been like two stubborn men standing back to back for more than forty years and complaining of seeing totally different landscapes. He knew that with a mere half turn by both they could rub shoulders and enjoy the same existing vista.

In the first months of his presidency he had townsmen and gownsmen shaking hands and building a mutually bright future. Such a turnabout took imaginative, creative thinking as well as hard work. The city's power structure had regarded the institution as of little economic

West Tennessee Normal School (now Memphis State University) under construction, *ca.* 1911. Scaffolding is visible on the entrance to the Administration Building *(right)*. Mynders Hall is on the left.

or cultural consequence from its inception as West Tennessee Normal School in an eighty-acre pasture beyond the east end of town near Buntyn Station. When the school held dedication ceremonies for its first three buildings on September 10, 1912, Mayor Edward Hull Crump, who would remain the city's political boss until his death in 1954, was in Charlevoix, Michigan. He did not think Normal School, one of three conceived on March 4, 1909, when the Tennessee General Assembly passed the General Education Bill, significant enough to interrupt a vacation.

Crump was not without company in his thinking. Several decades after Normal School began turning out school teachers, a newspaper had this single notation in a chronology of newsworthy Memphis events in 1912: "First public swimming pool opened."

In 1925 Normal became West Tennessee State Teachers College and was upgraded from a two-year to a four-year institution, but the ap-

The gaining of university status was a momentous occasion for Memphis State. Students join President Smith *(center)*, Humphreys *(rear right)*, and Dr. Heber Rumble *(front right)* in changing the name.

proaching national depression hardly gave the college time to catch its breath. To many people, closure seemed certain; but stronger figures prevailed. In the 1930s the college, through the tenacious leadership of President J. W. Brister, a Latin scholar, survived despite annual state appropriations of a little more than $50,000. Many legislators felt higher education was for those whose parents could afford it, and that view coincided with the thinking of many voters in Tennessee at that time.

The tallest building on campus—the library—honors the memory of John Willard Brister. It is noteworthy that he hired Cecil Humphreys as an assistant football coach and history instructor in 1937.

Even with Brister's success in the 1930s and the school becoming Memphis State College in 1941, history appeared to be working against it. The Japanese attack on Pearl Harbor on December 7, 1941, led to America's participation in World War II—and still another closure crisis for Memphis State. By 1943 enrollment dipped below 200, but, once again, the college skimped by. It had become a survivalist. It clung to life with severely tested fingernails.

After the Japanese surrendered on September 1, 1945, war veterans with federal GI Bill funds in their pockets helped to put the college on the road to recovery. Its future as a free-standing college faced one more obstacle, however. In the 1950s a plan was advanced to merge Memphis State with the University of Tennessee. The presidents of both institutions supported the idea, but a strong faction at Knoxville, including famed football coach Robert Neyland, struck down the branch campus proposal. In those days Neyland was the recognized leader in single-wing football, and that led to jokes about a merger bringing in "a Split T" formation.

An admiring dean once said, "Sonny Humphreys can look out a campus window and see ten years into the future." Many times in that first fateful decade of his presidency Cecil Humphreys would have settled for knowledge of what would happen the next day. In his 1972 "Closing Report" to the State Board of Regents, he wrote:

> For several years the chief administrative officer and his staff appeared to be moving from crisis to crisis; first providing faculty, classrooms, laboratories, living space for students, offices for faculty, parking spaces and other services for the extraordinary enrollment and program expansion.
>
> Then came the era of being confronted by the turmoil and violence which swept the nation's campuses.
>
> During the last five years of the 1960s the campus was caught up in both local and national issues, with students being most active, and sometimes violent, protestors against conditions over which the campus had little control.
>
> Such things as the Vietnam War, the draft, the assassination of Dr. Martin Luther King, Jr. in Memphis, the Kent State incident, the invasion of Cambodia and others were the issues which caused the campus to become almost a battleground.

There were months when it seemed that the Memphis State campus was in a state of siege.

Nevertheless, Memphis State under the presidency of Humphreys forged its greatness in the bellows of those events. His leadership was so effective that no damage was done to physical facilities and not a single day of classes was lost.

The reasons were many. Cecil Humphreys was of that middle-class persuasion willing to stand up for fairness and justice and law and order. He held the doors open by iron will, temperate talk and judicious decisions. He admits backing up a few times in building a university in a chaotic decade, but he never sold out, or even mortgaged, his principles. He simply had the good sense to relinquish an hour occasionally to save a day for his university.

Cecil Humphreys' power obviously lay in his purpose.

Looking back, of course, has few of the perils of looking ahead, but Humphreys' achievements on campus, downtown and in Nashville during legislative sessions may never be matched again, even in the most liberal of judgments. He, indeed, won friends and influenced people in behalf of Memphis State.

Few colleges faced an enrollment explosion rate comparable to that of Memphis State during the 1960s, but Humphreys managed to keep the university one step ahead of the astounding 245.9 percent increase. The increase was the second largest percentage growth in the country during the decade. There were students in the lofts and there were 7 A.M. to 9 P.M. classes, but the university met its challenge. In the 1959–60 school year, when Humphreys took control midway through it, Memphis State counted 4937 students, including eight blacks who had been admitted after five years of litigation. By 1972 there were more than 21,000 students, and 2198 of them were black. Halfway through the decade, in 1965, enrollment increased by an incredible 2500 over the previous year.

From 1960 to 1972 Memphis State awarded degrees to more than 21,000 men and women. It is of interest to view this "production record" in historical perspective. Those graduates represent a group nearly two and one-half times as large as all of those who earned degrees in the 48-year history of the institution prior to 1960.

Excellent work by search committees enabled Memphis State to find more than 500 new, and desperately needed, instructors and professors. Their numbers grew from 200 in 1960 to 725 in 1972. While managing this amazing bulge, Humphreys and his staff, which he credits for much of the university's success, never surrendered quality for quantity. Fine deans and excellent colleges surfaced, and the school never became an educational rogue elephant and diploma mill. Humphreys, unlike his predecessors, encouraged the formation of a Faculty Council and he welcomed its voice in university affairs.

Library volumes, always a yardstick to an institution's fealty to its students' needs, increased from 30,000 to 700,000 during the Humphreys presidency, and a twelve-story addition to Brister Library had everyone on campus looking up. To accommodate the growth in enrollment and new programs, campus building space increased from about 660,000 square feet in 1960 to more than 3,606,000 square feet in 1972. That translates into a growth from 20 buildings valued at $10 million to 176 buildings worth more than $76 million. Land holdings reached more than 1,000 acres as Memphis State dramatically broke out of an eighty-acre box. Although state appropriations never quite matched the needs, the university's operating budget jumped from $2,500,000 annually to more than $31,000,000 during this period.

Storytellers and historians have found that Memphis State, once a waif in a pasture out east, became a comprehensive urban university and a superb community asset between 1960 and 1972 because Cecil Humphreys, and the supporting cast he so ably recruited, broke the old mold in so many, many creative ways.

Perhaps some of the reasons can be discovered in the formative years. Cecil Clarence Humphreys grew up in a small town environment. In 1930 Paris, the county seat of Henry County, Tennessee, had a population of about 8000. It had the usual stores, banks, railroad machine shops, and rail facilities to ship cotton, tobacco and grain, and there was a town square. Three blocks from the square there was an attractive one-story house of Victorian architecture that had been built in 1880. Robert Lee Humphreys and his wife, Cecil Clare Huggins, liked it and bought in it 1904. It was in that house on May 17, 1914, that their fifth child, Cecil Clarence, was born just three months before the guns of August thundered Europe into World War I. Humphreys remembers the house at 107 McNeil with considerable fondness. He recalls it had "a lot of gingerbread trim, a full front porch, large rooms with fireplaces, and was very comfortable even for a large family."

Robert Humphreys was the coowner of Humphreys Bros. & Foster Men's Clothing Store, and he walked home for lunch every day. Mrs. Humphreys bought country produce and cooked three large meals each day.

The little West Tennessee town of Paris, 120 miles northeast of Memphis, offered pleasures reasonable to a healthy young boy who wanted to divide his time between vacant playlots and a library atop City Hall down on the square. For much of his life Cecil Humphreys, whom everyone in town called "Sonny," moved within two bookends—libraries and athletic fields. Sonny Humphreys, who learned to read well in the first and second grades, made a career walking back and forth between the two.

Miss Perry Alexander, his second grade teacher at Robert E. Lee Elementary School and later at the Campus School, recalled Sonny this way: "You just couldn't satisfy his desire for more knowledge. He wanted to know everything about every subject that came up." That insatiable quest for knowledge warmed when he was about ten years old. His brown eyes twinkled as he recalled the events:

> I was in the Henry County Library, which was located over the City Hall and next door to the fire station, on a Saturday afternoon, when the building caught fire and was destroyed. The fire truck was saved.
>
> I read everything I could understand, but enjoyed adventure stories with a historical background. A few years after the fire I read a book, God Wills It, about the Crusades, lent to me by a history teacher. It was history and adventure. A book could take you to any age, any place in the world and let you meet all kinds of people.

His family was Presbyterian, and Sonny Humphreys attended church regularly.

When he was twelve years old Cecil Humphreys began working as a soda fountain clerk in a drug store on the town square. He never drank coffee, but he developed what he called "a weakness" for Coca-

Cola. Somehow he always found time to play. His interest in athletics increased while he was a teenager at Paris' Grove High School.

As a 6–1, 170-pound performer he quickly made the varsity football, basketball, and baseball team. Humphreys displayed his basketball ability in the old tobacco barn that served as a gym in the late 1920s and early 1930s.

Neither of his parents had attended college, but they were proud of their son and his ambitions. They gave him love, not dollars. The Depression had brought reverses to his father's store, and one day in 1932 Mrs. Humphreys expressed dismay that the family would be unable to help him attend college.

"Your father hates it that he can't do more about college for you," she said. "Mama," young Humphreys replied, "you needn't worry. I'm going just the same."

Football would prove to be his ticket to three college degrees. In his senior year at Grove High he made All West Tennessee as an end, and Robert Neyland, one of the nation's legendary coaches, signed him to an athletic-work study scholarship at the University of Tennessee in Knoxville. While on the Hill he made his mark in football as the lightest lineman on the team, and he excelled in the classroom as a history major. Humphreys was where he wanted to be—between those beloved bookends, athletics and academics.

Throughout his days at Tennessee, there was the work-study aspect of Humphrey's scholarship. He met Fred Moses, a half-pint quarterback who would become his roommate, while painting. "First time I saw him was down at the field," Moses said. "I was down there to paint the under side of the bleachers at one end of the field.

"He was already there painting. I had never seen him before. I said, 'What are you, a track man?' He was so skinny. He said, 'Heck, no, I'm a football player'."

Moses, who became a lawyer, said he called Sonny Humphreys, "a pretty boy," for he was handsome and apple-cheeked. And a playful, but painful, incident crushed one of those cheeks. Humphreys, Moses and other athletes were working on the track one day when they began throwing cinders at each other.

"Somebody hit Bill Lippe pretty good," Moses said. "He picked up a pick handle nearby and flung it in the general direction of Bill Murrell.

"Somebody ducked. Sonny never did see the pick handle at all. It hit him on the cheek bone and shattered the thing. I remember that Dr. Bob Brashear worked on that cheek a long time to restore it."

Sonny Humphreys was not an All-American football player, but he was a team player with courage and determination. In the 1935 game with North Carolina, he received injuries to both shoulders. He could not raise his hands above his waist. Other players sent word to Coach Bill Britton, who led the Volunteers while Neyland was on active Army duty in Panama, to take Humphreys out. But the skinny athlete from Paris refused to leave.

"Sonny fought the blockers off with his body and did a good job of it," Moses recalled. "I don't think I ever saw more courage than that on a football field."

There were lighter moments. The well-groomed young Humphreys joined Sigma Chi and was well-liked by his fraternity brothers. He was a history major, but he liked journalism. Often after football games he could be found at the *Knoxville Journal,* writing a player's account of Tennessee football games.

After he received his bachelor's degree in 1936, Humphreys accepted an offer from Coach Everett Derryberry, a Rhodes scholar and head of the English Department, to become his assistant football coach at the University of Tennessee-Martin, a junior college not far from Paris. He also taught history, and immediately began work on a master's degree at Tennessee. Humphreys completed the work in 1938 with a thesis on "The History of the Reelfoot Region," a fabled area since the great earthquake of 1811 along the New Madrid Fault rattled the rib cage of the Mississippi River.

Martin fielded an undefeated team in 1936, and caught the eye of Coach Allyn McKeen, a Tennessee graduate who had taken over at State Teachers. He joined President Brister and Dean Jack Smith in recruiting Humphreys to become the line coach. There also was a little matter of delivering eight football players from Martin. When he recalls the event, Humphreys chuckles and says, "It was sort of a package deal." It was to be a pivotal move in Humphreys' career.

He remembers many things about 1937 other than the lingering

Depression. There was a great flood in the Ohio and Mississippi River valleys, West Tennessee State Teachers College was twenty-five years old, and a poorly paid faculty dug into shallow pockets to support athletics.

In the Buntyn-Normal area, the Reverend Alfred Loaring-Clark, a former Sewanee player and rector of St. John's Episcopal Church, and others formed a 150-member athletic association to support the Teachers. National Youth Administration (NYA) jobs also helped the scholar-athletes.

"Probably what convinced me to come to Memphis State," Humphreys said, "was that I discovered the commitment that was being made by the administration, the community and, surprisingly, the faculty to upgrade the football program. Even with the hard times, the low budget, and the uncertainty of the school's future, each faculty member pledged a week's salary to support the athletic program."

Humphreys looked forward to coaching and teaching history. There was much to do. The school had 698 students and the campus included five buildings, an increase of two since 1912. McKeen and Humphreys clicked as coaches. Their first team showed tremendous promise, and, in 1938, their football Tigers went undefeated. Acting on the recommendation of Coach Neyland at Tennessee, Mississippi State promptly hired McKeen to rebuild Bulldog football. McKeen wanted Humphreys to go with him, but President Brister asked him to stay in Memphis as head coach. Humphreys was hired and his salary raised from $200 to $225 a month. He also taught three history classes and summer school.

The talented seniors of the 1938 team had graduated, and the new coach faced the usual rebuilding task. Humphreys' third team in 1941, the year WTSTC became Memphis State College and branched into the arts and sciences, finished with an impressive 6–3–0 record. It would be his last football team; the winds of war were engulfing the world.

One day after the Japanese attacked Pearl Harbor on December 7, 1941, Coach Humphreys resigned at Memphis State and joined the Federal Bureau of Investigation. He recalled his days as a special agent with these handwritten notes:

I knew that I would be called into some kind of service for my country. Without previous military training I thought I could be of greater service in the FBI. I applied on Dec. 8 and was ordered to report to Washington for training on Jan. 2, 1942.

The work was hard, interesting and greatly added to my knowledge and education. The things I learned could not have come from textbooks and lectures.

I worked in the Seattle, Wash., office and after a few months was transferred to the San Francisco office. There I joined a small squad that was concerned with Communist activities.

Some dedicated members of the party had for many years been known to be engaged in espionage activities on behalf of the USSR, as well as "moles," underground agents serving the USSR intelligence organization: NKVD then, now KGB.

We learned that some Communist members or sympathizers had infiltrated a "top secret" laboratory at the University of California at Berkeley. After learning that the laboratory was an Army project (a part of the Manhattan Project) which was working on an atomic bomb, we became involved in covering the activities of a number of people who were a part of this project as well as the Los Alamos testing facility in New Mexico.

This became a major project involving the surveillance of CP members who were in contact with scientists such as J. Robert Oppenheimer, director of the U of C lab (Donner Laboratory) and of the Los Alamos project, and members of the staff of the Russian Consulate in San Francisco as well as some American citizens.

This was probably the most important espionage case in FBI history.

Meanwhile, World War II raged in Europe and Asia. Humphreys liked his work with the Bureau, but found himself repeatedly thinking that he should go overseas and join in the fight. In mid-November of 1943 American military forces in the Pacific were engaged in campaigns in the Gilbert and Marshall islands. One of them in the Gilberts would have a bearing later on Special Agent Humphreys. Among the atolls in the Gilberts were Tarawa and Makin. Makin was lightly defended and fell quickly to the 27th Infantry Division. Tarawa turned into another story, a bloody one. It had a long, coral reef apron and heavily fortified beaches. More than a thousand marines and sailors died eliminating 4000 Japanese troops who refused to surrender.

The lesson of Tarawa was that Navy intelligence needed scouts and raiders to take soundings, check tides, and scout beaches before landing craft and men were sent ashore. FBI Special Agent Cecil Humphreys would train to become a frogman and one of those rubber boat skippers so badly needed. He resigned from the FBI early in 1944 and accepted an ensign's commission in the Navy. He was twenty-nine.

After indoctrination at the University of Arizona, Ensign Humphreys went to gunnery school at Norfolk, Virginia. While there he volunteered for training with the scouts and raiders. Later, he jotted down these notes on an index card:

> I trained at Ft. Pierce, Fla., in rubber boats and swimming for use in taking soundings and scouting beaches prior to landings in the Pacific. I then went to the Advanced Naval Intelligence School at the Henry Hudson Hotel in New York—and then to the Pacific.
>
> I went out with a group of ships (staff) as a part of the Okinawa invasion, arriving there on D-day plus one; there were 65 ships in our group. I then went to Subic Bay in the Philippines and New Guinea. I didn't have to swim in to any hostile beaches, but if we had had to invade Japan they would have used all of us rubber boat skippers.
>
> Both FBI and Navy experiences were invaluable to me.

When the war ended Humphreys returned to the United States and served at the Navy base in Millington a few miles north of Memphis until he was discharged from service. He rejoined the FBI at Memphis in 1946, the year his old friend Jack Smith became president of Memphis State.

The school had given up football after the 1942 season, but there was student agitation in 1946 to renew the game. President Smith was sympathetic and promised to try to field a team the next year. Smith also wanted Humphreys to return to the college as athletic director when football was restored, but the school could not match his FBI salary. Cupid, along with Jack Smith's persistence, eventually helped Humphreys to take a $2500 pay cut and become an athletic director. In 1947 a mutual friend had introduced him to Florence Van Natta, and when the FBI told him he was to be transferred to Washington, he resigned to stay in Memphis.

President Smith had the man he wanted back on campus in 1947. And, on January 22, 1949, Cecil Humphreys and Florence Van Natta were married. When he became president in 1960 they had two sons, Robert Hunter, eight, and Cecil Clarence, Jr., five.

Memphis State as it appeared when Humphreys returned to the campus in 1947. There was to be little change until the 1960s.

George Peabody College, relied more and more on his athletic director. He also encouraged Humphreys to work for his doctorate at New York University. Humphreys' dissertation, "Financial Support for Higher Education by the State of Tennessee From 1930 to 1952," was completed in 1957.

On the flyleaf of a copy given to Jack Smith, Humphreys wrote:

To President Smith—
Without your encouragement and assistance
I never would have made it.
Cecil Humphreys.

The study has been described by Tennessee educators as one of the most comprehensive ever undertaken in the state. Four years of research had given Humphreys new insights into the attitudes of Tennesseans, particularly legislators, toward higher education, and the knowledge would aid his presidency.

Despite a less than traditional journey to such a post, Cecil Humphreys had prepared himself, without design and burning ego, to become a college president. In 1960, Humphreys knew his school and his city; he also understood that one can proceed but in his own way.

No one ever questioned Humphrey's sincerity, something that is not a saving grace in itself. A college president must know what he is doing if sincerity is to help him to success.

His record from 1960 to 1972 at Memphis State University suggests Humphreys knew.

2

"No, Sonny Humphreys is the One"

1959–1960

THE NEWS HEADLINES

President Eisenhower, in State of the Union address, predicts 1960 will be the most prosperous year in U.S. history...Two Americans training Vietnamese soldiers are killed...Mayor Robert Wagner of New York City tells the nation's mayors "the biggest challenge of the 1960s is to awaken fully to the fact we are an urban nation"..._Newsweek_ says the 1960s will be "The Decade of Man in Space."...Gary Francis Powers, piloting a U-2 spy plane, is shot down over Russia...U.S. Office of Education reports 3.4 million Americans are in college...Four black students in Greensboro, N.C., refuse to move from a Woolworth lunch counter when denied service, touching off sit-ins nationwide.

AND THE WAY WE WERE

Tigers pull big upset in downing Florida State before Homecoming crowd of over 15,000...Students get holiday after Homecoming win...Versatile coordinates, Italian collars and French cuffs, and ponchos are among the fabulous fall fashions for the chic coed...Students hear talk on the controversial topic of the formation of the state of Israel ...Haircuts—$1.50...1959 Cadillac—$4395...Five-year dream becomes reality as seven sororities move into the new Pan-Hellenic Building...Coach Zach Curlin retires after 36 years of service at Memphis State.

JACK SMITH HAND-DELIVERED A LETTER to Joe Morgan, chairman of the Tennessee State Board of Education (SBE), at his office in the Cordell Hull Building in Nashville on Monday, December 14, 1959. He summed up the burden of his message in two paragraphs:

> I hereby submit my resignation as President of Memphis State University effective February 4, 1960. It is suggested that you appoint an Acting President, effective January 1, 1960, since I have accepted another position beginning on that date. My accumulated leave of 24 working days will then extend to the effective date of my resignation.
>
> I have accepted an appointment as Regional Representative for the United States Commissioner of Education with headquarters in Atlanta, Georgia. The position is under Civil Service and does not provide a fixed age for compulsory retirement.

The resignation caught Morgan by surprise. Smith would be sixty-five on March 10, 1960, but under a board policy adopted April 6, 1959, the mandatory retirement age of sixty-five had been raised to sixty-seven with full knowledge the action would extend the tenures of Smith and President Halbert Harwell of Austin Peay State College.

A slight frown crossed Morgan's face as he looked at his old friend, a square-jawed man with a craggy face and iron gray hair characterized by a cowlick in perpetual conflict with a hairbrush. The SBE chairman, who also was state commissioner of education, began to offer protests about the decision. Smith shook his head and asked him to stop. For Smith, there would be no turning back.

Memphis State's president had guarded his hand well as Christmas approached in 1959, the nation's most prosperous year to that time and one of distinction for the university. Over the years the sixty-four-year-old educator had developed the temperament of a person who held his own counsel. Back on the campus, only Mrs. Virginia Brakefield Vickery, his secretary, knew of his plans. An educator out of the old school in the South, Jack Smith had learned the fundamentals of education the hard way, beginning his career in a rural elementary school before he had earned a college degree. But he had studied his lessons.

It is no easy thing to pinpoint the development of ideas and philosophies in an honest, practical man, but Smith, who held that school superintendents and college presidents had to be autocratic to survive, felt that no institution would run afoul of wrong methods if it hired the right teachers. He also held that presidents, rather than methods or measures, decided whether a university would be first class or second class. A sense of history always walked with Jack Smith, who was born at Stantonville, Tennessee, on the hallowed fields of Shiloh, only a little more than thirty years after a torn nation bled so profusely there. He never denied his roots and probably never entertained such an inclination.

When he met with Morgan on that December day Smith felt he was retiring from a state system that he had served to the best of his ability since the 1920s. In his long career he had been the principal at Memphis State campus school; a dean at Memphis State, his undergraduate alma mater; twice the state's commissioner of education; the president of Tennessee Polytechnic Institute at Cookeville; director of instruction for Memphis city schools; and for thirteen years, president of Memphis State. While Smith sat in Morgan's office in Nashville, 4973 students—a record number—were attending classes at Memphis State. Smith felt the school was on the threshold of accelerated growth just two years after it had achieved university status in 1957.

Smith and Morgan soon turned their attention to the future leadership of the university. The State Board of Education would not meet until February 5, 1960, and Morgan was empowered to name an acting president. Morgan brought up the names of several highly qualified educators. Smith listened politely but shook his head. He looked Morgan in the eye and said, "No, Sonny Humphreys is the one."

Morgan, who had known Humphreys for many years and held him in high esteem, agreed with Smith. Then the SBE chairman asked, "When would you like to make the announcement of your retirement?" Smith replied, "The day after Christmas."

The two friends shook hands, and Smith returned to Memphis.

The announcement plans quickly fell by the wayside. Morris Cunningham, the Washington Bureau chief for *The Commercial Appeal* in Memphis, learned of Smith's resignation from a source in the U.S. Office of Education and alerted his newspaper the day after Smith got back from Nashville. Reese Wells, education editor of *The Commercial Appeal*, called Smith for confirmation. Smith did not want the story to come out at that time, but he knew he had to be honest. Immediately after he completed his interview with Wells, he asked Mrs. Vickery to get Humphreys to his office as soon as possible.

Humphreys was at work in his little cubbyhole that was the size of an elevator shaft and eventually would serve just that purpose. It was across a hall from the president's second-floor office in the Administration Building, and he was in Smith's office within a minute. As usual, Smith was direct. "Sonny," he said, "I have resigned to join the U.S. Office of Education as regional representative in Atlanta. Joe Morgan will ask you to serve as acting president. He will be calling you. I would like for you to succeed me as president, but it will be up to the board."

Smith also told a stunned Humphreys that a photographer for the newspaper was on his way to the campus. It was Tuesday afternoon, December 15, 1959. *The Commercial Appeal* gave the story front page play, with a picture of Smith and Humphreys. The afternoon newspaper, the *Memphis Press-Scimitar*, came back with a strong story on the surprising development. The lead editorial in *The Commercial Appeal* on Thursday morning, December 17, had a "University Milestone" headline. It said, "The resignation of J. M. (Jack) Smith as president of Memphis State University and naming of C. C. (Sonny) Humphreys as acting president marks a milestone in the development of an institution of higher learning which enjoys a vast potential for the whole region." The editorial also said Humphreys, "groomed as a presidential successor by the retiring administration," faced a challenge to develop research and encourage the quest for truth. It spoke of "a potential population thirsting for opportunities in higher education."

Humphreys liked the tone of the editorial, and he sensed that Frank R. Ahlgren, editor of *The Commercial Appeal* and a University of Tennessee trustee, and Edward J. Meeman, editor of the *Memphis Press-Scimitar*, would be crucial allies in his desire to sell the city on the potential of the university to the community.

But there always was Smith's role in his personal advancement to be remembered. "The sudden resignation was a great shock to me," Humphreys said. "I suppose that somewhere in the back of my mind I knew that someday he would leave the university, but we had all been so busy and he was such a strong and dynamic person that his leaving seemed a long time in the future."

Upon reflection, though, Humphreys knew his mentor had struggled through four debilitating years involving desegregation of Memphis State. Smith and the State Board of Education had been in and out of federal court since 1955 as defendants in a suit vigorously pushed in behalf of student plaintiffs by the National Association for the Advancement of Colored People.

Initially, Smith had advanced a "step by step" plan whereby the university would admit black students one class at a time, starting with graduate school. The Federal District Court approved the plan, but it was overruled by the Sixth Circuit Court of Appeals in Cincinnati. After that, the State Board of Education decided integration would begin in the fall of 1958. The Little Rock riots and other events bothered Smith. Acting on a request from the Memphis State president, the SBE voted to delay integration one year.

That decision promptly put Memphis State, the SBE, and Smith back in court, with Mrs. Constance Motley, legal counsel of the NAACP, seeking an injunction against the delay. Under questioning by Federal District Judge Marion Boyd, Smith testified that he had no plans to seek delay beyond the 1958–59 school year. "I don't think it would do any good," he said.

Judge Boyd denied the injunction, and at the university's winter graduation exercises on January 30, 1959, President Smith reiterated that the university would be integrated in the fall. "I trust the citizens of this area...will accept the inevitable which has been forced upon us," he said.

Smith, who was approaching his sixty-fourth birthday, expressed hope that "the last days of my tenure will not be fraught with problems which have been encountered on many other college campuses." That desire was met. Integration began in the fall of 1959 in a quiet, peaceful process by eight black students, whose performance matched those of white students.

A generation younger, Cecil Humphreys had foreseen, and accepted,

Unlike other schools, in 1959 Memphis State University was peacefully integrated.

certain changes easier than his good friend and mentor, Jack Smith. "I would be less than honest to say that I agreed with him on all things over the years of our association," Humphreys said. "The world was changing rapidly; he had grown up in a different era.

"I knew I would miss him, and thought about him often a few years later when society and higher education were caught up in even more dynamic changes in an even shorter period of time.

"It was as hard for me to meet some of the changes that came as it had been for Jack Smith."

The Christmas break ended and classes resumed on January 3, 1960, the day a young senator from Massachusetts, John F. Kennedy, announced that he would seek the Democratic nomination for president on a "New Frontier" platform.

At Memphis State a forty-five-year-old "acting" president set about enlarging Memphis' concept of what the university could be to it. Along with that, Humphreys would work to continue improving the school's image of itself. He had a long memory. In 1956–57, a time when Memphis State was achieving university status, its Bulletin had printed this negative placement advice:

> MSC cannot guarantee positions to its graduates. It endeavors, however to place students with satisfactory records in good positions.
> It invites county and city school authorities and business organizations to make use of its Placement Service in securing desirable teachers, office assistants, and salesmen.

An embarrassed Humphreys had placed this cryptic note in his files about the advice: "A limiting concept in view of the changes taking place and reveals the institution's self-image."

In 1960 the image had improved, and the broadening base of the university could be detected in the majors of its 4973 students, an increase of 638 over the previous year. The School of Arts and Sciences claimed 2396 students, the School of Business 1181 and the School of Education only 933. There were 315 in seven master's degree programs in the Graduate School, and the remainder were in a general college program. Memphis State had no doctoral programs.

The academic schools and divisions were headed by directors in 1960, the State Board of Education being reluctant to change to deans. Dr. W. P. Carson directed the School of Arts and Sciences; Dr. Edward I. Crawford, the School of Business; Dr. Heber E. Rumble, the School of Education; and Dr. Calvin M. Street, the Evening Division. In the coming months Humphreys would name replacements for the three posts he had held: director of the graduate school, athletic director, and assistant to the president. Serving in general administration offices were R. M. Robison, dean of the university; Lamar Newport, bursar; George Pratt, dean of students; Miss Flora Rawls, dean of women; and R. P. Clark, registrar.

The state funded $1,257,931.73 of Memphis State's $2,613,778.95 budget. Ten years earlier, in 1949–1950, the state appropriations had been $555,403.60 for an enrollment of 2368. Humphreys realized he would have to fight for additional dollars. In a decade there had been little increase on a per-student basis. In a time when a rapidly growing fast-food franchise named McDonald's sold burgers for fifteen cents and Memphis State tried to run a news bureau on $8 a week, the president of the university drew an annual salary of $10,500. The average monthly salary (on a 10-month contract) for a professor was $669, associate professor $572, assistant professor, $531, and an instructor $467.

Since the news broke on December 16, 1959, that President Smith would resign and Cecil Humphreys would become acting president, it had remained the number one topic on the campus and in the community. At a surprise faculty-student assembly on December 18, Clyde Ford, Student Government Association president, gave President Smith and his wife gifts of luggage and a silver punchbowl.

To Humphreys, a smiling Ford presented an extra large pair of brogans. Smith told the audience Humphreys would fill his shoes nicely: "I trust and fully believe the State Board will name him as your new president."

A realist, Humphreys knew he held an interim appointment. He made no immediate plans to sell his year-old Williamsburg style house at 5496 South Angela Lane and prepare to move into the president's house on campus. "I knew I had made contributions to the university," Humphreys said, "but I did not actually seek the presidency. It was not a life or death thing."

Humphreys said he never talked to Ernest Ball, an old friend who headed a search committee for the State Board of Education. Others, however, spoke in Humphreys' behalf. Both Memphis newspapers gave him solid endorsements. So did the university newspaper, *The Tiger Rag*. And, by February 5, when the SBE met in Nashville, almost 50,000 Memphians had signed petitions supporting Humphreys' appointment. Greater Memphis State, Inc., a nonalumni support group Humphreys had helped to organize in the 1950s, and its president, P. K. Seidman, sent telegrams to the board.

There was speculation in the newspapers that a permanent appoint-

ment would come at the SBE session, but Chairman Joe Morgan decided to proceed with usual precedents and named Ernest Ball to head
a search committee. Serving with Ball were Judge W. R. Landrum of
Trenton, James Williams of Henderson, J. Howard Warf of Hoenwald,
and Mrs. Sam Wilson of Loudon. Morgan told them to report on or
before the May meeting. In other action the SBC officially accepted
President Smith's resignation and named him president emeritus of
Memphis State.

A touch of nervousness hit Memphis on Feburary 9 when the *Memphis Press-Scimitar* reported that Humphreys was a leading nominee
for the presidency of Texas Technological College in Lubbock. But no
serious candidate other than Humphreys ever surfaced for the Memphis State job, and in a specially called SBE meeting on March 29,
1960, he was chosen president by unanimous vote.

In actuality, the new president had been on the job since January 3,
when he immediately became a super-salesman for the university and
began a personal shuttle downtown.

His goal involved a delicate balancing job. There are theoretical demands of college disciplines derived from inner logic, and it requires
careful charting for a curricula to also meet society's social demands.
Humphreys, the historian, once felt that a knowledge of history and a
competency in writing and speaking English were the basic subjects to
be taught, but he had come to attach an asterisk to that viewpoint.
Humphreys drew three conclusions in 1960:

1) A majority of the students at Memphis State, most of them first
generation college students, were motivated by a desire to improve
their economic status and enjoy a better life.

2) A public institution is obligated to prepare students to take their
place in a rapidly changing and complex society.

3) By making the resources of the campus available to the community, its value would be enhanced in the eyes of the public.

In his note files are these thoughts: "The esoteric knowledge and
areas which had enjoyed the greatest academic prestige, but insufficient support, would benefit from the exoteric knowledge which was
more involved in the economic or industrial life." That may come
across as a bit academic, but Humphreys knew the value of an urban
university and what the payoff could be. "I knew that if a local com-

munity would support anything in the university, then English and history and other basic academic subjects would benefit, however indirectly," he said. "The key then, it seemed to me, was to enlist the aid of the community: Show it that the university offered it something that would help it and it would respond with support of the total institution."

By February Humphreys could be found downtown almost daily. In a speech to the Shelby County Council of Civic Clubs he said there was a critical need for a branch of study, an industrial management program, and he put in a plea for $100,000 from the city to support it. The new president also graphically depicted how he once needed data on the forestry and wood products industry in Tennessee, went downtown in search of it, and returned to campus empty-handed. He suggested a bureau of economic research at Memphis State would be an asset for the region.

Humphreys had a torch in his hand, and the community response astonished him. He soon was overwhelmed with speaking engagements, but he accepted most of them. In addition to economic subjects Humphreys spoke on brotherhood, military service, and law. He was not selling himself; he was selling Memphis State University.

On April 20 it was announced that Greater Memphis State, Inc., and the Downtown Lions Club would hold a "MSU Appreciation Dinner" on May 3 in the Balinese Room at the Claridge Hotel. For that event Humphreys took a large supporting cast downtown to reveal "the changing concepts of university service." Among speakers from the university were Dr. John Richardson, education; Dr. Walter Smith, pre-professional programs; Dr. Calvin Street, adult education; George Harris; arts activities; Cadet Colonel Richard Koepke, Air Force Reserve Officers Training; Clyde Ford, president of the Student Government Association, student activities; Dean R. M. Robison, athletics; and Dr. Herbert Markle, Dr. Wayland Tonning, and Professor Charles Spendler, programs of the School of Business.

A capacity crowd of 500 business, industrial, and governmental leaders attended, and *The Commercial Appeal* reported the next morning that Humphreys spoke last, saying: "This community has enjoyed an educational economy of millions of dollars....This, plus, the presentations you have heard are the arguments why Memphis should be interested in providing support."

His plan had not been fleshed out fully, but Humphreys wanted Memphis State to provide the intellectual resources for an urban area that land grant colleges and universities had done so effectively for rural sections. Political machinery moves slower than a man with ideas, and there was mixed feelings on the Memphis City Commission about using municipal tax dollars to support a state institution. Late in 1959 Mayor-elect Henry Loeb, a graduate of Brown University, and Public Works Commissioner William Farris, a Memphis State alumnus, had voiced support for aiding Memphis State. Others said the Tennessee General Assembly would have to authorize financial grants by the City of Memphis.

Meanwhile, the public response told Humphreys he was on the right track. The Memphis Sales Executive Club, which had been contributing $4000 annually to the university, announced plans to endow a distinguished professorship in sales. The $100,000 for the university's first chair came just four years after the School of Business pioneered the nation's first sales major.

Humphreys always seemed to be looking ahead to diverse projects that would benefit Memphis State and the community. He had been a good football coach, and coaches always take a schedule "one game at a time." Humphreys, however, was a master juggler; he kept three or four ideas up in the air at all times.

As usual he read many reports and books; he wanted to know trends at their beginning. In a newspaper interview the day after he became president, he said, "Our growth at Memphis State is assured, provided we get money to provide staff and physical facilities, because young people who want a college education to face modern living are passing through our high schools in increasing numbers." Demographics dictated part of the Memphis State story in the 1960s. However, enrollment figures would mushroom far beyond the estimates made in a state legislative study. Memphis State would have to reach out as it never had to do before, and it would require dynamic leadership from its new president for more than twelve exciting years.

Many of the highly publicized activities of President Humphreys kept him in downtown Memphis, or in Nashville, the state capital. He could have lost sight of his primary role as a college administrator. Somehow, though, he found time to see that Memphis State provided a quality education for its students, built a highly professional faculty, and carried out the mandates of the State Board of Education.

From January 3 to June 30, 1960, he faced many new chores, including the preparation of a budget for the 1960–61 school year. At the May 6 meeting of the SBE he presented an operational budget totaling $2,651,853. Included in this was a state appropriation of $1,257,922. In April and May Humphreys made key academic and administrative decisions. He announced the appointment of Dr. John W. Richardson as director of the Graduate School, the changing of the status of George Pratt from dean of students to dean of men, and the hiring of Dr. Eugene Lambert as athletic director. Early in the 1950s Humphreys had hired Lambert as basketball coach. It was Lambert who started Tiger basketball on the road to national prominence before moving to the University of Alabama.

To meet the school's rapidly growing enrollment, Humphreys launched a search for 16 new faculty members. Humphreys also enlisted the aid of highly qualified business and professional people in the private sector to come to the campus on a part-time teaching basis. He then struck a deal with WKNO, the educational television station operated by a private foundation, to offer math classes in the evening.

As the 1959–60 year closed, it appeared that Jack Smith had been eminently right when he told Chairman Joe Morgan of the SBE, "No, Sonny Humphreys is the one."

3

Reaching for Greatness

1960–1961

THE NEWS HEADLINES

John F. Kennedy wins Democratic presidential nomination on first ballot, saying his New Frontier platform "sums up not what I intend to offer to the American people, but what I intend to ask of them"...Vice President Richard Nixon, the Republican nominee, and Kennedy appear in the first live TV debates...President Eisenhower says farewell, warns of the increasing power of a "military-industrial complex"...U.S. breaks diplomatic relations with Cuba ...Russian cosmonaut Yuri Gagarin orbits earth in Vostok I...Fidel Castrol's forces defeat CIA-trained Cuban refugee force at Bay of Pigs...Kennedy commits U.S. to "landing a man on the moon and returning him safely to earth" by the end of the decade.

AND THE WAY WE WERE

Girls win three out of four contests in freshman elections...Richard Nixon wins the two-day MSU presidential opinion poll, defeating John F. Kennedy by only 52 votes...Senior rings—$28.50 plus tax...MSU is no longer just a commuter school as students from 43 states, the District of Columbia, and 10 foreign countries are attending ...Cafeteria service is the object of criticism...The Brothers Four star at the annual spring concert...Shakespeare Festival stages "Julius Caesar"...Rent a complete formal outfit including accessories for only $6.95.

A HALF-YEAR INTO HIS PRESIDENCY in 1960, Cecil Humphreys initiated steps to try to get Memphis State out of a nightmare scary enough to challenge the ablest of city planners. He felt that the university had been swallowed, then ignored, by a city galloping eastward into Shelby County farmland. Access to the campus was a joke: it exemplified that "you can't get there from here" saying attributed to savvy old farmers when asked for directions by a lost motorist.

Memphis State, basically a commuter school gearing for a student population explosion, was squeezed into an eighty-acre box. It had few of the amenities needed in the age of the auto. The school had a couple of small lots and campus streets for parking, and in 1960, for the first time, designated parking zones by color and charged $2 for color-coded auto decals.

In the beginning, back in 1912, the founders of West Tennessee State Normal School had carved a pleasant, tree-shaded campus out of an old plantation known as the W. D. Dunn tract. The Creath Land Company donated forty-eight acres to the fledgling school, and an additional thirty-two acres were purchased through donations by citizens, led by former Governor Malcolm R. Patterson, a Memphian. He had been a leader in a six-year fight in the Tennessee General Assembly to build three normal schools in the state.

Masons and carpenters built a president's home, a women's dormitory, and a stately Administration Building facing south toward the tracks of the Southern Railway, which put up a little depot and called it Normal Station. The school's nearest neighbors were farmers. A short distance to the west, toward Memphis, were Buntyn Station and Messick, then a county high school. In Normal's early years male students lived on the fourth floor of the Administration Building or in private homes in the area. The school opened its first dormitory for men (Scates Hall) in 1923.

Problems associated with urban growth had developed in the intervening 48 years before Humphreys became president in 1960. A unit of city government, the Memphis Light, Gas & Water Division built

Sheehan Pumping Station along a cinder lane cul de sac on the east border of the campus. It effectively walled off growth to the east. The railroad tracks and a deep gully prevented an entrance from Southern Avenue, and the north edge of the campus ended at the backyards of houses on the south side of Norriswood Avenue. Appropriately named but not a major traffic artery for the city, Patterson Street offered access on the west side, along with limited help from Walker Avenue. Walker had a bus turnaround at the southwest edge of the campus a short distance from where it met Patterson.

An escape from this aspect of the university's traffic plight was plotted on the Fourth of July. As Humphreys recalls the incident:

> I called City Commissioner of Public Works William Farris on July 4, 1960, and asked him to come to discuss a matter of great importance to the university.
>
> He said he would come out right away, despite the holiday. When he arrived, I explained that there was no entrance to the campus on the north, east, or south sides of the campus. Better access had to be provided.
>
> I felt a dedicated street extending Walker east along the campus' southern border to the cinder road known as Normal Street and then north to Central Avenue would not only alleviate the campus traffic problems but also would open up that entire section of the campus for development of needed buildings for classroom space. I explained that I believed that I could get the state to deed the necessary land if the city would construct and maintain streets on the east and south sides of the campus.
>
> Bill Farris took a look and agreed with my idea.
>
> I mention the meeting with Farris because his was one of the first positive responses the university had received from local officials. True, he was an MSU alumnus, but too often in the past local officials had found reasons why assistance could not be given the university.

Farris delivered. Walker was extended and the cinder road on the east became Normal Street and later Zack Curlin Drive, named in honor of the school's coach and physical education teacher from 1924 to 1960.

Humphreys' initiatives in 1960 did not always elicit such positive response, as many urban institutions discovered when they tried to expand. A simple Memphis State suggestion that women physical education students might use the parklike grounds of Sheehan Pumping

The Humphreys family early in the presidency of Dr. Humphreys. Hunter is to the right, Cecil, Jr., to the left of Mrs. Humphreys.

Station for classes drew immediate opposition when it was advanced at the beginning of the fall semester.

Residents of the Grandview area east of the pumping station objected. They retained a lawyer, who maintained that Major Thomas H. Allen, late president of the Memphis Light, Gas & Water Division, had given "solemn assurances to property owners when the station was built that the surrounding area would be kept as a park, and that nothing would be done to depreciate the value of the land."

President Humphreys met with Grandview homeowners on September 3 and left saying, "I'm hopeful that a misunderstanding has been cleared up and good neighborliness will prevail."

Downtown, Mayor Henry Loeb indicated that he was sympathetic to the university's request.

A reporter for *The Commercial Appeal* put a touch of humor to a story about a protest meeting, mentioning that Grandview homeowners, "who regularly walk their dogs through the wooded lot without objection," expressed fear that use of the area would pollute their water. The news account pushed in a wry stickpin or two for the Grandview residents: "They reasoned that boys and girls in rubber-soled tennis shoes would jar the ground and shake dirt into the pipes beneath." The writer added that the area was "kept mowed by a heavy tractor."

Grandview homeowners remained firm in their opposition, and a hearing before the City Commission was scheduled for September 20. Memphis State appeared to have enough votes to win, but Humphreys pulled a surprise. He told the commissioners MSU was withdrawing its request. He said the university did not want to be the reason for a test of power between the City Commission and one of its boards. The Light, Gas & Water Division had opposed the school's requests after complaints arose. Actually, Humphreys made a strategic withdrawal. His notes suggest that he felt a generous gesture would strengthen the university's drive for community support on more important matters in the future.

The new president got in a few substantial licks, however. In his statement he said: "We state emphatically that we do not think there are any valid grounds in opposition to our request. The important question this case has raised is the extent to which the City Commission should exercise its power in reviewing actions taken by one of its boards."

Humphreys then raised a significant question about Major Allen's promise to the Grandview residents, asking: "Can any official, elected or appointed, make a personal promise, that has no legal basis, with any individual or group of individuals that binds the government in perpetuity? Such a practice, if accepted from the past and followed in the future, would eventually lead to a paralysis of government."

Humphreys also said the university, which was drafting plans to reach for greatness as an institution of higher learning, was withdrawing its request because its building program would be "severely handicapped when state leaders, knowing of our limited land area, learn that a minor request that would have helped us meet our land needs has been objected to so strongly." He concluded his statement with a plea for community support. There were other cards in his hand to be played.

A "For Sale" sign in front of a modest house on .17 acre of land at 3663 Norriswood caught the eye of Humphreys during the time of the pumping station controversy, and it turned a college president into an extraordinary land developer. It would be the first small step in adding 104.5 acres to the campus' original 80; a house-by-house approach to growth had begun.

It would end with giant leaps to both sides of Central Avenue and beyond to Poplar Avenue to the north and across the Southern Railway barrier to expansion on the south covering four and a half blocks. By the end of Humphreys' administration in 1972, some 314 individual parcels of land adjacent to the campus had been acquired for $6,847,114. Only $1 million came from the state, and that just before Humphreys moved to a higher post in Nashville.

Looking back, Humphreys is not sure how he conceived the idea to buy the house on Norriswood with borrowed money, get it off the tax rolls, rent it, make payments on the loan and launch campus expansion. In any event, he shared his thoughts with friends. "I took the idea to Ernest Ball, always a wise counselor, supporter of the university and longtime State Board of Education member," Humphreys recalled. "He thought it worth exploring."

Humphreys next sought advice from a banker, John Brown, president of Union Planters National Bank. His bank had a branch in the neighborhood and had handled the financing of the Panhellenic Building which opened in 1959. "I timidly approached him for advice as to where and how money could be borrowed to buy a house without even a down-payment," Humphreys said. "I really just wanted advice. I explained the idea to Mr. Brown and he listened patiently."

Brown asked him how much money would be needed.

"I decided that as long as I was dreaming I might as well dream big," Humphreys said. "I told him that all the houses on the south side of Norriswood would eventually be needed, and, over a period of years, at least $200,000 would be needed."

A good banker, Brown calmly responded, "We will lend you the money." Up until that time the university president thought he and Brown were just exploring an idea. "I was speechless," said Humphreys, who had begun a real estate saga highly unusual for a university president.

The banker explained to Humphreys, who had bought only one house in his life, that with State Board of Education approval a bond could be issued by the university for the amount of the purchase price, plus real estate agent fees and closing costs, and the bank would make the money available at 4 percent interest. Humphreys placed his proposal before the SBE in Nashville on November 11, 1960, and won approval. The board knew Memphis State would have to expand to serve its growing student body, and it opened the door for the university.

An exuberant Humphreys returned to Memphis and bought the house at 3663 Norriswood for $14,076.10. The transaction was duly recorded, but Memphis State made no public announcement. It was not until August 26, 1961, when two additional houses were acquired, that the morning newspaper learned of the acquisitions.

"We're buying the land only as the owners put it up for sale with an eye on future expansions," Humphreys told *The Commercial Appeal*. He said this was a "common practice" by urban universities. Humphreys emphasized the university had "no intention of building a parking lot on the property next year, and we are not going to try to drive the property owners out."

Some objectives would change rapidly as Memphis State bought houses. It would, in times of critical need for space, hire real estate agents to solicit sales from homeowners. The temperament of Humphreys was such that, in his own words, "our transactions with neighborhood residents were quite pleasant."

They must have been. The university never once used, or threatened to use, its power of eminent domain.

There may have been a slight twisting of arms in one case after Memphis State decided in 1964 to jump its campus over the railroad and acquire more than a hundred homes from Southern to Spottswood between Goodman and Houston. A target date of two years was set because MSU needed the property for parking, intramural activities, an athletic field, and an ROTC drill field. Humphreys wrote:

> One house we needed was owned by a railway postal clerk and his wife whose two children attended the campus school. They loved the house and steadfastly refused to sell, even though Memphis State owned the property all around the house.
>
> We had plans to build the parking lots and tennis courts there, and I directed the crews to begin construction. It turned out that all the land surrounding that house was excavated for the parking lots off Southern. The house was left on a little spit of land about six feet above the surrounding area.
>
> The wife came to me practically crying about what to do. I offered again to buy the lot, and told her she could keep the house and have it moved to a new lot. She and her husband jumped at the chance. They moved the house and enlarged it with the money while the university saved the cost of razing a house.

Aside from the money his daring plan saved the state over the years, Humphreys said the land acquisitions reflected proudly on the school.

In the fiscal year 1963–1964 the university began a push toward Central Avenue, and it had been in Humphreys' mind all along. He knew that a new "front door" with a row of impressive buildings on Central would be a visual declaration to Memphians of the expanding role of their university.

After acquiring the property on the south side of Central, a main east-west thoroughfare, Humphreys turned his eyes to the north side.

> We already owed a lot of money for our recent expansion, and had no prospects of state help. Then we learned that an apartment builder had

gotten options on several houses there. I knew we couldn't wait or we would be permanently blocked from expansion in that direction. We went to the Planning Commission and explained that we would need that space for parking to take care of the buildings to be built on the south side. They denied the permit for apartments and we began to acquire the large houses and lots north of Central. Our borrowing limit with the bank had been increased from $200,000 to $750,000.

There were protests from citizens and letters to the editors that the state should not be buying the fine houses on Central to use for student parking. I published the cost figures of past acquisitions that showed the land costs per square foot were less on Central, because of the size of the lots, than they were between Southern and Spottswood on the south side of the railroad. The criticism stopped.

There was one ticklish issue in the university's growing campus and educational opportunities that never seemed to go away—parking. Everyone, students and neighboring residents, complained.

"I don't know what we're going to do with all the cars this year," Humphreys said in 1961. "It'll be one of our biggest problems." One problem stemmed from old attitudes. Many Memphians who lived beyond the Memphis State area, including some who should have known better, never understood the role of a car at a university in an urban setting. They had little sympathy for college students who owned 5000 parking decals costing $2 each and a red-faced university with space for only 2500 cars.

Many of Memphis State's neighbors understood and were more sympathetic. But on October 1, 1963, *The Commercial Appeal* ran a lengthy story headlined: "Sympathy is Wearing Thin of MSU Car Swarm."

"I attended MSU and felt sorry for the students," the newspaper quoted one resident on Patterson Street, "but when they block your driveway and you can't get out, you get pretty mad." An apartment dweller on Mynders also was quoted: "We can't even use our clothesline anymore because students park their cars under it all day. If we ask the kids to move their cars, they said they are late for class and will be back in a couple of hours. By the time they come back another student has his car ready to take over that parking place." A routeman in a delivery truck shook his head and told the newsman, "I don't know what can be done, but they are going to have to do something. I have to double park in the street. I don't dare pull in a driveway for fear I would never get out again."

President Humphreys told the newspaper the university would work with anyone to try to solve the problem. "It is a matter that has concerned us for some time," he said, "and the situation is going to get worse before it gets better. We can't disqualify a student from enrolling just because he does not have a parking place."

Humphreys was ahead of his time in knowing that parking space should be provided but he had to be cautious. In an editorial after its news stories, The Commercial Appeal called for "a long-range solution that would not wind up putting a burden on taxpayers, who need not be expected to finance parking lots for college boys and girls."

Humphreys had heard that before, especially in the rural-dominated Tennessee legislature, where he found many members actually hostile when the need for parking was mentioned. Their thinking was tied to forty acres and a mule—and the little red schoolhouse down the road—concept. "They would quickly tell you how many miles they had had to walk to school," Humphreys said.

Editors of the student newspaper, The Tiger Rag, did not go along with rural logic. They were in tune with Mayor Robert Wagner of New York, who had called for an urban nation to understand urban problems. Humphreys knew parking space should be provided by an urban school, but he realized it would take a little time to win converts. In an interview with Tiger Rag reporters, he said, "If a choice has to be made between academic buildings and parking lots, we'll build classrooms. MSU's main concern is education."

Eventually urban thinking would help the parking situation, with the university owning a large lot on the north side of fashionable Central Avenue. When the parking lot was being planned, Humphreys told the designers, "I don't want a shopping center parking lot. Leave a setback and some trees and shrubbery." But in the first years of the 1960s public parking lots for students fetched apoplexy for many Memphians. Times change, though, and so do attitudes.

In many ways the 1960–61 school year, with a record 5279 enrollment, was a time for firsts other than color-coded parking decals and limited on-campus parking areas.

Humphreys became a master at politicking. Greater Memphis State sponsored a luncheon on July 25, 1960, for nineteen Memphis and Shelby County candidates for the state legislature, and Humphreys brought up the question of city and county financial support for a state institution. He told the office seekers that Memphis State deserved the same hometown support that was being given other Tennessee institutions, which often benefitted from their more apparent contributions to the cultural, social, and economic life of the community.

The legislative candidates pledged their backing, and in March, the bill was passed in the General Assembly. Newspapers reported Humphreys said the first $100,000, if voted by the local governments, would be used to establish a Bureau of Economic Information at Memphis State. "The bureau would be of tremendous help to both local governments and to the community," Humphreys said.

The wooing of state legislators became a consistent thing for Humphreys, who liked to invite them to the campus. On November 12, 1960, William D. Baird, speaker of the senate, and James L. Bomar, house speaker, with twenty-nine other legislators from West Tennessee counties, came to Memphis State for lunch and a football game.

"I detailed for them my belief in the regional role Memphis State could play," Humphreys said. "I pointed out that all but three counties in West Tennessee had lost population during the last ten years. The loss consisted of young people in their most vigorous and productive years."

The university president was planting fertile seed in the minds of political leaders who knew their counties needed economic aid and advice. They also had fun and enjoyed watching Memphis State's football Tigers thump the University of Chattanooga, 42–0.

Humphreys held to the belief that visitors to the campus would sense the vibrancy in its mission, and he seized each opportunity to add to the lures. Goodwyn Institute's free public lectures had been held in downtown Memphis since 1907, providing enlightenment and entertainment to thousands. A member of the institute's board, Humphreys offered to hold the lectures in the university's auditorium, and the move was made.

"It made the nonstudents, many of whom had never been on campus, aware of the university," Humphreys commented. And it did not cost the school a penny.

Another major coup would follow. One of the nation's oldest non-commercial television stations soon would be at Memphis State. WKNO, an educational television station which went on the air on June 25, 1956, in an old school building at 268 Jefferson in downtown Memphis, needed new quarters. Humphreys became aware of this need when he visited Ernest Ball, who had become director of the station following his retirement as superintendent of the city school system. Humphreys knew of a development on the campus that might be the answer to WKNO's space need. The Memphis State Training School was changing from 1–9 to 1–6 grade system, and the old gymnasium would be available.

"I envisioned the mutual benefits of having WKNO located on the campus," Humphreys recalled. "I suggested to the station's board that the gymnasium would be available if it assumed the cost of installation, any needed alterations, and utility costs. The board lost no time in making a formal request," On March 9, 1961, Julian B. Bondurant, president of Memphis Community Television Foundation, wrote asking if Memphis State could house its studios and "join the exclusive group of universities which have a television station located on their campus."

The State Board of Education approved. One immediate result was the addition of broadcast production to the offerings of the Journalism Department, which used WKNO facilities. "A fine and beneficial relationship was begun," was Humphreys conclusion.

Somehow, for a freshman president, Humphreys managed to mix personal charm and an intelligent grasp of ideas with an ability that seemed uncanny. He did not always win all that he wanted for Memphis State, but he came close repeatedly.

With the biennial session of the General Assembly coming up in 1961, Humphreys appealed to Greater Memphis State to throw its support behind a record request of $2.5 million for a campus building program. The list included an addition to the library and two new dormitories. He told the group that 481 students had been turned away because of lack of dorm space that fall.

The organization unanimously pledged its support and went to work. In its wisdom the legislature appropriated $7.2 million for the six schools under the SBE, and MSU received $1,671,170 for the next two years instead of the needed $2.5 million. In addition to the library expansion and the dormitories, the funds would be used for a new classroom building for the School of Business.

The School of Business would get its share of newspaper ink early in 1961 as students at Memphis State began to speak out more and more on campus and academic issues.

In Humphreys' files are these comments about attitudes toward traditional roles: "There were indications that campuses were going to be affected in a number of ways by the great social changes taking place.

"Memphis State, with a high percentage of its students living at home and commuting to the campus, coming from middle class families and conservative backgrounds and many working part-time to pay college expenses, would be slower to become involved in various protest movements.

"But they would become involved."

In January of 1961 the Student Government Association passed an "Academic Freedom" bill, challenging the administration to permit more individual expression by students and faculty members. Humphreys wrote:

> I was a little hurt by the action but should have known that with the administration strongly advocating many changes to meet new conditions and relationships with the public the internal campus would not remain unchanged.
>
> Students arriving on campus at this time were not children of the Depression, but products of the more affluent '50s and were well aware of the role being played by black students in the swelling civil rights movement.
>
> With growing enrollments and college teachers in great demand, many positions were filled with recent graduate students who wanted to be involved in the changes taking place.
>
> They were not adverse to making tentative alliances with students to bring about campus changes.

The first challenge by this new attitude came in March 1961, when President Humphreys announced that economics courses were being moved from the School of Arts and Sciences to the School of Business. The business faculty had urged such action for two years. Before the announcement Humphreys checked with the major state-supported universities in the Southeast and found that economics was taught in the business schools of all of them.

Twenty students who opposed the change met with the president on March 7. They presented him with a petition signed by 654 students who felt the School of Business would teach economics "to the ring of cash registers" and would only "deal with making money."

Humphreys heard the students out and expressed appreciation for their sincere interest, but he told them the issue already had been settled.

Although he never was given to flippancy, Humphreys added this retort that he regretted immediately and even more so the next morning when he read it in *The Commercial Appeal:* "We think that it is a little beyond your depth to settle academic affairs."

In one of the notes in his extensive files, Humphreys wrote, "I would have to learn during the next few years to be more diplomatic and that you should develop methods and measures for providing communication between students and the administration."

Cecil Humphreys could never be accused of being a slow learner and he remained convinced that his decision was correct. Economics came to be accepted as a business rather than a classics course, and eventually the business school became the School of Business and Economics. It was there, too, that Humphreys' long-sought Bureau of Business and Economic Research would be placed.

There were many other developments in the first full year of Humphreys' presidency. He walked the campus many times with Dr. Calvin Street of the Evening Division and they sketched a master plan for new building sites and a mall stretching from Walker Avenue, which was being extended, to the Administration Building.

In cooperation with Dr. Herbert Williams of the Journalism Department and Frank R. Ahlgren, editor of *The Commercial Appeal,* he approved an internship program for students. This was a wise decision because Ahlgren, in addition to being editor of the city's largest newspaper, was a driving force in the national accreditation of journalism schools. With 250 students and ranked twenty-first in the nation on an enrollment basis, Memphis State's Journalism Department wanted to be accredited. In a few years that would come. One paternalistic note, something the new president was trying to avoid, crept into the announcement of the internship program: "Because of the late hours they must work, selections will be limited to men students."

By the end of his first year in the president's office, and with a number of projects under way to prepare for the anticipated growth and development of the university, Humphreys was ready to propose a plan to involve the faculty in an expanded role in the academic affairs of the institution. For the past several years the only organization involved in academic matters had been an administrative council composed of the administrative officers, school directors, heads of academic departments, and chaired by the president.

With the anticipated growth in enrollment and the expansion and improvement of the academic programs, it was felt that a broader based involvement of the faculty would improve communications between faculty and administration, and strengthen the academic programs.

At the last general faculty meeting of the 1960–61 academic year Humphreys proposed a committee to draw up a constitution for a faculty council with members elected on a proportional basis from each college, and serving three years on a staggered basis.

The proposal was well received and the appointed committee worked during the summer on the proposed plan. At the first faculty meeting of the 1961 fall semester the new constitution was presented and with some minor adjustments was adopted. On November 6, 1961, the newly elected council in an organizational meeting elected Dr. Lawrence Wynn, chairman; Dr. Aaron Boom, vice chairman; and Dr. Jae Riggs, secretary.

The administrative council, reduced to a more workable size, was continued and was composed of operational officers, directors of the schools, the chairman of the Faculty Council, and was chaired by the president.

The new arrangement did improve communications, developing a better flow of ideas and a stronger feeling of involvement by the faculty. As was expected, and as was happening on most campuses, there was the continuing question as to the responsibility of the faculty in matters extending beyond the academic area.

During the 1961–1962 year a number of changes were made in the administrative positions on the campus. Dr. W. P. Carson, the first director of the School of Arts and Sciences, and an outstanding teacher and scholar, reached retirement age and was succeeded by Dr. Walter R. Smith, a professor in the English Department. In the rapidly growing School of Business, Dr. Herbert J. Markle was named director to succeed Dr. Edward Crawford, the first director of that school, who had reached retirement age.

In his personal papers it is evident that President Humphreys was proud of his efforts to offer a doctorate in education in cooperation with the University of Tennessee. The West Tennessee Education Association on October 7, 1960, adopted a resolution urging such a program. Copies were sent to all legislators in the twenty-one counties in West Tennessee and to the presidents of Memphis State and the University of Tennessee.

"I decided to be aggressive in pursuing the matter," Humphreys wrote. "I wrote a letter to my good friend, President Andrew Holt of the University of Tennessee. I made the point that greater cooperation between the institutions was needed to ensure the best use of meager funds."

Humphreys suggested that UT offer the first year of a doctoral program in education on the MSU campus, with MSU providing classroom and office space, library resources, and some faculty. The students would be UT students and complete their work on the UT campus in Knoxville. Humphreys felt that this plan would provide a much-needed opportunity for teachers in Memphis and West Tennessee, although it meant going to Knoxville for the second year. In a few years when the need had been demonstrated and Memphis State would be better prepared, the West Tennessee institution could take over an on-going program.

His files reveal some faculty members in the School of Education were upset by his letter. They apparently felt Memphis State should undertake the program immediately. "They overlooked the fact that no institution under the State Board of Education had the authority to offer such a program," Humphreys said. "Furthermore, the accelerating growth of Memphis State severely strained the school's limited funds."

At its next meeting the State Board of Education approved Humphreys's proposal to work toward a doctoral program with UT.

In his letter to President Holt at the University of Tennessee he brought up other matters, noting that UT had recently employed a full-time person in its Extension Division to establish an Industrial Management Program in West Tennessee. He pointed out that Memphis State was close to receiving local financial support for a similar program that he had been seeking for almost a year. In his notes he placed this comment: "Protection of a traditional role by another institution, as well as apathy by much of the public, is a continuing barrier to the efforts to realize the potential of Memphis State."

Humphreys was a new president building a sound base for a school's potential. He wanted Memphis State to become a university in more than name. In his voluminous notes he never jotted down comments on accolades that came his way between 1960 and 1972. He left those clippings for others to evaluate.

At the time he was exchanging letters with Andy Holt at the University of Tennessee, *Sports Illustrated* named Cecil C. Humphreys to its 1960 Silver Anniversary All-America team. He was in the company of John Hersey, who wrote *A Bell for Adano* and other widely acclaimed novels; Jay Berwanger, the first winner of the Heisman Trophy; Paul (Bear) Bryant; and twenty-one others who played college football in 1935.

In its announcement *Sports Illustrated* said: "The twenty-five men have these things in common: twenty-five years ago they earned varsity letters in football; over the intervening quarter of a century they have acquitted themselves in careers and public service with outstanding distinction. This is how they were chosen: more than 200 colleges and universities were asked to nominate one senior from their 1935 varsity football squads whose career, after twenty-five years, has shown the most accomplishment." Retired University of Tennessee Coach Bob Neyland, who had recruited a tall, skinny athlete out of Paris, Tennessee, during the Depression and made a college education possible for him, nominated Humphreys.

Memphis basked in the national spotlight from the honor Humphreys had brought to the city. Most of the citizens, however, had no way of knowing that his greatest accomplishments were still to come.

A few with their fingers on the pulse of Memphis State might have been able to predict such a future for a one-time coach who organized the university's "Scholar Scouts," a recruiting team looking for brain instead of brawn in Memphis and West Tennessee high schools.

4

The Launching of a Law School

1961–1962

Berlin Wall goes up as East Germany closes border between East and West Berlin in an effort to stop exodus of East Germans from Communist rule...President Kennedy signs an Act of Congress establishing the Peace Corps...Astronaut John Glenn becomes the first American to orbit the earth, circling it three times in Friendship 7...Supreme Court in *Baker* vs. *Carr*, a reapportionment suit brought in Shelby County, Tennessee, rules for one man, one vote...American military advisers in South Vietnam number 2000.

AND THE WAY WE WERE

The city is still surveying the traffic situation at the corner of Walker and Patterson and plans to install traffic signs within the next three or four weeks...Sigma Pi Epsilon and Alpha Epsilon Pi move into houses which brings to 8 the number of fraternity houses owned or rented by Greek groups...630 are expected to attend the twelfth annual Military Ball...Half a century ago 19 students received teaching diplomas from West Tennessee Normal School; 50 years later more than 300 are candidates for degrees.

THE SCHOOL YEAR was only two days old when on July 2, 1961, John Eubank, who headed the Scholar Scout team, revealed that he had signed 16 valedictorians in West Tennessee high schools to academic scholarships at Memphis State. It was noted in news stories that MSU's "brain scouts" held a comfortable lead over Vanderbilt, UT, Ole Miss, Southwestern, and Mississippi State.

That same July at a meeting of the West Tennessee Alumni Association in Jackson the need for academic scholarships was pointed out, and this led to the creation of a Foundation Board as a part of the MSU Alumni Association. It set an initial goal of $10,000. In an address to the group Humphreys said, "Your project is in keeping with the needs of the university, and you could have chosen no project of greater benefit to the school."

When fall classes began on September 11, the enrollment reached 6284, an increase of 1005 students over the preceding year. Twenty-seven new faculty members had been added to handle the crush.

The Commercial Appeal described efforts by university officials to provide space and facilities for an ever-increasing student enrollment and quoted Humphreys as calling it "a gigantic Chinese checkers game. In this game, however, we're using people, money, and buildings instead of colored marbles."

A conversation between Humphreys and Richard Nichols, district manager of the Tennessee Employment Security Office, at a breakfast for newcomers to Memphis had unusual results. Humphreys asked Nichols if he could extend the services of his office to students seeking part-time jobs. "I don't know of any office anywhere in the country offering such service," Nichols replied.

That did not deter MSU's president. He offered office space, equipment, and a telephone on campus. Nichols queried his superiors in Nashville, and they approved the idea. It is believed to have been the first such campus office in the nation.

Some 213 students were placed in jobs the first year. So successful was the service that in a few years four full-time employees were needed, and by 1975 the number of Memphis State students placed reached 24,555.

With its 50th anniversary only a year away, Memphis State made what Humphreys called the university's first "horizontal" expansion. It obtained Chucalissa Park and Museum from the Tennessee Department of Conservation and Commerce.

Chucalissa had been the site of an Indian settlement 14 miles southwest of the Memphis State campus. When Humphreys suggested to the State Education Board that the park, which was on a 75 acre tract, and an adjacent 100 acres of undeveloped land were available, the SBE told him to move ahead, if the parcel could be acquired without cost. "This is a good thing," the *Memphis Press-Scimitar* said in an editorial. "Chucalissa is one of the most exciting spots in the Mississippi Valley to anthropologists and archaeologists....We commend SBE for letting MSU extend its campus...and President Humphreys for his vision." Humphreys said the 100 acres near the park would be utilized as a biological field station.

Back on the campus, each day seemed to bring a new development. Early in September WKNO with its new manager, Howard Holtz, and a 23-member staff started telecasting from Memphis State.

The new women's dormitory opened, and the SBE approved Humphreys' recommendation that it be named for Dr. Nellie Angel Smith, a member of the faculty from 1927 until her retirement in 1952. She had served as dean of women for 20 years.

"She wisely counseled and was a friend of thousands of young women, even to the extent of personally helping many who needed financial assistance," Humphreys said. "She was one of the truly dedicated teachers of our times and is an important part of the heritage of the institution."

Usually, Humphreys could be a patient man, but there could be spontaneous sparks from him too. In February 1962 he announced that Memphis State would establish a Bureau of Business and Economic Research by July 1, even though funds and personnel were not available. "I decided to take the bull by the horns," he told *The Commercial Appeal* on February 17. Humphreys said the bureau would compile data on natural and human resources; analyze economic and

Chucalissa Indian Village about 10 years after it was acquired by Memphis State. Visitors, seated before the replicas of native dwellings built by the university, are enjoying a Choctaw stickball game.

marketing data; and provide speakers, short courses, publications, and other forms of information.

The City Commission held a hearing on Memphis State's request for $15,000 to help support the bureau, but postponed approval when the Planning Commission said the bureau might duplicate what it was proposing to do. Memphis State's vigorous president was not overly dismayed. He put this into his records: "The obtaining of local govern-

Commissioner of Education Joe Morgan *(left)* and Humphreys expressed their appreciation for the many years of service of Dr. Nellie Angel Smith when a women's dorm was named in her honor.

ment support for this project was to be delayed, but it was only a temporary setback. The acceptance of new ideas is seldom easy."

Memphis and Shelby County soon realized what Humphreys was trying to do and provided financial assistance; it takes time to climb out of political webs. Meanwhile, the SBE could see where the energetic president of Memphis State wanted to go. While the city was waffling over the Bureau of Business and Economic Research, the State Board agreed to his plan to hire an expert land planner to assist him in completing a master plan for the Memphis campus.

"There are many things to be done," Humphreys wrote. As early as

1961 he advanced the idea of Memphis State establishing a junior college for high school students who could not meet entrance requirements to the university. At the time Tennessee did not have a junior college system. Later, he was a leader in the establishment of Shelby State Community College.

Humphreys said his thinking had been influenced by the depressing experience of talking to parents of high school graduates who had been denied admission to Memphis State, which had instituted entrance tests in 1958 to hold down enrollment, necessary due to the lack of funds.

"The parents of those young people would come to my office and plead for a chance for them to continue their education," he said. "It was the path to a better life. These conferences were very sobering. I knew that in our changing society an eighteen-year-old with a high school diploma was unskilled labor, and our area had an overabundance of that. Two years of specialized training could make them employable. However, I decided that we were probably overreaching and couldn't meet every need. But in a few years the state did establish a system of community colleges."

The year had many interesting turns and achievements. Perhaps the best of them, a law school, had a link to an event as early as 1941, and it involved a debate. On the surface it appeared to be an unlikely debate—a young college football coach going against an articulate young Memphis lawyer.

Cecil C. Humphreys was not out of his element, however, in August 1941 when he took on Lucius Burch at the Memphis Public Forum on this question: "Are civil rights inviolate in times of emergency?" Law and its historical application interested Humphreys.

In his arguments Humphreys cited historical precedents where civil rights had been suspended in national emergencies in the nation's past, including use of the Alien and Sedition Law in the War of 1812 and the suspension of rights by President Lincoln during the Civil War. Burch spoke of constitutional guarantees to rights which should never be surrendered. The debate ended in a draw. Both were right, one from a philosophical viewpoint and one from a historical and practical viewpoint.

Neither debater had an inkling that four months later there would be war with Japan and President Franklin D. Roosevelt would issue a presidential order that led to the relocation of Japanese-Americans on the West Coast to internment camps. That action, which suspended their legal rights, remains a significant American legal issue.

Humphreys was taking night courses at the Southern Law University after his afternoon duties of coaching football, but the attack on Pearl Harbor by the Japanese on December 7, 1941, ended his law studies.

That the debate even took place suggests that Humphreys was more than a ex-athlete become coach. It reveals how intellectually involved he was in community affairs taking place far from the Memphis State campus.

When he became president of Memphis State, Humphreys, who had retained his interest in law, believed that a fully accredited law school would be a major community asset. There were two night law schools in the city, Southern Law University and the University of Memphis Law School. Neither was accredited by the American Bar Association, but many of the graduates passed the State Bar Examination.

It turned out that the first academic addition of President Humphreys would be a law school. Some luck may have been involved, but Humphreys, a tireless worker, had an unusual talent for making things happen. This is reflected in his detailed monograph on "The Establishment of the Law School at Memphis State University." His treatise, with only minor editing to personalize and condense, reveals much of the man, his ability to communicate, and his presidency:

On May 4, 1961, the evening before the quarterly meeting of the State Board of Education, I was invited to have dinner with Dr. Athens Clay Pullius, president of David Lipscomb College, at his home in Nashville.

The reason for the invitation was not explained, but upon arrival I found that several trustees of Cumberland University at Lebanon, Tennessee, were gathered. They said their law school was in difficulty. Enrollment had been declining, there were financial problems and the school was in danger of losing American Bar Association approval. The board members were interested in seeing the law school become part of Memphis State University.

Founded in 1847, Cumberland Law School quickly became the South's leading law school, pioneering the two-year law course. From its 6000 graduates, had come 15 governors, more than 100 congressmen, and two United States Supreme Court justices. Its most famous alumnus was Cordell Hull, a United States Congressman and Senator from Tennessee and Secretary of State, 1933–1944.

The addition of the Cumberland Law School to Memphis State would make available a needed educational opportunity to the region.

The trustees told me that because of its financial plight, the law school would not be able to open for the fall term. Immediate action was needed. If Memphis State would pay the outstanding debt of about $80,000, the board would transfer the library, records, and name of the Cumberland Law School to Memphis State. Judge Sam Gilreath, dean emeritus and highly respected professor at Cumberland, offered to come to Memphis for one year to help get the school started.

I said that I was interested in establishing a law school at Memphis State that could become approved by the ABA and would serve the Memphis metropolitan area and the surrounding region. I had previously discussed the matter with the heads of the two unapproved evening law schools in Memphis, and they indicated they would close their schools if Memphis State would start a law school and offer evening classes in addition to a daytime program.

I told the Cumberland trustees the purchase of the library would be a problem for Memphis State because the legislature would not meet again until 1963, and thus no additional funds could be obtained from the state before that time. The State Board of Education (SBE) also would have to approve the addition of a law school to Memphis State. I said I thought I could raise the money needed for the transfer from sources in Memphis, and I would ask the SBE for time in executive session the next morning to present the Cumberland proposal.

Everyone agreed that the proposal would be held in confidence until I could get a reaction from the SBE and could have an opportunity to seek funds in Memphis.

The next morning, in closed executive session of the SBE, I presented the Cumberland proposal. The offer on such short notice was not discouraged or encouraged, but there was interest. The board decided that no action should be taken at the open meeting that day; rather it was agreed that I would seek the necessary funds upon my return to Memphis, and if successful, would advise the SBE chairman, Joe Morgan.

I decided that the prospects for obtaining the money were better from the city and county governments than from private sources. I knew that since Mr. Crump's death in 1954, the political power in the city and county governments had been in the hands of Claude Armour, commissioner of fire and police and vice mayor of the city, and Dave Harsh, chairman of the Shelby County Court. These two had control of most of the old Crump organization and had more influence with the city and county governments than any other persons. Fortuitously, Harsh was also an alumnus of the Cumberland Law School. By working through these men I could avoid premature publicity.

I arranged a meeting with Armour and Harsh, and they both agreed that moving the law school to Memphis State was desirable. They gave assurance that $75,000 could be provided from the city and county governments if the SBE approved the move. Although the Cumberland Board had asked for $80,000, I felt sure it would accept $75,000.

With a commitment in hand, I notified Commissioner Morgan that the funds were available. I reminded Morgan that Cumberland was going to have to move quickly, and action could not wait until the August meeting.

A few days later, Morgan advised me that the addition of the law school at Memphis State would have to be considered by the Joint Committee on Higher Education before any action could be taken by the SBE.

The Joint Committee had been established by an executive order of Governor Buford Ellington earlier in the year in an attempt to coordinate the programs of the University of Tennessee with those of the colleges and universities in the SBE system in order to avoid duplication. The committee was to be composed of three members of the SBE, three members of the University of Tennessee Board of Trustees, and was to be chaired by the Commissioner of Education. The introduction of the Joint Committee into the picture meant that approval of the Cumberland proposal would not be a simple matter.

The Cumberland Law School was offered officially to the State of

Tennessee in an emergency meeting of the Joint Committee on Higher Education in Governor Ellington's office on May 16, 1961.

Dr. Ernest Stockton, president of Cumberland University, said the law school could not continue beyond the summer term. The committee considered first, whether the state should take over the Cumberland Law School, and second, whether the school should be attached to Memphis State University, or to some other school under the SBE, or to the University of Tennessee. The committee decided to have Commissioner Morgan appoint a subcommittee to study the proposal and report back on July 17.

The subcommittee which the Joint Committee mandated was composed of Dr. Andrew Holt, president of the University of Tennessee; Harry Laughlin, Memphis attorney and member of the UT Board of Trustees; Ernest C. Ball, former superintendent of the Memphis City School System and a member of the SBE for many years, and me. This ad hoc committee was to meet on May 24 in Nashville.

Both Memphis newspapers carried stories about the Cumberland proposal the next day. The *Memphis Press-Scimitar* reported that the University of Tennessee had been offered the first opportunity to acquire Cumberland but had not been interested. *The Commercial Appeal* reported that one state official was "strongly opposed" to the proposal of moving Cumberland to Memphis State. He was said to have pointed out that only three states operated more than one law school, and that the University of Tennessee Law School was well below its capacity of 400 students. The next day, the newspaper reported that Cumberland also was negotiating with several out-of-state institutions to take over the law school.

Considerable interest was aroused in Memphis by the prospect of a law school at Memphis State. Cumberland alumni in Memphis immediately began organizing a campaign to bring the law school to Memphis State. The alumni began a huge letter-writing effort urging the governor and the members of the Joint Committee to relocate Cumberland at Memphis State. Sidney G. Surret, vice president of the Shelby County Cumberland Alumni Association, firmly stated, "We want Cumberland to stay here in Tennessee where it belongs." A *Memphis Press-Scimitar* story reported that 90 percent of the prelaw students at Memphis State when polled said that they would prefer to attend law school in Memphis.

It was learned the night before the meeting of the ad hoc committee in Nashville that Ball, a strong Memphis State supporter, would not be able to attend. His absence would be a serious blow to Memphis State's hopes.

On the plane to Nashville the evening before the meeting, I had an opportunity to discuss the proposed move with Harry Laughlin, a graduate of the University of Tennessee Law School. He seemed to be favorable to the move, reflecting somewhat the feeling expressed by other lawyers in Memphis who had graduated from ABA-approved law schools. Their feeling was that the discontinuance of the two unapproved evening schools and the establishment of a law school in Memphis that required three years of undergraduate prelaw preparation and three years of law school, over a period of years, would lead to a strengthening of the legal profession in Memphis and Shelby County.

My slight optimism after my conversation with Laughlin did not last long. A delegation from the University of Tennessee met Laughlin when the plane landed. The next morning at the meeting of the subcommittee in the governor's office, I found myself very much alone.

A plan to deal with the question had already been developed and agreed upon. No one from Memphis State had been consulted. A study would be made by the Southern Regional Educational Board and its report would be made to the Joint Committee on Higher Education on July 17. I pleaded with other members of the subcommittee to reconsider their plan, pointing out that Cumberland had publicly stated that it could not operate the coming fall, that it already was rumored that Cumberland was negotiating with an out-of-state institution, and that the $75,000 offered by Memphis sources could be lost. The pleas were to no avail.

The plan, on the surface, seemed reasonable and logical. However, everyone knew that Cumberland would not wait until after July 17 if it had a chance to move the law school to another institution that would meet its offer. I also was concerned about how Memphis State would fare in an SREB study.

The SREB had been created on February 8, 1948, by the governors of Tennessee, Florida, Maryland, Georgia, Louisiana, Alabama, Mississippi, Arkansas, North Carolina, South Carolina, Texas, Oklahoma, West Virginia and Virginia, to provide a full range of higher education programs on a regional basis. Certain states would offer programs to students of other states in certain specific specialized fields, on a prearranged basis, with each state paying the host institution the equivalent of the out-of-state fee.

The SREB staff was professional and competent, but none of the State Board institutions was included in this interstate agency. On the other hand, the University of Tennessee was one of the major participants in the SREB, and, at that time, Governor Ellington was its chairman.

The SREB was asked to make a fact-finding study as to whether Tennessee needed a second state-supported law school. Dr. Winfred L. Godwin, director of the SREB, would direct the study, with the results due July 17. The Joint Committee would require additional time to analyze the results before it could make its recommendations. The time that would be needed for the prescribed procedure was simply not available in view of Cumberland's situation.

On May 30 John Folger, associate director of the SREB, wrote to me asking for the results of a compilation I had made of the educational background of Memphis lawyers. Further, the SREB arranged for two consultants, Russell N. Sullivan, dean of the law school at the University of Illinois, and Charles Turck, former dean of the University of Kentucky Law School, to accompany Dr. Folger on visits to Memphis, Nashville, and Knoxville, June 27–30.

In the interim there was a groundswell of support in the Memphis area and across the state for moving the Cumberland Law School to Memphis State.

The Shelby County Cumberland alumni met in Memphis on June 5 and passed a resolution saying, "Cumberland men have a duty to use their collective and individual influence in behalf of Memphis State."

The alumni decided to mount a letter-writing campaign to reach 800 Cumberland alumni both in Tennessee and elsewhere urging them to write to Governor Ellington and Andrew Holt, president of the University of Tennessee, in support of the Cumberland proposal. The letters that were sent out on June 12 bore the caption, "This Is Not A

Plea For Money, But Your Moral Support." In response, Governor Ellington received numerous letters from Cumberland graduates across the South.

Many prominent citizens wrote to the governor. Judge A. B. Neil, a retired Chief Justice of the State Supreme Court and a former dean of the Cumberland Law School, urged him to "use his influence to transfer this great school to Memphis." Harry Phillips, a prominent Nashville lawyer and later a judge of the United States Court of Appeals for the Sixth Circuit, was personally visited and wrote on behalf of a statewide committee of Cumberland alumni which had been organized to support the move.

Leroy Collins, former Governor of Florida and a Cumberland graduate, was the subject of a lengthy interview by the *Memphis Press-Scimitar* on May 20 in which he said that he had spoken with me and that he was "very much interested in moving Cumberland to Memphis." William A. Klutts, executive secretary of the West Tennessee Mayors Conference, wrote to the governor on behalf of 40 municipal officials in the area expressing "their strong feeling that West Tennessee is gravely in need of fully accredited law-school facilities, such as the transfer of Cumberland University to Memphis State would provide."

In Memphis a group of lawyers mounted a drive to promote the transfer of the city's two evening law schools to Memphis State. They supported a plan to combine all three schools, the Cumberland Law School and the two evening schools, to provide full-time legal instruction at Memphis State. This group said that if the Cumberland proposal should fall through, plans should continue to bring the evening law schools to Memphis State. In previous efforts to expand the educational programs of Memphis State to meet the needs of the area it served, there had been no great interest or support outside of Memphis and West Tennessee. The support of the Cumberland alumni and lawyers from all parts of the state and nation was a significant development and undoubtedly made an impact upon the governor.

On June 16 I sent a lengthy report to the SREB that I felt would help justify the transfer of Cumberland to Memphis. Included in the material was data showing the legal education of 904 lawyers in Memphis as listed in the most recent edition of Martindale-Hubbell, the national directory of lawyers. Sixty-nine law schools were represented in the survey of the legal education of the lawyers of Memphis; the seven with the largest number of graduates were Southern Law University (Memphis)—181; Vanderbilt—119; University of Memphis Law School (Memphis)—90; University of Tennessee—73; Cumberland University—54; University of Virginia 43; and University of Mississippi—41.

This seemed to indicate that a relatively small percentage of attorneys in Memphis had received their legal training at the University of Tennessee, and that with three years of prelaw training required (subsequently increased to four years), plus three years of professional training, fewer students from the Memphis area would be able to travel 425 miles and pay the cost of residence away from home for legal training at UT Knoxville.

The report also pointed out that in a questionnaire completed by 87 prelaw students at Memphis State, only three indicated that they planned to attend the University of Tennessee Law School. When asked how many would attend Cumberland Law School if it were located in Memphis, all 87 indicated that they would follow that course.

In the report, it was noted that both Southern Law University, which provided the legal training for more members of the Memphis bar than any other law school, and the University of Memphis Law School, which provided the legal training for the third largest number of lawyers in Memphis, had indicated in letters to Memphis State that if an approved law school should be established on the campus, they would be interested in consolidating their resources with this law school and ending their operations.

The owners of both of these schools made their offer contingent upon the offering of evening classes.

Dr. Folger, Dean Sullivan, and Dr. Turck, the SREB consultants, were to arrive in Memphis on June 29. I made arrangements for them to meet with prominent Memphis attorneys Walter Armstrong, Walter Chandler, Shepard Tate, William Farris, Sam Margolin, Judge John E. Swepston, and Chancellor Robert A. Hoffmann.

On June 27, just two days before the SREB team was to arrive in Memphis, the feared but not unanticipated blow fell. The *Memphis Press-Scimitar* headed a front-page story, "Alabama College Gets Cumberland." The story reported that "MSU's hopes to acquire Cumberland Law School were dashed today with the official announcement that the law school would be moved to Howard College in Birmingham."

I called it "a tragic loss for Memphis and West Tennessee," and the story quoted me further as saying,

> Memphis has the need and the money to buy the law school, but delaying tactics used by those opposed to Memphis and West Tennessee having a fine accredited law school such as Cumberland were successful.
>
> Cumberland, unable to wait out this tactical delay, had no choice but to take the only definite offer made.
>
> This example of selfishness by those opposed to Cumberland coming to Memphis has resulted in denying of a great opportunity to the youth of Memphis and West Tennessee.

I requested that the SREB study not be made because the risk of an unfavorable report would prejudice any new effort to establish a law school at Memphis State without Cumberland. The procedure prescribed by the subcommittee and its schedule, from the beginning, made it inevitable that Cumberland would have to seek another affiliation.

A battle had been lost, but not the war.

A number of allies in Memphis and West Tennessee had been won over to the idea that Memphis State could, with sufficient support, provide many missing educational opportunities for West Tennessee.

Numerous letters were received at Memphis State from Cumberland alumni, educators, and others across the state expressing disappointment that the Cumberland Law School had been lost to Tennessee. Memphis State had made many friends by its efforts to keep Cumberland in the state. There is little doubt that Governor Ellington and officials of the University of Tennessee were made aware by their friends that Cumberland should not have been lost to Tennessee.

Interest then shifted toward consolidating the two evening law schools into a full-time law school that would open at Memphis State in the fall of 1962. Chancellor Robert A. Hoffmann, head of the 62-year-old University of Memphis Law School which had 48 students, reported to *The Commercial Appeal* on July 3 that he was "ready to see his school move to the Memphis State campus, but (that) night classes should be continued there, in addition to day classes." In the same news story Sam Margolin, head of Southern Law University, also gave his support to the establishment of a full-time law school at Memphis State. He too felt that classes should be offered at night.

In July, the University of Memphis Law Alumni began developing a plan to raise money to buy that school and make it a part of Memphis State. Abe D. Waldauer, attorney and alumnus of that law school, was named chairman of an alumni committee. Waldauer told the *Memphis Press-Scimitar*, "The alumni are organizing to make a gift of the law school to the State of Tennessee to be part of MSU."

No official action regarding a law school was requested or taken by the SBE at its August or November meetings in 1961. However, conversations continued in Memphis with representatives of the two evening law schools.

Waldauer, with members of his committee, had raised most of the $5000 needed to purchase half of the stock of the University of Memphis Law School. The other half was owned by the widow of S. Walter Jones, the dean of the school for many years, and the grandchildren of the dean, who donated their stock to the group. Sam Margolin agreed that Southern Law University would not start a new class and that he would close his school within two years and donate its library to Memphis State if a law school was established there.

Of great importance in the continuing effort to obtain a law school at Memphis State was the widely expressed disappointment across the state by highly regarded citizens at the loss of Cumberland. The influence of this feeling could be detected in a statement by Governor Ellington, in which he made no mention of the Joint Committee, that legislation was not necessary to establish a new law school and that a decision as to whether Memphis State should establish one was up to the State Board.

Many people, particularly in West Tennessee, blamed the University of Tennessee, rightly or wrongly, for the loss of Cumberland. President Holt also received such criticism. Because of this criticism it was believed that a new effort to establish a law school at Memphis State would meet with little opposition from UT.

At the SBE meeting on February 9, 1962, I recommended that a law school be established at Memphis State. A comprehensive justification was presented, including a review of the Cumberland effort, interest shown in Memphis and West Tennessee, and excerpts from a report by the American Bar Association that indicated that the nation's law schools were not graduating a sufficient number of qualified students to meet the needs of society. I told the board that action should be taken quickly if the program was to be started in the fall of 1962.

Chairman Joe Morgan named a five-man committee to study the feasibility of establishing a law school at Memphis State in September. The committee included James Williams of Henderson, Ernest Ball of Memphis, W. R. Landrum of Trenton, Edward F. Jennings of Liberty, and Thornton Strang of Chattanooga. It is noteworthy that three members were from West Tennessee.

On April 3, a special session of the SBE considered Chairman Morgan's recommendation that the board authorize a law school to be established at Memphis State University. The committee which had been appointed at the February 9 board meeting presented a comprehensive report. It closed with a unanimous recommendation that a law school be established at Memphis State University, beginning with the fall term of 1962–63. Morgan reported that the Joint Committee of the State Board of Education and the University of Tennessee recommended its establishment on March 14, 1962. No study by the SREB had been required this time.

The Board adopted the motion by a unanimous voice vote.

I was well aware that the attitudes of Governor Ellington and UT President Holt toward a second state-supported law school had been swayed by the tremendous response across the state to the loss of Cumberland; thus, I had anticipated the approval of the school by the Board, and had prepared certain proposals for the beginning operation of the school.

I requested that the Board establish a fee structure for the law school students on both a full-time and part-time basis, explaining that since there was a demand for evening classes and the offering of evening classes was a condition placed by the Southern Law University on its offer to phase out its operation, a fee schedule for part-time students would be necessary.

The fee for full-time students was set at $225 per year, $112.50 per semester, and this fee was prorated on a per-hour basis for part-time students. This was the same fee that was being charged at the University of Tennessee Law School. The dean of the law school was to be classified on the same basis as the academic dean for salary rating purposes. Projected enrollment for the school was 100 students. There was to be a faculty of two full-time instructors, one of whom would serve as dean, and a number of part-time instructors, who would be practicing attorneys, for the evening division.

In a little less than 11 months since the effort had started, the goal had been achieved. It had been a hard fought battle. Memphis State now had a law school on paper, authorized to open in five months.

All that needed to be done was to obtain a dean and faculty, find space for the new school on an already overcrowded campus, acquire a library, establish a curriculum and academic requirements, arrange for the acceptance of students, and "scratch up" the funds with which to operate the school. Also, I implied, but not promised, to the board that the school could get approval by the American Bar Association within three years. There was little time and much to be done in preparation for the opening of the law school in September.

I conferred with President Stockton of Cumberland, who suggested I contact Dr. John G. Hervey of Oklahoma City, the regional representative of the Legal Education and Admissions Section of the American Bar Association. I wrote to Dr. Hervey on April 11, explaining the authorization by the SBE to start a law school and the proposal to absorb the two privately owned evening law schools. I asked Dr. Hervey to visit Memphis State to discuss the steps that would be necessary to establish the school. He was extremely helpful with his suggestions and encouragement.

I also visited Dean John Wade and Professor Elliott E. Cheatham of the Vanderbilt School of Law, seeking advice and information. Both were quite helpful. Professor Cheatham, especially, seemed intrigued by the audacity of trying to establish a law school from scratch and with so little time to do it. He was willing to help and suggested prospects for a dean for the new school.

John Porter, president of the Memphis and Shelby County Bar Association, was asked by me to appoint a committee to assist Memphis State in establishing the law school. Members of the committee were Harold Streibich, chairman; Elmore Holmes, III, secretary; Abe Waldauer; Thomas Turley, Jr.; J. Woodrow Norwell; Charles G. Black;

and Hall Crawford. They also served on various subcommittees that were called on for advice and assistance in getting the new school into operation.

The involvement of the local bar association was important in the planning stage, and it continued to serve with dedication for many years. There were other indications of support for the new law school. The family of Judge John D. Martin, who served as judge of the United States District Court in West Tennessee and of the United States Court of Appeals for the Sixth Circuit, requested that memorials to Judge Martin be sent to the Memphis State Law School. Milton Fortas sent a contribution of $500. Leo E. Levy left $5000 in his will to Memphis State, and the SBE approved the use of these funds for the law library. Abe Waldauer, as chairman of the trustees of the Kahn Trust, provided $2000 for a salary supplement for a law librarian.

The most important step at this stage was obtaining a dean who could pull together all the pieces that were needed for the opening of the school in September. Many names were submitted by interested persons, and there was a frenzy of telephone calls and letters to those who had been recommended. Two broad categories of prospects emerged: Those with established names and reputations in legal education who could take their retirement from their present positions, and those younger and less well known, but highly regarded by the profession, who were brave enough to undertake the tremendous challenge of starting a new school of law in a few months with limited resources.

In early June, Robert D. Cox, a young member of the faculty of the school of law at the University of Tulsa, was employed as acting dean. Because of teaching commitments in Tulsa, he could not report to Memphis State until later in the summer. However, he came to Memphis almost every weekend. On these visits and with the able assistance of Dr. Calvin Street, the director of the Evening Divison, the many arrangements necessary for the opening of the law school in September were begun.

On June 20, a petition for approval of the law school was submitted to the Board of Law Examiners of the State of Tennessee. The petition said classes would begin September 17, 1962, and provide for both a day and evening division.

The day division would offer only the first year of law school, but would add the second year in 1963–64, and the third year in 1964–65. The evening division would begin the fall term of 1962 with a complete schedule of classes. The courses of study in both the day and evening divisions would be the same and would meet the minimum standards of the ABA for a law library as soon as possible. There would be a full-time teaching staff of not less than two law professors and a law librarian for the fall term, 1962, and additional teaching members of the faculty would be part-time instructors from the local bar who were lawyers of known ability and integrity, and who had been enrolled members of the Tennessee Supreme Court Bar in actual practice for at least five years.

Physical space for the new law school on the Memphis State campus had to be found during the summer months. Enrollment at the university had increased from 5279 in 1960 to 6284 in 1961, and was expected to reach almost 8000 for the fall term of 1962, creating a severe academic space problem. However, arrangements were made for offices and classrooms in Johnson Hall, and a reading room in the Old Library was converted into a law library. These were not fine facilities, but they were all that were available.

On September 24, 1962, the law school began operations a little more than five months after official approval. The law school was a reality.

Its birth had not been calm, nor easy, but it represented the hopes and dreams of many people to provide another needed educational opportunity at Memphis State.

Dean Robert Cox wrote a letter of appreciation to the Memphis and Shelby County Bar Association Special Committee on Law Schools and Legal Education on September 27, 1962, describing the law school at the beginning of its first year:

> We have begun operations with an excellent beginning library of approximately 10,000 volumes and an initial enrollment of more than 140 students. There is no reason to believe that the quality of instruction for which we have arranged will be less than excellent.
>
> Our facilities now are adequate and will improve at the end of the present academic year. We have active plans for the institution of student

organizations and publications in the near future, as well as for the expansion of the curriculum and faculty.

In short, we have the foundation upon which an outstanding Law School can be built.

President Humphreys' monograph handled a severe tiff with the University of Tennessee accurately, but with more diplomacy than might be expected.

When he returned from the SRB meeting of May 24, 1961, where Tennessee, his alma mater, had stacked the deck against moving the Cumberland Law School to Memphis State, his secretary Mrs. Virginia Vickery, took one look at him and asked, "Are you sick?"

He shook his head; he was sick at heart.

Early in 1965, exactly three years after he won the law school, the American Bar Association's House of Delegates accredited the Memphis State University Law School, fulfilling one of Humphreys' "implied" promises.

The University of Tennessee may have fought a native son in opposing Cumberland Law School moving to Memphis State, but its respect for Cecil Humphreys never diminished. It grew. On May 5, 1978, the University of Tennessee Center for Health Sciences in Memphis, at the suggestion of Abe Plough, who had given the Center $1,000,000, named a new $15 million structure the Cecil C. Humphreys General Education Building.

One day later, May 6, the Memphis State Law School unveiled a portrait and plaque naming the facility the Memphis State University Cecil C. Humphreys School of Law.

These were only two of many honors. In June of 1966 Rhodes College, then Southwestern, a prestigious liberal arts institution, conferred an honorary Doctor of Laws degree on Humphreys. On January 25, 1973, Christian Brothers College of Memphis also presented him with a doctoral degree, a Doctor of Pedagogy. His educational peers knew— and acknowledged—his outstanding achievements.

5

Fifty Years Beyond Normal

1962–1963

Troops from the 101st Airborne Division sent to Oxford after rioting breaks out over admission of James Meredith, a black student, to Ole Miss...President Kennedy announces U.S. has photographic evidence Russia is building missile bases in Cuba, orders naval blockade. Russia says it will remove missiles; U.S. promises not to attack Cuba...Stamps for first class letters raised to five cents ...Two black students enroll at University of Alabama despite Governor Wallace's vow to stand in the doorway... Supreme Court rules that Bible reading in public schools is unconstitutional.

AND THE WAY WE WERE

Total teaching staff numbers 302, 58 new...Special for MSU–Ole Miss game: large football mum corsage—72¢ ...Tempers flared high over the proposed consolidation of Memphis and Shelby County in debate on campus...The MS Cub Club, in conjunction with the Highland 100, is sponsoring a project to buy a live tiger as a MSU mascot...Students fire complaints at cafeteria...Approximately 38% of freshman class fail English classes...Cafeteria manager cites several major improvements...300 students are recognized in Honors Assembly.

STUDENTS STACKED THE CRATES AND BOXES and lit the campus bon fires to happy shouts of approval. The MSU Marching Band, a resplendent 100 strong for the first time and labelled "the Pride and Joy of the Southland," turned loose its horns and drums in musical celebration. In the Claridge Hotel downtown, alumni danced the anniversary waltz. The city's two daily newspapers, *The Commercial Appeal* and the *Memphis Press-Scimitar,* published special sections saluting the occasion.

Memphis State University was 50 years old, and it had a lot of Homecoming help in putting the candles on its birthday cake in the fall of 1962, a momentous time for the nation and world. Havana and Oxford became datelines around the globe, one for its missile base crisis and the other for an integration riot. Life goes on in narrower spheres, however, and the anniversary celebration proceeded. It was due.

In halving a century the university had shown a little steel in its backbone; it would have perished otherwise. In time's scheme of things, Memphis State's Normal School beginnings were only 50 years distant. In a modern educational sense the university could have considered itself a world away from its origin, but the supposed normal school stigma had only been in the eyes of a few Memphians, certainly never in the minds of the Blue and Gray standard bearers. Ernest Ball, a celebrated educator, was one of those.

When Normal School opened in 1912, Ball had enrolled as a lower school student. In 1926 he was in the graduating class that received West Tennessee State Teachers College first baccalaureate degrees. Later, he would head the largest public school system in the state. Ball, a member of the State Board of Education, was a staunch supporter of his alma mater and a confidant of Cecil C. Humphreys.

The measure of an educational institution rests with the quality of its graduates, then and now, and Ernest Ball exemplified the mission of education in Humphreys' mind.

All the indices suggest Memphis State was not a comprehensive uni-

The construction program under Humphreys is evident in this 1962 view of the campus. The first "new" building, Business Adminstration (now Mitchell Hall), is completed while the Campus School (*extreme right*) is under construction.

versity in 1962, but it was an emerging one with a 48-year-old president who also was a rising star on the state scene. Cecil Humphreys was at the right place at the right time.

The tip of the 1960s enrollment iceberg hove into sight dramatically in 1962 with a record headcount of 7529, an increase of 1284 over the previous fall. Instead of the projected 100 students, the new Law School enrolled 258 students in both day and night classes. Long sought by West Tennessee schoolteachers, the MSU-UT Center for Graduate Education opened with 112 students enrolled in doctoral programs.

With 58 new professors and instructors aboard for the first time, the faculty counted 302 members, who noticed an expanding physical plant. They found Smith Hall, East Hall (later named Browning Hall), and the School of Business building ready for occupancy. Typical of the university's growth was the art department. In 1954, when Dr. Dana Johnson came to Memphis State as department head, it was a one-man show. There were 13 faculty members in 1962 and 1500 students enrolled in art classes. More than 300 students were art majors.

The cultural role of the university broadened each year in the 1960s, and in 1962 Eric Salmon, an English actor and director, became Artist in Residence in the Speech and Drama Department. Salmon directed the eleventh season of the Shakespeare Festival, an annual event which had great support in the community and on campus.

Intercollegiate football took the spotlight in October as the Memphis State Tigers defeated Mississippi State at Starkville. It was the first triumph over a Southeastern Conference team, and a giant pep rally celebrated the achievement.

So expansive were the feelings that the Highland 100 Club and the Cub Club spoke of buying a live tiger as MSU's mascot. The administration wondered what was wrong with a Tiger suit worn by a student, but the boosters would win this one.

When the 1962–63 basketball season got underway, the sports momentum continued. Crowds in the university's Field House, which seated 4500, had to take to the aisles. The crush for the University of Dayton game was such that the fire marshal delayed the contest and threatened to arrest Dean Robison unless the aisles were cleared.

Growing pains affected all areas of the university.

Memphis State, one of the first all-white state institutions of higher learning in the South to admit black students, was doing well in race relations in 1962, its fourth year as an integrated school. There had been no major problems since five young black women and three black men began classes in 1959.

That was not the case at the University of Mississippi in the fall of 1962, and MSU's president kept a wary eye on events unfolding at Oxford where tensions built throughout September. Memphis served as a base for federal officials involved in the struggle with Mississippi officials, and Cecil Humphreys knew Memphis State students were watching the legal skirmishing with strong, and perhaps mixed, feelings.

The Ole Miss riot broke out on Sunday night, September 30, over the admission of James Meredith, its first black student. Two men were killed and the campus became a small battlefield as hundreds of U.S. marshals tried to hold a line in front of the Lyceum. President Kennedy sent in Mississippi National Guardsmen to assist as Army troops rolled south from Fort Campbell, Kentucky.

Federal forces headquartered at the Memphis Naval Air Station in Millington faced white pickets waving Confederate flags and holding up signs saying: "Troops for Cuba, si; for Mississippi, no."

President Humphreys watched the Sunday evening news on television. There was full coverage of the Ole Miss riot, with gunfire, burning of cars, tear gas, and jeering mobs of students and others.

The next morning on campus Humphreys received disturbing information: A number of Memphis State students had been in Oxford on Sunday. In its Tuesday editions *The Commercial Appeal* ran a story under a headline saying, "Memphis students stream to Oxford." It reported two Southwestern students had been held for questioning on Monday. The story quoted one Southwestern student as saying that 40 percent of the school's freshman class went to Oxford during the weekend.

A paragraph about "scores of students" from Memphis State being in Oxford or shouting at troops along highways leading out of Memphis grabbed Humphreys' attention. He did not want that virus on his campus. Humphreys immediately sent out an announcement—to be read at each class that Tuesday—that if the university learned that any student went to Oxford that week, either as a spectator or participant in the troubles there, he would be expelled. "MSU should have no part in adding to these troubles," Humphreys' statement said.

The directive apparently worked, but it raised a question or two. "A couple of days after the announcement," Humphreys recalled, "I had a conversation with Professor Larry Wynn. He asked, in his usual polite manner, 'How could you expel a student for going to Oxford, Mississippi?' I replied that I didn't think I could, but that by the time they found out that I couldn't, the danger to them and to our campus would be abated."

Humphreys, upon reflection, knew that he was being a surrogate parent, as in the old days. He also knew that time had passed; it just happened to work in 1962. Notes in his personal file said, "With the changes coming in the next few years the principle of 'in loco parentis' would be obsolete, and the expanded rights of students would have prevented such action."

In truth, there would be a complete reversal of attitudes. In the "good old days" parents thought college campuses had to be protected from outside forces. But in the 1960s cities and towns with universities feared student demonstrations and other encroachments into their lives and businesses.

Accreditation is more than a buzz word in institutions of learning, and much of the evaluation in that process begins at home. In 1960 the Southern Association of Colleges and Schools, the accrediting agency for schools in the South, began a new program of evaluation. Under it, each institution made a comprehensive self-study preceding a visit from the association's evaluation committee.

President Humphreys directed that Memphis State should be one of the first to take part. "All segments of the university were involved," Humphreys said, "and a very comprehensive and objective report was prepared after considerable work by the faculty and administration in the 1961–1962 school year."

The Southern Association's evaluation committee came to the campus in November of 1962. One of the conclusions of the visiting committee was that Memphis State needed a separate governing board rather than being included with five smaller colleges under the governance of the State Board of Education. "It must be recognized that in the past few years the institution has changed from a relatively small college to a large and complex urban university," the committee said.

Another finding was that salaries "of administrative officials are inadequate and the total amount of money for administration is inadequate." The chairman of the committee told the campus newspaper, "MSU is growing rapidly, is in crowded facilities and is in urgent need of better financial support." This was not news to Humphreys.

For Humphreys, there was no off-season in pleading the need for increased financial support, and a biennial session of the General Assembly was coming up in 1963. "I knew every legislator from West Tennessee was important to Memphis State," Humphreys said, "but the support of the Shelby County delegation was crucial." After the November general election Humphreys entertained the Shelby delegation, all Democrats, at a dinner on campus. He pointed out what the state was doing and what it should be doing for Memphis State and other institutions. Humphreys noted that neighboring Mississippi with a per capita income of $1173 spent $15.39 per capita on higher education while Tennessee, with a per capita income of $1545 provided $10.52.

As it turned out, higher education had a major friend in Nashville— Governor Frank Clement. Shortly after the opening of eighty-third General Assembly he presented a budget with increases for most state operations, but education was the pacesetter. His recommendations included $3,404,000 for Memphis State in 1963–64 and $4,142,000 in 1964–65. The 1962–63 appropriation had been $2,198,245. This increase of more than a million dollars for the first year was the largest in any one year period in Memphis State's history.

"We were pleased with the recommended increase for the first year, but this was not assured," Humphreys said. "The governor did not say where the funds for the increased state budget would come from, saying only that taxes would have to be increased and that he would suggest a plan later."

When Clement revealed that the major source of new revenue would be a 3 percent sales tax on utilities, a legislative fight started immediately.

Cecil Humphreys did not sit on the sidelines. Too much was at stake

Assisted by Bill McElroy, president of Highland Hundred *(center)*, and President Humphreys, Governor Frank Clement dons a MSU jacket to become a "Tiger." Clement was a strong supporter of higher education throughout the state.

for Memphis State. *The Commercial Appeal* headlined his views: "Humphreys Voices Support for Governor's Tax Plan." For 19 out of 19 years Memphis State had been shortchanged on per-student appropriations compared to other state-supported institutions. "This is the first time in years that we have had what approaches equal treatment," Humphreys told the newspaper. He added that the public schools in Memphis and Shelby County, as well as the University of Tennessee Medical Units in Memphis, would suffer if the proposed funds were not made available.

There were other revenue measures suggested by Clement, but opposition focused principally on the utilities tax. Nashville's morning newspaper, *The Tennessean,* vigorously opposed it, claiming in almost daily editorials the utility tax would drive industry out of the state and hurt the development of new industry. Joining with *The Tennessean* in the political battle were the Tennessse Public Power Association, the Memphis Light, Gas & Water Division, and others. Many rural legislators strongly opposed the tax.

Lining up with the governor was the Tennessee Education Association. It called on teachers to let their legislators know of their support. Under the proposed funding for education, public school teachers would receive a $500 increase in pay.

College officials joined the fray. Humphreys' primary lobbying was with the Memphis and Shelby County members of the General Assembly, but he also worked West Tennessee.

"Considerable preliminary work had been done with the legislators," Humphreys said, "but the effort now shifted to a one-on-one situation in Nashville. We worked the corridors of the Capitol and even the floor of the Senate and House chambers. At that time you could go into the chambers and sit with a legislator at his desk. For several weeks I spent more time in Nashville than on campus."

In February the Senate passed the utility tax bill after a hard-fought political battle, 18–15. Humphreys and others quickly turned to lobby work in the House; he expected an even harder fight there. *The Tennessean* on February 20, 1963, reported: "The toughest legislative battle in years is predicted for today." The story said both sides claimed enough votes to win. It said there were fourteen legislators who were undecided.

The following day, after much oratory and complicated parliamentary skirmishing, Governor Frank Clement's forces won over most of the uncommitted legislators. Others, noting the swing, decided to get aboard. Clement's utility tax was approved, 63–34.

Humphreys said a utility tax was not the most equitable tax with which to provide funds for public services, but noted that an income tax was prohibited by the Tennessee constitution.

All thirteen representatives and the four senators from Memphis and Shelby County supported the revenue bill. Only three votes from all of West Tennessee were cast against the bill in the House. Cecil Humphreys, other educators, and the forces of Governor Clement had struck a significant blow in behalf of higher education.

Memphis State gained much more than the one-million-dollars increase in operational funds. There was a major increase in capital funds to relieve crowded conditions at all the schools. The six institutions under the SBE received $11,869,000. The board, recognizing that Memphis State was its fastest growing school, allocated it $3,352,934.

"There were only 18 months before the opening of the 1964–65 fall session," Humphreys said, "and the crowded conditions on campus during the current year were difficult. With a projected enrollment increase of over 30 percent by the fall of 1964, we knew that without more physical facilities for students and faculty we faced a chaotic situation."

He went before the State Board and received approval for a $950,000 Biology Building, a $750,000 School of Education Building, and $1,800,000 for two new residence halls. The one for women students would be six stories, the tallest building on campus. Both it and the new men's residence hall would be the first to have air conditioning. To assist in building the dormitories, a $1,440,000 loan would be obtained from the federal Housing and Home Finance Authority, with the loan to be repaid from rental revenues.

In addition to these projects $100,000 would be spent reworking the campus electrical system, $250,000 for an addition to the Physical Education Building and $175,000 to add a floor to the School of Business Building. The SBE also approved the addition of two suites to the Panhellenic Building. It would be financed by the sororities requesting the new space.

Humphreys could feel that he was on a bit of a roll in 1962–63; he edged tradition several times. One of his triumphs involved the SBE's stand against more than one dean other than a dean of women at the six universities under its jurisdiction. The presidents had recommended in 1958 that the titles of directors be changed to deans. A board committee recommended that action be deferred, and it was.

At the November 9, 1962, meeting of the SBE Humphreys recommended that directors become deans. He pointed to the growth of the four schools at Memphis State and said the title of director created confusion for students, the public, and people in the academic world.

In a bit of surprise the board agreed with Humphreys, and Memphis State had four new deans.

At its May meeting in 1962 the State Board of Education had approved the position of Academic Dean, and Humphreys had launched a search for one. In addition to the usual qualifications President Humphreys wanted another quality. "The additional quality that was needed for leadership in the academic area was the ability to apply the tools of research to the solving of institutional problems," he said. "Higher education had become heavily involved in many kinds of research in recent years, but had been slow to apply research techniques to its own decision making. This was needed to achieve the orderly and maximum development of the university."

It involved good management, but Humphreys avoided the word. "The word 'management' as applied to the academic area was avoided because many with a traditional academic background would have concluded that business methods were being usesd to make academic decisions and resent it," he said.

A smart man, Humphreys turned to the euphemistic term of "institutional research" instead of management, and he picked Dr. John Baird Morris to be the new academic dean. At the time of his appointment he was a professor in the department of psychology at the University of Mississippi and director of institutional research. Earlier, Dr. Morris had served as director of institutional research at the University of Minnesota.

During the school year Greater Memphis State, Inc., named Cecil Humphreys Educator-of-the-Year at its annual meeting at the University Club, and he won an ovation from the 300 persons in attendance. A former winner of the coveted award was Ernest Ball.

Cecil Humphreys always sought ways to tell the Memphis State story. Perhaps it had to do with his sense of history. Back in the 1950s when President Jack Smith felt comfortable with Humphreys as athletic director, head of the Graduate School and as his assistant, the tireless Humphreys also directed public relations for Memphis State.

Surprisingly, for he was a master at it, Humphreys considered communications as one of his weaknesses. He was wrong. When he did not know how to handle a certain point involving the media and the public, Humphreys had a knack for cultivating friends who did. In the early 1950s he often turned to Harry Woodbury and Gene Roper to help tell Memphis State's story. Woodbury, a former reporter for *The Commercial Appeal,* was an advertising and public relations executive in a firm, Archer & Woodbury, with Ward Archer. Woodbury also served in the administration of Mayor Henry Loeb, who took office the same year Humphreys became president of Memphis State. Roper, who had worked at the university as alumni secretary and in other capacities, later became a television executive in Memphis and Boston.

Early in the 1960s Humphreys detected that a growing university needed a different approach to public relations. The time when a news bureau had to operate on $8 a week, with $5 going to a student assistant and $3 for stamps, had passed. In 1962 he hired a director of public information, Charles F. Holmes, an MSU graduate who was a reporter for *The Commercial Appeal.* Holmes was an aggressive newsman who had been editor of *The Tiger Rag* when he graduated in 1957. For many months Holmes directed a one-man operation from the third floor of the Administration Building. His office was a revamped women's lounge. It was a humble beginning, but, as Holmes was to say later, it gave him time to learn about public and community relations.

Humphreys and Holmes made a good team in telling the Memphis State story. And, as the university grew, so did its public relations staff. Today Holmes heads a staff of 20 professionals and 20 student assistants as director of community relations.

In the summer of 1963 Humphreys was among 40 educators and religious leaders across the country who were invited to Israel. Abe Waldauer, the Memphis attorney who had aided Humphreys in his fight to establish a law school at Memphis State, nominated Humphreys. Waldauer was a member of the Inter-University Committee on Israel, and he would be instrumental in future academic expansions at Memphis State.

The trip abroad began on July 17 and ended on August 15. Humphreys, who had been turning in 15-hour work days consistently, needed the break. It would be one of the few he would be able to take during the rest of the 1960s. The momentous days in a university's growth were just beginning.

6

The Herff Connection

1963–1964

More than 200,000 civil rights activists march on Washington, and Dr. Martin Luther King, Jr., delivers his "I have a dream" speech...South Vietnamese generals kill President Ngo Dinh Diem and his brother, overthrowing the government...a sniper assassinates President John F. Kennedy; police arrest Lee Harvey Oswald, an expatriate to Russia, and charge him with the crime; Jack Ruby shoots and kills Oswald in Dallas police station...President Lyndon Johnson declares national "war on poverty" in State of Union address...Authorities discover the bodies of three young civil rights workers near Philadelphia, Mississippi.

AND THE WAY WE WERE

A new self-service bookstore which replaces the old counter-style business is now open; students must possess integrity if the new bookstore is to succeed...the new $250,000 academic computer center begins operations in five areas ...Students circulate petition favoring live tiger mascot... The student section in the Fieldhouse is being enlarged for basketball...Memphis' finest bar-b-que sandwich—25¢... President Humphreys reports MSU has finest record of any southern institution of higher education in the integration of student body...Student leaders meet and discuss efforts to quell growing racial tensions.

SYNERGISM, AN OLD WORD OF GREEK AND LATIN ORIGIN, worked its modern magic in behalf of Memphis State University in the 1963–1964 school year.

Separate activities and initiatives coming together simultaneously produced a greater total effect than the simple sum or list might suggest. Internal and external forces contributed, and the university's bonding with the city strengthened. The city and county voted to give funds to university research. To the elation of the community, Coach Billy (Spook) Murphy's football Tigers went undefeated and enjoyed a Main Street parade. Abe Waldauer, an old friend of Cecil Humphreys and the university, built the bridge for Herbert Herff's remarkable connection with Memphis State.

New names with new missions appeared on campus: Ronald Carrier, R. Eugene Smith, Paul Lowry, Haskell Harrison, and F. H. Kellogg, among many others. Mostly administrators, they mixed in with 42 new faculty members.

Cecil Humphreys' dream of building a comprehensive university tied closely to its community and region had reached the front door in 1963. The key was in his hand.

Ending more than two years of indecision, Memphis and Shelby County governments committed $35,000 a year for the university to operate a Bureau of Business Research. President Humphreys promptly filled the top post with Dr. Ronald E. Carrier, associate professor in the School of Business at the University of Mississippi. Barely in his 30s, Carrier brought Paul Lowry, who had been with the Bureau of Business and Economic Research at Ole Miss, with him as associate director. Also coming with Carrier was Van N. Oliphant, a graduate student who worked part-time in the bureau. Oliphant is now vice president for advancement and continuing education. A whirlwind of activity followed.

At a breakfast meeting with 36 government and business leaders in the University Cafeteria, Carrier outlined the bureau's services and announced that a quarterly publication, *The Memphis Business Review,* would survey business conditions in the city and county. He said there also would be an annual publication reviewing economic conditions and making forecasts for the coming year.

Early in November Carrier invited business and civic leaders to help organize a Research Roundtable, and the first volume of *The Memphis Business Review* appeared on November 17, 1963.

The Commercial Appeal gave a strong editorial endorsement to the new bureau. It said, "No one firm is prepared to look at the broad business picture of Memphis and the Mid-South so comprehensively as the Bureau of Business Research will." Carrier, whose star would rise rapidly at Memphis State, closed the calendar year with plans for a Business Outlook Conference for Mid-South business leaders.

Aiding Carrier and others was the opening of a new computer center on campus, with its equipment valued at $250,000. It would be used for research, computer classes, and administrative record keeping. The computer also would be available to Mid-South industry on a time-rent basis.

Another step was taken to improve the efficiency and effectiveness of university operations. But, as usual, Humphreys had to convince the State Board of Education that an internal auditor was needed. "There had been no serious problems in the routine audits of the university's financial operations by the State Comptroller's office," Humphreys said, "but the funds accountable for by the university had doubled in the past three years." A somewhat reluctant SBE agreed with Humphreys' view that growth dictated a need to improve the business structure of the school. For this key post President Humphreys selected R. Eugene Smith, director of the audit division in the state comptroller's office.

Haskell Harrison also came aboard to fill a need. Harrison, a retired Army major, joined the administrative staff as the first personnel officer for nonprofessional employees, including clerical and maintenance workers.

One of the unusual stories in the school's history began in April with, in collegiate football parlance, "a walk on." That's when an athlete who is not on scholarship walks up to the coach and asks for a chance to make the team.

Dr. F. H. Kellogg, if not a "walk on," was a "walk in." Unannounced,

Kellogg and two colleagues came to President Humphreys' office and said they would like to help establish a graduate program in engineering at Memphis State. Kellogg happened to be the dean of the University of Mississippi College of Engineering, which was fully accredited. Memphis State did not have even an undergraduate engineering program.

Kellogg suggested the university offer a master of science in engineering in its Graduate School. "It was an interesting proposal," Humphreys said. "There was a need because there were about 800 licensed engineers in the largest metropolitan area of the state, but I was not too optimistic because of the recent expansion of academic programs and limited resources."

He reported the proposal to the SBE in an executive session in May of 1963, and, shortly before he left on his trip to Israel, he told Abe Waldauer about Kellogg's visit.

The morning mail on September 20 brought a letter from Herbert Herff, a Memphis businessman and philanthropist, with a completely unexpected proposal: He and Mrs. Herff were prepared to make a gift of $100,000 to start an engineering program at Memphis State.

The letter to President Humphreys asked that the proposal be presented to Governor Frank Clement for acceptance on or before December 1, 1963, and that the SBE approve the proposed school as a permanent part of the academic program at MSU.

"Mr. Waldauer, a close friend and legal adviser to Mr. Herff, undoubtedly instigated the offer," Humphreys said. "The offer was timed to coincide with a visit to Memphis by Governor Clement on September 21.

A committee named by Herff met with the governor on that day. It included several movers and shakers in Memphis, Waldauer, chairman; Frank R. Ahlgren, editor of *The Commercial Appeal;* General Everett Cook, chief executive of a worldwide grain company; John Brown, president of Union Planters National Bank; S. Toof Brown, a printing company executive; Joseph Lewis, Dr. Henry Rudner Jr., and Morrie Moss, who had been finance chairman of Clement's gubernatorial campaign.

Clement, an effusive man, expressed gratitude for Herff's offer,

The support, both in hard work and philanthropic gifts, of several individuals helped make the university's academic and physical growth possible. Pictured are Abe Waldauer *(top left)*, Edward J. Meeman *(top right)*, and Herbert Herff *(left)*.

said it had merit and told the committee he would give it serious consideration.

In Humphreys' words, "It appeared to be a very unusual way to start a new engineering program, and perhaps a little foolhardy when one considered the limited funds available and the cost of engineering education. But it was believed that a state-supported engineering program was needed in West Tennessee, and this unusual opportunity could not be ignored."

Humphreys went to work on a detailed justification for a master of science in engineering and recommended acceptance of the Herff offer to the SBE on November 8, 1963. The board, with no signal from the governor, deferred action.

Governor Clement, who had helped Memphis State obtain university status in his first term as the state's chief executive, apparently needed time to discuss the matter with officials at state institutions already offering engineering–the University of Tennessee, Tennessee Polytechnic Institute, and Tennessee State. "Each institution jealously guarded its territories," Humphreys said, "and he didn't want criticism for what could be said was unnecessary duplication of expensive programs. His political acumen and leadership skills were too great not to prepare the way for acceptance with as little controversy as possible."

Late in November Clement announced the state's acceptance of the Herffs' gift. Support grew immediately. The Memphis Society of Professional Engineers was enthusiastic and presented Humphreys a resolution saying a graduate engineering program would "greatly enhance the city's chances of acquiring new industry and would increase engineering knowledge within existing industries."

An unexpected boost came on December 2 when President Andy Holt of the University of Tennessee made a speech in Memphis and said, "I personally feel there is sufficient demand to justify some type of engineering program at MSU."

There would be no intrastate battle similar to the Cumberland Law School controversy. At the February 7, 1964, meeting of the State Board Ernest Ball introduced a resolution authorizing Memphis State to accept the Herffs' gift and start a master's degree in engineering science. It was approved unanimously.

Dr. Kellogg received a call from Humphreys, and the two began immediately to face the challenge of building a program from ground zero.

The Herff connection would not end with the gift. When the Memphis auto dealer and investor died on December 31, 1966, he left the bulk of his estate in a trust with the State of Tennessee for the benefit of Memphis State. Income from the trust would be used for the colleges of law and engineering. Trustees would be the president of Memphis State, William B. Rudner, Abe Waldauer, William A. Loewenberg, and the chairman of the state board of education. The court transferred the trust's assets of $1,307,511 to the trustees in 1970. In March of 1987 the assets had a market value of $10,517,581.

In addition to the trust Herff had established the Herff Foundation to handle bequests to relatives, friends, and associates, including a $60,000 lifetime annuity to Mrs. Herff. After the bequests were made the income from the principal was to be used for academic scholarships at Memphis State. The Herff Foundation board in 1971 approved the transfer of $982,833 in assets to the Memphis State University Foundation. In March of 1987 the assets of the Herff Foundation had a market value of $1,082,566.

A major use of the funds had been the establishment of chairs in engineering and law. The chairs in each school have each received $2,250,000 from the funds. Income from the monies makes it possible to attract distinguished professors in these fields.

Humphreys said, "The total value of the contributions of Mr. Herff for the benefit of Memphis State was by far the largest contribution ever made to the university, and likely the largest ever made to a public-supported institution of higher education in Tennessee."

He pointed out the engineering and law schools have advanced because of this private support and hundreds of students have received scholarships. The *Memphis Press-Scimitar* said in an editorial, "Memphians unborn will have reason to thank Herbert Herff for his generosity."

Herff was born in Michigan and had never attended a college or university, but he recognized the value of education. Several years before he and Mrs. Herff offered money for the engineering school, the Herff Foundation provided support for the J. P. Young Lectures in American history. The aid came after Enoch Mitchell, head of the MSU history department, told Abe Waldauer about the need. Waldauer called on Herff and his interest in Memphis State increased.

Kellogg had walked in; Humphreys had passed the word to Waldauer and he got a sympathetic ear from Herff. Eventually, there would be a Herff College of Engineering fronting on Central Avenue, a front door for the institution, and *The Commercial Appeal* commented on the university's evolving image as a urban university.

"The new image is that of a thriving business with a product that has suddenly caught on and is striving to keep up with consumer demand," it wrote. Humphreys was quoted as saying, "A university today, especially in an urban center, can and should be a vital force in helping the community meet the many changes in our society." He added a warning, however, about the danger of huge enrollment numbers causing a university to become impersonal. Humphreys liked to walk about the campus and talk with students. He sought their views about world and national events as well as campus issues. As student numbers grew he fretted about having no personal contact with so many commuting students.

The headcount reached 8697 in 1963–64, and the crest of the enrollment tide was still to come. The faculty had increased to 350, but there were retirements that took away familiar faces.

One of them was Dr. Rayburn W. Johnson, who was 70 and had been on the faculty since 1925, when Normal became West Tennessee State Teachers College. *The Commercial Appeal* put this headline on his retirement story: "Tireless Teacher Will Leave a Void."

"He and his wife, Ethel, were vital members of the campus community," Humphreys said. "In 1958 Dr. Johnson made a contribution of $100,000, a amount equal to his earned salary from the university during his career, to the construction of a building which bears his name. His contributions were many and his retirement did leave a void at the university and in the lives of those with whom he had been associated—students, faculty, and staff."

Johnson, head of the geography department, had served many years as chairman of the athletic committee. In 1937 he had joined President Brister, Dean Smith, and O. H. Jones, the bursar, in trying to revitalize the football program after it won only two games in the previous two seasons. Humphreys remembers that Johnson cast careful eyes at the meager funds for athletics.

"He was well remembered by the players of those days," Humphreys, a new assistant coach at the time, said. "He accompanied the teams on bus trips and stood at the door of the bus, handing out a dollar bill to each team member as the bus stopped at a small-town restaurant for meals. On one memorable occasion the players opened the back door of the bus and after receiving their dollar circled back through for a second dollar. He never let that happen again."

In his spare time Johnson became an expert on East Memphis real estate. Money made there led to Johnson Hall.

Another professor, Dr. Chester Peter Freeman, a biology teacher from 1934 until his retirement in 1959, remembered MSU in his will. He left it $505,841. Dr. Freeman, who had bought land in Mississippi over the years, also gave the university $26,396 for scholarship loans in memory of his wife, Bess Henderson Freeman, who had been head of the Home Economics Department.

"Freeman gave Memphis State much more than he earned," Humphreys said. "He should be remembered by the university."

The school year began with the usual invitation by Humphreys to state legislators to tour the campus. Later, the State Legislative Study Council visited and heard an unusual appeal from Humphreys. "We would like to get a pork chop instead of a pig's foot from the next General Assembly," he told the group, pointing out that enrollment would reach 10,000 in 1964–1965. "We hope to impress on you how crowded we are. During the regular school year we start classes at 7 A.M. and run til 9 P.M, even eliminating the lunch hour, and this is equivalent to 12 percent more space."

He told the legislators Memphis State ranked seventh among the seven state-supported institutions in appropriations per student. With a smile, he added, "Some day we hope to work our way up to at least sixth place."

When the tour ended, Lt. Govenor James L. Bomar, chairman of the council, said, "I wish every member of the legislature could visit here and see the progress that is being made." Humphreys never let up in his selling job, and his efforts did not go unnoticed.

Following in the footsteps of two widely acclaimed business leaders,

Abe Plough of Plough, Inc., and Kemmons Wilson, founder of Holiday Inns, Inc., Cecil Humphreys was the recipient of the Memphis Sales Executives Club's third annual Community Salesman's Award.

In an editorial the city's morning newspaper said, "Dr. C. C. Humphreys, at first glance, seems an unlikely choice for the Memphis Sales Executives Club's annual Community Salesman's award. The president of MSU is concerned about things academic and administrative rather than selling a product. But the fact is that he is an ideal recipient. And he does a purvey a product, which is the good reputation of the community. What Dr. Humphreys has done is to recognize the needs of Memphis and the surrounding area and provide the services that only a university can."

A busy spring for Humphreys and the university progresssed nicely until April 18, when the nation's racial problems cast a shadow on the campus.

Four black Memphis State students, joined by one white student from Southwestern and another from Memphis State, entered the Normal Tea Room on South Highland Street near the campus. They refused to leave when the restaurant owner said he would not serve the black students.

The owner called police, who arrested the students on the charge of "interfering with trade and commerce." On May 1 the students were indicted by the Shelby County Grand Jury. One of the black students also was indicted for extortion because of a letter he had written the restaurant owner.

White and black pickets with protest signs began walking in front of the restaurant the next day. A crowd, most of them Memphis State students, gathered and began to jeer and throw sticks and fruits at the pickets. The scene grew increasingly ugly, and some in the crowd physically attacked the pickets. Chased by jeering students, the pickets ran toward the campus to the Newman Catholic Student Center where they found refuge. Police came and dispersed the mob.

Humphreys, who had seen integration work at Memphis State for almost five years, realized that the expulsion threat he had used in 1962 to keep Memphis State students away from Ole Miss would no longer work. "Student attitudes had changed," he said.

The refusal of the Normal Tea room to serve four black students led to picketing of the restaurant and campus tension.

Students were no longer willing to accept the traditional patterns of institutional control off campus. This was a new kind of problem for the university that involved a strong emotional element that had not surfaced on the campus before. Solutions for the needs of an expanding institution had been pursued vigorously, some successfully, some delayed. But regardless of the outcome, you could move on to the many other things that needed to be done. Open hostility and physical violence between students created a volatile situation that posed a real threat to the basic purposes of the university. It was small comfort that this scene was being played on campuses across the nation with disastrous effects upon educational institutions and educational programs.

Tension on campus increased. The Memphis Committee on Community Relations was called into action, and Humphreys met with it and the restaurant owner to seek a solution to the threatening situation. Saying he personally had no objections to serving black people, the restaurant owner said he would be happy if all students stayed out of his place. He added that most of his business came from blue collar workers who told him they would go to other restaurants in the area if he served blacks.

Little progress was made at the meeting, and comforting news was hard to find for Humphreys. He conferred with Claude Armour, commissioner of fire and police, and Armour said he considered the situation volatile. He also said he did not have enough policemen to control a serious outbreak of violence involving a large number of students and still handle regular police work.

Humphreys decided the solution rested with the student body.

> On Sunday evening, May 10, a meeting of student leaders was called at the university cafeteria to discuss what the student body could do to quell the growing tension. A presentation was made to the group that the good record of the student body since the integration of the institution and the overall progress of the university was at stake. Regardless of their personal feelings concerning the rights of the pickets and the restaurant owner, they were being called upon to demonstrate that campus student leaders could set an example of calm and mature judgement in meeting the crisis.

The president's call for leadership led to a long discussion. Viewpoints were exchanged, and sometimes heatedly so. The idea that a university should provide leadership in a community prevailed. It was decided that a student petition would be circulated the next day. It read:

"We the undersigned students of Memphis State University respect the right of all groups and individuals to pursue their objectives by lawful and peaceful means.

"We pledge ourselves to avoid violence, to influence others to avoid violence and to preserve the dignity of our university."

The student leaders also decided, with the cooperation of student editors of *The Tiger Rag,* to put out a special edition Tuesday morning. It came out with statements endorsing the petition from President

Humphreys, the student government president, and presidents of other student organizations, including fraternities and sororities.

Students flocked to sign the petition, and the campus calmed down. In a story in its June 7, 1974, edition, *The Commercial Appeal* reported that blacks were "served politely at the Normal Tea Room" on the day before.

"The meeting with the students and their action was one of the most gratifying experiences of my career at the university," Humphreys wrote.

It was crisis that had a real threat of violence and chaos, with the outcome entirely in the hands of the students. I was never prouder of any group of students.

The threat of racial violence involving Memphis State students which could have spread to a whole community, has been forgotten by most. But, placed in the historical context of events of the preceding three years—the Freedom Marches and Freedom Riders in Georgia, Alabama, and Mississippi which were met with bitter hostility; the murder of civil rights workers; and the more than 750 riots that had taken place in 187 cities in the summer of 1963—a critical problem was resolved peacefully. Given the mood of the country and the widespread resort to violence, the action of the Memphis State students deserves to be remembered.

And Memphis State's astonishing growth, in numbers and in leadership, would continue.

7

"The Tigers can have Claws"

1964–1965

Warren Commission concludes that Lee Harvey Oswald acted on his own and was not part of a conspiracy in assassinating President Kennedy...Red China explodes its first nuclear bomb at Lop Nor...Democratic ticket of Lyndon Johnson and Hubert Humphrey wins in presidential landslide over Republican candidates Barry Goldwater and William Miller...700 arrested as students riot at the University of California at Berkeley, and President Clark Kerr offers to resign...Dr. Martin Luther King, Jr., leads civil rights march in Alabama from Selma to Montgomery...U.S. Marines land combat forces in Vietnam.

AND THE WAY WE WERE

Variety of items, from lipstick to garters, has been added to books and supplies available at bookstore...A new era begins for MSU basketball as Tigers take the court for the first time in the Mid-South Colisum; largest crowd ever—8763—watches MSU defeat Texas A&M, 82–73... Student dress rules such as "women should not wear shorts, slim jims, slacks, unless engaged in active sports" and men "should not wear bermuda shorts when calling on a date at the Women's Residence Halls" need to be changed... Religious Emphasis Week has been abolished because of lack of attendance...Week of tension and controversy ends when Free Speech Movement leader speaks to capacity crowd of 200.

PERHAPS AN ATTORNEY'S REMARK best reflected Memphis' changed attitude toward Memphis State in the 1964–65 school year when it welcomed 10,975 students, 70 new faculty members and a 400-car parking lot south of the railroad tracks.

"Being against Memphis State these days is like being against mother," said Ralph Farmer. He represented citizens opposed to rezoning a stretch of Highland Street a few blocks west of the campus to enable a private company to build twin high-rise student residence halls. The lawyer was correct in his assessment. The City Commission approved the rezoning, although it accepted a compromise suggested by Commissioner Hunter Lane, Jr., that the rezoning be limited to the site of the two buildings.

The college waif out east had become a towering figure in the life of the city. The views of Memphians had turned 180 degrees, a dramatic about face from the days when many townsmen thought of Memphis State as a "teachers school" and athletic boosters of other colleges referred to it as "Tiger High." Athletic success, particularly in basketball and football, contributed heavily to the change. Tiger teams had proven they could win, and win big, against major schools, and Memphians rallied to their cause.

In 1964 the Memphis and Shelby County governments, in a 60–40 cost agreement, opened the Mid-South Coliseum and its more than 11,000 seats as the home court of the Tiger basketball team coached by Dean Ehlers. The city built Memphis Memorial Stadium (later renamed Liberty Bowl Memorial Stadium) with the football Tigers in mind as the principal tenants. A sellout crowd of 52,000 saw Memphis State play Ole Miss in the inaugural game in 1965. These excellent new facilities built for $8.8 had not cost Memphis State a cent in capital outlay. The city and county had awakened to the economic assets inherent in a major university.

Traditionally, Memphis had imported its big-time collegiate teams, in both basketball and football. Ole Miss–Arkansas or Ole Miss–Tennessee games had been the big attractions at antiquated Crump Stadium, a depression-era WPA project, before the Tigers showed their claws and Memorial Stadium became a gleaming reality. In basketball in the early 1950s, a Memphis State game with Delta State served as a preliminary event for a big crowd awaiting an Arkansas–Ole Miss game in Ellis Auditorium downtown.

Memphis State's ascendancy in the athletic world evolved out of seventeen years of key decisions by Cecil Humphreys. He was the catalyst. Humphreys was still in the FBI in 1947 when President Smith asked him to help find a man to revive football at Memphis State after a five-year absence.

Humphreys suggested Ralph Hatley, the coach at Christian Brothers High School in Memphis. Hatley had been a senior guard and captain of the 1934 University of Tennessee team when Humphreys was a junior living in Knoxville's Farragut Hotel with other Vol athletes. Smith hired Hatley, and, shortly thereafter, Humphreys declined an FBI transfer to Washington and accepted Smith's standing offer to become athletic director at Memphis State. Hatley would spend 10 years building a solid base for Memphis State to start reaching for NCAA Division One football stature in 1958, and Humphreys would come up with the idea of first building a nationally prominent basketball program.

The thought came to him as he watched Memphis State in that warm-up game before the Ole Miss–Arkansas finale. "Delta State just beat the hell out of us in front of a big crowd in our hometown," Humphreys said. "It was embarrassing."

 · The next day the athletic director was in the president's office with his plan, and Smith listened as Humphreys spelled out the ways and means—and what a topflight team could do for the college. He also presented his major selling point: It would not cost much. President Smith, who believed that athletics should pay its own way and had a convert in Humphreys, liked the basketball idea. Athletic director Humphreys hired Dr. Eugene Lambert, who had done well coaching the Arkansas Razorback basketball team, to launch the campaign. Coach Lambert's recruiting and his decision to enter tournaments around the nation proved effective. Crowds began to increase in the 3800-seat Field House on campus.

When the University of Alabama lured Lambert away in 1955,

In the late 1950s and in the 1960s an invitation to the NIT was a glorious climax to Memphis State's basketball season.

Humphreys turned to Bob Vanatta to keep up the momentum. Vanatta accelerated it, and Memphis State clawed its way to the finals of the National Invitational Tournament in New York's Madison Square Garden in 1957. Bradley nicked the scrappy little Memphis State team, 84–83, in the NIT championship game, but the crowd in Madison Square Garden and a national television audience found themselves cheering a team they hardly knew.

The NIT performance caused Humphreys' two young sons to re-name the family cat Nit, and, in Nashville, Governor Frank Clement dashed off a telegram immediately after the game: "I was never prouder of any representatives of Tennessee than I was today of the Memphis State University basketball team. They were glorious in a technical defeat and so far as I am concerned they were the cham-pions....It is obvious that the spirit of Memphis State University was of such a wonderful degree that the name of Memphis and Tennessee has now become synonymous with sportsmanship and ability throughout the country."

In a reply wire two days later—by a less expensive night letter—President Smith said, "Read your wonderful telegram to the student body at assembly today. They simply went wild. We not only appreciate your thoughtful message concerning our basketball team but are also very grateful for the many other evidences of your sincere interest in our college (university July 1)."

Other NIT and NCAA invitations to Memphis State would follow. In 1973 Coach Gene Bartow's Tigers, with Larry Finch one of the stars, reached the NCAA finals in St. Louis. Coach John Wooden's UCLA team, led by seven-foot Bill Walton, won the title, but Cecil Humphreys' basketball dream had long since been realized.

In the days preceding its NIT invitation in 1957 the University of Louisville's nationally ranked Cardinals met the Tigers in Ellis Auditorium. Coach Vanatta's team won.

"It was a big upset and a very exciting game with lots of time-outs and tension toward the end," Humphreys recalled. "Everybody was standing and cheering for our Tigers. A lot of townspeople who never attended Memphis State events had turned out for the evening, and one of them was Mayor Edmund Orgill."

The next morning the mayor called Humphreys. "Sonny," he said, "I have never seen any group of people this large stand up and agree on one thing as long as I have been in Memphis. Why don't we do the same thing for football that we are doing for basketball and let tens of thousands attend?"

A surprised, but elated, Humphreys told the mayor that was what he would like to do, but he added that it would take a lot of community support and a lot of money. Orgill said he thought his office could help. Humphreys suggested that the mayor convey his feelings to President Smith. Orgill followed through and the first match had been struck for the public fire that lit the way for big-time football at Memphis State. Much of Humphreys' time in 1957 was spent downtown working with Sam Hollis, the mayor's administrative assistant, and Forrest Ladd, vice president at the Chamber of Commerce, to reach a goal of $100,000 from business interests.

Mayor Orgill, on April 2, 1957, sent a letter to W. O. Galbreath, Jr., chairman of the Planning Commission, and Fred Davis, its director, which said it is "entirely possible that Memphis State will embark upon a stepped-up major league football program—it is my hope that it will decide to do so this year. This would require a new stadium correctly located and with ample parking space." The letter also suggested "a modern stadium might be a great asset to our Mid-South Fair, if it could be located there." A copy of the letter went to President Smith. After consultation with Humphreys, Smith wrote to Orgill on April suggesting that first priority should be given to "a field house large enough to accommodate some 10,000 spectators for basketball and other contests."

A coliseum and a stadium would be built at the Fairgrounds, but not during Mayor Orgill's tenure in office. Memphis does not rush to judgment with ease or speed. It would be seven years before the Mid-South Coliseum opened and eight years before the dedication of Memphis Memorial Stadium.

Meanwhile, the drive to build a major program at Memphis State picked up strength. On June 5, 1957, *The Commercial Appeal* said, "Memphis State and the Memphis Chamber of Commerce formed a team yesterday for the greater glory of football at the soon-to-be university. The Chamber of Commerce, cooperating with Mayor Edmund Orgill, has obtained the guarantee of 22 scholarships from business people of the city. They will be the equal of grants made by the Southeastern Conference and will be on a five-year basis. Inspiration for the movement to bolster MSU football came from the tremendous success of the basketball team, which went to the finals of the National Invitational Tournament in Madison Square Garden and brought a wave of enthusiasm in Memphis and throughout the nation."

The newspaper quoted Humphreys as saying, "We had looked at this as a long-range program for increasing football prestige, but people came to us and said, 'Now is the time to move into the major football picture,' and we are certainly agreeable."

Six days later the City Commission adopted a resolution approving of Memphis State's efforts and listed three benefits:

(1) the crowds attracted will bring in additional business and money, and
(2) a successful team will boost the morale of the community and give us something to cheer for, and
(3) a Memphis State University team will advertise Memphis as the location of a university and thus help attract additional residents and additional industry.

Coach Billy (Spook) Murphy, who had been an assistant coach with

Ralph Hatley, was called home from the University of Minnesota on January 13, 1958, and given a mandate to field a major college football team in five years. A graduate of Mississippi State and a tough ex-marine, Murphy met the goal Humphreys had set. In 1962 the Tigers claimed their first victory over a Southeastern Conference team, whipping Mississippi State, 28 to 7, in Starkville. Memphis State never was a member of the SEC, but it followed its guidelines.

A few days after the triumph over Mississippi State, George Bugbee, sports editor and columnist of the *Memphis Press-Scimitar,* wrote that Humphreys had been right back in 1958 when he had insisted that "the Tigers could one day have claws."

The 1963 team—five years after Murphy's return—tied Ole Miss, 0 to 0, in an epic defensive struggle at Crump Stadium and went through the season undefeated. The Highland 100 Club, a strong Tiger support unit, and fans began to cast eyes at the University of Tennessee as a football opponent. Murphy liked the idea himself, and games with the Vols would come to pass.

In one of his personal notes, Cecil Humphreys wrote: "This is a country that has had a great interest in athletics and sports. Since its earliest history physical prowess has been admired—qualities that were so needed in conquering and developing a wilderness into a new nation. This interest has continued as organized athletic competition has been incorporated into the programs of educational institutions....A well-managed athletic program can be an asset to an institution, particularly an emerging institution, if kept under the control of the university."

Humphreys, a former athletic director, kept athletics in perspective. Memphis State teams paid their own way, and in the middle 1960s had built a million-dollar reserve.

When fall classes began in 1964 Memphis State's athletes moved into a new 150-bed Tiger den—Robison Hall. The athletic department paid the usual student rental fees. Two other new buildings also were ready for occupancy, a new women's dormitory to be named in honor of Dean Flora H. Rawls and the School of Education Building.

The school years at Memphis State run on fiscal year budgets—from July 1 to June 30, and in mid-July of 1964 Greater Memphis State, Inc., hosted a dinner on campus for 58 legislative candidates and several hundred other guests. The meeting centered around five-minute talks by civic leaders on what the university means to the community. Speakers included Wallace Witmer, president of the Memphis Area Chamber of Commerce; Walter Armstrong, attorney and a leader in cultural affairs; William T. Ross, executive director of the Memphis AFL-CIO Labor Council; Morgan Christian, assistant superintendent of the City School System; and Gloria Datson, a June graduate of Memphis State. All the political candidates got the message: Give a high priority to the increasing needs of the university.

That summer Memphis State bought its first house on Central Avenue, the new front door envisioned by Humphreys. "The expansion of the campus by having to purchase the homes of old friends and neighbors was not pleasant, but was necessary," Humphreys said. "One of them wrote, 'We are proud of our big neighbor, Memphis State, but we sincerely believe that you can expand in other directions.' "

Forty-two residents on Central signed a protest petition. It said, "Funds made available for the acquisition of property do not belong to MSU to do with as it sees fit." The petition stooped a bit and suggested that it was not in the best interest of the university "to pay premium prices for Central Avenue land" while land on campus had not been fully utilized, noting "the president's home occupies a good deal of land" which might be used.

The petitioners had not done their homework. Humphreys quickly pointed out that MSU had not used state money for campus expansion but bank loans. He also presented data showing that the big lots on Central cost less on a square-foot basis than the land being acquired south of Southern Avenue beyond the railroad tracks. Humphreys also had announced earlier that the stately old President's Home, which fronted the campus mall and had its back to Patterson Street, would eventually give way to academic buildings. It would take time for some alumni to forgive Humphreys' views on the president's house, but Memphis State had broken through to Central and was there to stay.

The student avalanche forced the expansion. Memphis State, with almost 11,000 students, was the largest of the six institutions under the State Board, and it was within striking distance of the University of Tennessee, which had an enrollment of 14,000.

A headline in *The Commercial Appeal* on October 12, 1964, said,

"MSU Reaches Its Limits, More Students on the Way." The story said that with 2000 more students already seeking admission in the fall of 1965 the university faced a desperate situation and "with the projection of 16,000 to 17,000 students within the next three to four years" major steps would have to be taken.

President Humphreys suggested the university might have to raise its admission requirements, make afternoon classes mandatory and move some functions to the Kennedy Hospital complex, if arrangements could be made with the federal government. "These suggestions were partially strategic," Humphreys wrote. "I knew that if Memphis State, which already had the highest admission requirements of any of the state-supported institutions, increased the differential for admission, parents and students would feel that their local representatives were ineffectual in serving them. The full extension of the academic schedule would bring a strong protest from students who had to work part-time, and we were interested in getting on the Kennedy Hospital property and establishing a "best use" for it when the new Veterans Hospital was completed and the Federal government would make some disposition of it."

As usual, Humphreys' plan worked. A week later eleven Democratic legislative candidates toured the campus to see the needs first-hand. Among the things they saw were recently installed laboratory tables of 1918 vintage that had been given to MSU by Vanderbilt University after it modernized its chemistry labs. The candidates also were told again about Memphis State's funding being at the bottom on a per-student basis. The SBE did not have a formula based on enrollment.

During this period the West Tennessee Education Association adopted a resolution asking that a doctoral program in education be offered by Memphis State separate from its joint endeavor with the University of Tennessee. Humphreys took the matter to the SBE at its November meeting. The board took no immediate action but passed a motion asking the next session of the General Assembly to approve doctoral degrees at schools under SBE supervision "when such programs could be offered within existing facilities and appropriations are available."

Many other significant developments were taking place. The Mississippi Valley Collection of historical documents—published works,

Meeting the needs of the rapidly expanding number of students and faculty was a major concern during the Humphreys' presidency.

manuscripts, journals, diaries, and transcribed interviews—was begun at Brister Library, with Dewey Pruett in charge. At the Downtown Center, the first of five courses for law enforcement officers was offered and 40 officers registered. One police lieutenant, a veteran of 17 years, said, "We have the actual policing, but no theory. For the first time in a long time I'm starting to crack books and dictionaries. It better prepares a policeman to do his job. It gives him a different outlook."

The widening scope of the university's academic objectives brought additional financial pressures on the administration. "It had been recognized that the university, if it was going to grow in ways other than enrollment, was going to need more financial support than would be provided by state appropriations," Humphreys said.

The answer, in his mind, was a foundation to give Memphis State a vehicle to seek funds from sources other than the state. As a prelude to this, Humphreys hired Frank Holloman, who had retired from the FBI after 25 years and held a law degree from Ole Miss, to become director of development in July of 1964. One of Humphreys' goals in setting up the Memphis State University Foundation was to be able to supplement state-mandated salary levels and bring in nationally known professors and researchers. A full professor's pay was limited to $11,000 in 1964–65, and no one at Memphis State made that much.

At the November meeting of the State Board of Education in Nashville, President Humphreys won approval for a state-chartered foundation, and he quickly turned to the city and country for contributions. He wanted $50,000 from each. Both governmental bodies indicated interest, and as expected, the question of legality came up. With the unanimous backing of the Shelby County delegation, a bill authorizing such grants breezed through the General Assembly. The idea had received an excellent press throughout the state.

The Commercial Appeal on consecutive days carried editorials strongly supporting financial aid. The second editorial, headed "To Build for Greatness," said, "President C. C. Humphreys has a good idea when he asks for Memphis-Shelby County funds to start a chartered foundation for adding big names to the MSU staff."

Across the state *The Chattanooga Times* splashed the Memphis State story on page one. It also had this comment: "Those concerned [with such college programs] warn that cities and metropolitan centers without commitment to methods for special enrichment of urban universities and faculty additions of some leading figures in research and scholastic fields are likely to fall behind in economic growth and the building of an elite segment of leadership in the future."

In carrying his proposal to the County Court President Humphreys said "a community service division" would be established that would benefit county government through off-campus extension programs to update the skills of county employees and to provide research and special services for its operating departments. The city and county quickly contributed $50,000 each and when the Memphis State Foundation elected officers in March of 1965 its assets totalled $116,973.26. In one of his notes Humphreys commented, "As with most of the other projects started in these years, there was more hope than resources." But it was a beginning.

Humphreys was elected president. Other foundation officers included Frank Holloman, executive vice president; Harry Woodbury, secretary; and Eugene Smith, treasurer. Also chosen as directors were Ed Thompson, president of the Alumni Association; Ernest C. Ball, a member of the SBE; Dr. John Morris, academic dean; Dr. John Richardson, dean of the Graduate School; Dr. Ford Haynes, School of Education; Dr. Ronald Carrier, director of the Bureau of Business Research; Allen Morgan, president of First National Bank; John Brown, president of Union Planters National Bank; and Lewis McKee, president of the National Bank of Commerce.

Other strong leaders serving on the board were Charles H. Schneider, editor of the *Memphis Press-Scimitar;* Frank R. Ahlgren, editor of *The Commercial Appeal*; Hoyt Wooten, radio and television executive; Walter Armstrong, Jr., attorney; Morrie Moss of Moss Enterprises; Julian Bondurant; Abe Waldauer; Everett Pidgeon, Sr.; Nat Buring; S. L. Kopald; S. L. Kopald, Jr.; P. K. Seidman; Dr. Roy Tyrer; Dr. John J. Shea; Dr. Steve Bledsoe; and S. Toof Brown. In picking the board Humphreys revealed how well he knew the community power structure.

At the annual meeting of the Alumni Association on November 14, 1964, Humphreys pledged to "forcefully present" the university's financial needs to the state legislature in January. In its January 9 editions *The Commercial Appeal* reported that 185,000 students were enrolled in Memphis and Shelby County schools from grade one to college graduate school, and it pointed out that Memphis State had enrolled 10,900 the past fall, which was a 2200 increase over 1963, and the university anticipated 12,500 students in 1965 and 15,000 by 1966.

Humphreys had promised to be a tiger in the legislature, but Governor Clement made his lobbying easy. He proposed a $1,563,000,000 budget for the next two years, including $13.7 million for Memphis State. That was almost double the $7.5 million of the past two years. In his budget message, Clement said, "This means

this year alone the number of new students at MSU, our fastest growing institution, equals the total student population there just ten years
ago."

"I am pleased with the support which has been recommended,"
Humphreys told the *Memphis Press-Scimitar.* "It will enable us to
continue to grow and make progress."

Clement's budget also included $6,737,000 for capital improve-
ments. With money that could be borrowed for dormitories, which
would pay for themselves by rental fees, and federal assistance for a
new chemistry building, about $10 million would be available for
physical expansion. A generous General Assembly passed the governor's budget. It also removed the legality question about the Memphis
State Foundation receiving city and county monies, and it approved
the beginning of doctoral programs at Memphis State. When the idea
of doctoral programs at Memphis State first surfaced, the other five
universities under SBE governance objected, but their opposition faded
as it had when Memphis State sought university status in 1957. They
realized that they would have a better chance of getting programs beyond the master's level after one of the institutions had broken the
barrier.

Excited about Memphis State's successes in Nashville, Humphreys
looked ahead to a quiet spring of planning for the fall crush. It would
prove to be anything but quiet. In the wake of the riots at the University
of California, *The Commercial Appeal* made a survey on the Memphis State campus to try to determine whether student unrest was
widespread or Berkeley was an isolated case. A story in its January 3,
1965, editions said, "The quiet tread of student feet toward MSU classrooms may never shift to the riotous clamour for more student freedom as it did at the University of California last month. A combination
of student apathy, influential campus leaders, family ties, and university restrictions would probably prevent it."

Opinion sampling of students and faculty members found no large-
scale restrictions of student rights, but apathy kept students from
speaking out on many issues. Jim Cochran, president of the Student
Government Association, said, "We have about as many freedoms as
we need. But many students don't take advantage of the freedoms they
have."

April brought rainshowers, flowers, and the announcement that Steve Weissman, one of the leaders in the University of California "Free Speech Movement," would speak on campus. Weissman, according to a news story, was to "defend" the group's role. It also said that Steven M. Shiffrin, MSU's debating team coach, had asked the administration to allow Weissman to explain the Free Speech Movement. The report indicated President Humphreys was interested in having both sides of controversial issues presented.

"This statement was not true," Humphreys said. "The administration was not aware that such a meeting was planned."

Memphis State had a policy that faculty members could invite a speaker to discuss class-related matters, but any campuswide meeting had to have approval of the administration. "I was 'set up' and realized it, as did Shiffrin and others who had knowledge of the planned speech," Humphreys said. "The worst action that could have been taken was to cancel the speech." He said cancellation would have given credence to the rhetoric of campus activists that all colleges were repressive and represented only the establishment.

There would be occasions during the next five years when student actions, often violent and unlawful, held the nation's attention. A college administrator stood alone much of the time. Boards, alumni, politicians, and others were on one side, and students, some of them astute in the manipulation of their peers, were on the other.

Humphreys got a lot of advice on how to handle Weissman and the Free Speech Movement. Many telephone calls and letters suggested a simple remedy: "Fire the Commie professors and kick out the long-haired troublemakers."

The president had more sense than that.

In one news story Weissman was described by California reporters who had covered the sit-in at the president's office and subsequent arrests at the University of California as "almost the No. 1 man in the Free Speech Movement." They said he had been among those who took over the Administration Building when more than 700 students were arrested but "had escaped by climbing out a window." Memphis newspapers gave extensive coverage to the budding campus story, as did *The Tiger Rag.*

Dr. Harry Ausprich, chairman of the Speech and Drama Department, which was sponsoring Weissman's appearance, told *The Commercial Appeal* a major function of his department was "to provide a framework within which ideas can be tested—to promote critical thinking, responsible debate, and the interchange of ideas." Ten women leaders in Memphis came to President Humphreys' office and urged him to cancel the speech. He declined, saying it "would create future problems of greater significance and would be the best way to attract attention to the Free Speech Movement."

A few days earlier in a talk to about sixty students at Vanderbilt University in Nashville, Weissman said the nation's university system was nothing more than "an assembly line to train students for large corporations." He also claimed the right to break any law if he had no part in making it. In responding to a student's question asking why demonstrators at Berkeley had blocked police cars for thirty-two hours, Weissman said, "You can't have social change without being outside the channels."

The Memphis newspapers reported that Weissman's appearance had been arranged in March by a student at Loyola University in New Orleans and said she represented the Southern Student Organizing Committee (SSOC). They also said Weissman's tour of southern colleges was financed by Students for a Democratic Society (SDS).

Public opposition to the scheduled speech grew, and one group, most of whom lived near the campus, planned to assemble on the lawn of the president's home. Humphreys, upon learning of this, invited the area residents to meet with him in the university cafeteria. A spokesman for the residents said Weissman's appearance was opposed because "the texts of his speeches have been based on lawlessness. We want to prevent him from speaking, or at least from speaking on a state-supported campus." *The Commercial Appeal's* account of the meeting said Humphreys told the group cancellation of the speech could inflate the issues beyond its worth. "Simply shutting people up won't cure problems," Humphreys was quoted as saying. "You've got to use a little bit of intelligence."

The president also nixed the suggestion that a person be named to debate Weissman, especially an older person with a conservative viewpoint. In the presidential files is this further comment: "the phrase 'you can't trust anybody over thirty' had not become a slogan with college students, but the attitude was developing, and I didn't want to encourage it at Memphis State."

Weissman spoke on May 3, 1965, and the morning newspaper reported, "A bearded, self-styled prophet of the Free Speech Movement sounded a battle cry for civil disobedience last night before several hundred students at Memphis State University." It said there were cheers and boos during the address. The speech in the auditorium of the School of Education Building lasted from 8 to 9 P.M., the allotted time. Afterward, Weissman was invited to the home of a young faculty member, but just beyond the campus Weissman resumed his comments. He contended that all university regents are autocratic, and he said he felt President Humphreys "has been a kind of horse's neck about this."

Weissman proposed a student protest movement in Memphis. He followed up with a request for donations, a suggestion "met with small response," according to *The Commercial Appeal*.

"One clear remembrance I have of this event was meeting Dr. Harry Ausprich, the head of the Speech and Drama Department, the morning after the meeting," Humphreys said. "His eyes were sparkling and he was literally dancing on his toes as he greeted me with the statement, 'Isn't this exciting?' I counted to ten slowly, then counted to ten again, keeping both hands in my pockets, and, still not trusting myself to answer, smiled weakly and walked away."

Both city newspapers editorially supported the way Humphreys handled the issue. The headline on the *Memphis Press-Scimitar* commentary said, "Dr. Humphreys Did Right." The Faculty Council by unanimous vote adopted a resolution that said it "would like to express particular confidence in the President of Memphis State University relative to his stated policies in support of the free expression of popular and unpopular ideas before the university at large."

Many citizens in the private sector had other thoughts. One letter to a newspaper said, "Dr. C. C. Humphreys evidently thinks he can 'vaccinate' MSU students against Communist endoctrination by giving them a small dose of communism in the person of Steve Weissman...Humphreys does not learn from the experience of others, such as Dr. Clark Kerr, president of the University of California." Another writer, complaining that Humphreys had disregarded the advice of concerned Memphians "to prevent a potentially dangerous speaker from spreading his evil," added: "Now Dr. Humphreys is going to have to live with the result. His headaches have just started, and frankly I feel sorry for him."

Humphreys' own notes said, "There were many divisive questions and elements in the country at this time. These, plus the growth and increasing importance of higher education, would keep college administrators caught between divergent elements, most of them presented with emotional involvement. The maximum support of the public was sought, but decisions had to be made on a rational and personal judgment basis rather than a consensus of any particular element, which could turn hostile the next week."

Under heavy public pressure, however, the State Board of Education on May 21 adopted a new "Statement of Policy" on university speakers. Mainly, it put the burden of approval on presidents, who were directed "to establish adequate procedures to insure that those invited to speak on campus or in a college facility...shall be known to be of such reputation and character that their appearance will make a positive contribution to the cultural benefit of the institution." The original draft said "subversive" speakers must be barred, but President Humphreys, a former FBI agent, warned of the problems of identity and definition. The word was not used in the final draft.

In the middle of all this Humphreys received the American Bar Association Liberty Bell Award for community service from the Memphis and Shelby County Bar Association. Since the ABA was not generally thought of as a radical organization, the honor came at an opportune time for Humphreys.

"It helped," he said.

The Normal Tea Room confrontations in the spring of 1964 and the Weissman agitation at Memphis State in 1965 were just the beginning of a campus war that was a national phenomenon not predicted by social scientists. Yet, hardly a major university escaped at least one sizable student revolt in the 1960s.

Sit-ins, strikes, marches, the systematic disruption of classes, bombing of university buildings, and the counter use of police, tear gas, mass arrests, university closures—sometimes for weeks on end—became quite common. "There was no end of explanations and little agreement among the expert explainers," Humphreys said. "Most explanations were too simplistic and, even years after, it must be concluded that no one, two, or three causes are likely to explain this phenomenon completely."

Cecil Humphreys relied on his best judgment and tried to personalize his relationship with students despite the increasing numbers. He reminded his staff that a student headcount in the thousands began "with a unit of one." Under criticism he did not panic; he always took the time to count to 10. At an adminsitrative council meeting on April 11, 1965, complaints arose about the campus newspaper, *The Tiger Rag,* which had become quite critical of some university operations—and sometimes inaccurately so, presidential files indicate. There were suggestions of greater supervision, but Humphreys stood firm: There would be no administrative control of the newspaper's editorial policy.

His long view of First Amendment rights would serve him well in darker days to come.

8

"Wall-to-Wall Students"

1965–1966

THE NEWS HEADLINES

President Johnson announces U.S. strength in Vietnam will be increased to 125,000 men and draft quotas will be doubled...Rioting in Watts, a black neighborhood in Los Angeles, leaves 34 dead and $40 million in property damage ...In his third State of the Union address Johnson sticks to a guns-and-butter program, saying commitments to South Vietnam will be kept as well as his Great Society programs...Demonstrations are staged in San Francisco, Chicago, Philadelphia, and Washington in nationwide protests against the Vietnam war...Unmanned Surveyor I makes soft landing on the moon...Secretary of Defense Robert McNamara reports 285,000 American troops are in Vietnam.

AND THE WAY WE WERE

Total enrollment is approximately 13,500...Hiring of 96 new professors brings number to high of 483...The campus police force is doubled to 12 men...1150 parking tickets have been issued this year compared to 800 at this time last year...A majority of students are dissatisfied with cafeteria service; faculty agree...New policy governing speakers on campus requires students to secure approval before issuing invitation...Probably the busiest instructor at MSU teaches in almost every department, is scheduled for more than 400 courses—his name is STAFF...100% pure beef hamburger—15¢; old fashioned shake—22¢.

FOR EDUCATION PER SQUARE INCH of classroom space, Memphis State can probably contend for all time that it set a national record in the 1965–66 school year. The fall semester opened with an enrollment of 13,561, including a record freshman class of 2745. And, while the student body increased by more than 2500 over the previous year, not a single new classroom building had been completed. During the year nine new buildings worth $18 million would be on planning boards or in various stages of construction, but Memphis State faced its largest single-year jump in enrollment with exactly the same space it had when 10,975 students showed up in 1964–65.

The corridors of campus buildings resembled the entrance to a Beatles' concert. The English department had to teach 8000 students in six buildings scattered across the university; here and there, a classsroom was divided into four parts to provide office space for almost 100 new faculty members.

The Commercial Appeal in early September of 1965 reported the frantic scramble for space. It said university officials had "thrown walls up around once-dark corners and moved in a desk, a chair, and a filing cabinet. They've taken over the foyer outside the women's lounge and even set up tables in hallways. Old storage rooms, some little bigger than closets, have been refurbished."

The news report said a place for the new office of the assistant dean of men had been jammed under a busy stairway, adding that it "is little more than a paneled box about the size of two telephone booths which previously occupied the space." Returning to the campus in October, the reporter described classrooms with "wall-to-wall students."

The Commercial Appeal in a long editorial said, "A Madison Avenue public relations genius would be needed to think up superlatives to describe MSU's phenomenal growth." It also said such mass education might "look like a mill" to boost the economy, but suggested that one had to look beyond sheer numbers: "It [the university] serves the age-old function of nurturing the creative spirit of man. When we look at the future of Memphis, we can see much potential for good. Memphis State, in meeting the needs of the present, is providing the base for a dynamic tomorrow."

In the thinking of President Humphreys, the needs of 8000 students enrolled in English classes became more important than a president's home of admitted grandeur. Midway in the school year the SBE approved a new $1,200,000 four-story Humanities Building. It would be built at Patterson and Walker near the site of the president's home, the first building constructed at West Tennessee Normal School.

"The original president's home represented memories of older alumni of when the institution was small, and students would gather on Sunday evenings around the piano in the living room and sing hymns," Humphreys said. "But respect for the past and its heritage reluctantly had to give way to the pressures of new needs."

A wry twist might be detected in the new presidential house at 4035 Grandview, which was occupied in the summer of 1966. In 1960 Grandview residents had opposed the university's use of Sheehan Pumping Station grounds for physical education classes, and Humphreys withdrew his request. Times change, of course, and the new home cost only $82,000. It had an appraised value of $120,000, but its owner, William N. Fry, vice president of Home Federal Savings and Loan Association, contributed $38,000 of the value to the university.

The physical face of the campus lagged behind in meeting the enrollment crush, but throughout the year masons and carpenters were tripping over surveyors in the rush to catch up. A law school building soon would join a fine arts complex in dressing up Central Avenue, and work had begun on the Humanities Building and a $2.2 million, 12-story undergraduate addition to Brister Library. Extra rooms were added to the School of Education Building to provide space for newly approved undergraduate engineering courses, and one of the university's greatest needs, a student center, would soon be remedied by a $3.8 million Student Service Center.

All this activity did not stem from a splurge of tax dollars, as one might suspect. Memphis State still used bank loans to acquire property adjoining the campus, and, with the rising costs, the SBE had raised the borrowing limit to $1 million. Another progressive step had been the creation of the State School Bond Authority which made possible the borrowing of funds for campus construction. The sorely needed

Student Service Center, for example, would repay its costs through a small increase in student fees.

"The adminstration shared the reluctance of the SBE to increase the cost of education to the student," Humphreys said, "but there was no other alternative available. This would not be as great a hardship on Memphis State students as on others since 80 percent of them resided at home and did not have as great a cost for room and board as did most students on other state campuses."

It might be said that Memphis State was a state-assisted university. In 1965–66 the school had acquired 92 pieces of property at a cost of $1,429,906.38 since its first $14,000 purchase on Norriswood. Sixty parcels with a valuation of $943,323.95 had been paid off. There remained 32 pieces of property valued at $486,582.43 which had been bought with bank loans, but they were bringing in $42,480 annually.

The interest of private developers in building and operating residence towers for students led President Humphreys to tell the Memphis and Shelby County Planning Commission that additional campus housing would not be needed except for married students. "I hope we never have to spend any more state tax money for student housing," he said. He added, however, that if Memphis State should obtain the Kennedy Veterans Hospital after it moved into a new facility in the Medical Center married students would be housed there.

The university's students could see the future of the school's physical plant and their lamentations about their current crowded plight were remarkably light. Perhaps they were too busy trying to find a place to park and wend their way through the crowd to class.

Acting as a collective student voice was *The Tiger Rag,* which had become a twice-weekly publication and had earned an All-America rating by the Associated College Press Association in competition with other newspapers across the nation. In its October 1, 1965, edition *The Tiger Rag* reported Memphis State had 3104 students enrolled in the AFROTC program, the third largest in the nation. In some years it was the largest. A contributing factor was that it was compulsory in the freshman and sophomore years, but it had an obvious popularity of its own.

In sharp contrast to scattered demonstrations by college students in other parts of the country against the nation's Vietnam policy, the In-

Perhaps the most dramatic structure of the 1960s was the John Willard Brister Library Tower.

tercity Council, made up of student body presidents at Memphis State, Southwestern, LeMoyne College, Siena College, Owen College, and Christian Brothers College, organized a campaign to send food and gifts for Christmas to members of the 101st Airborne Division in Vietnam.

Widespread community support was offered by church, social and civic organizations, and individual Memphians. Goldsmith's Department Store provided gift wrapping, and the Air Force provided transportation. John Houseal, Jr., president of the Student Government Association at MSU, said, "Many students and student groups had asked me what they can do to show our servicemen that we are aware of their work and that all students are not demonstrating against the government."

The Tiger Rag polled 180 students and 150 said they preferred a heavier military commitment in Southeast Asia. Thirty said they felt America had no real obligation to help the South Vietnamese fight communist aggression.

Other issues were closer to Patterson and Central. The newspaper, long a leader in the struggle for more parking space, reported on October 14 that 1150 parking tickets had been written, 350 more than during a comparable period the year before. It noted that the security force had doubled in size to 12 members.

It reported on October 29 that two university doctors had announced that "giving birth control pills to any student, married or not, is forbidden on campus." In one editorial it said, "MSU women live under archaic rules of residence. These rules make us wonder how women can find college the 'happy and worthwhile experience' which the residence hall handbook calls it."

Vet Village, where old War War II barracks provided housing for married students, did not avoid the newspaper's eye. It said, "Seventy-five feet from almost new Rawls Hall stands Vet Village, the name given the living facilities for married students on campus, which might well be termed the campus slums."

Lighter moments received their share of ink. *The Tiger Rag* reported that Alpha Epsilon Pi won $100 and first place by packing 31 men into a 1958 Ford. One of its feature stories noted that the school had become "a city within a city, boasting everything from a shoeshine boy to a sophisticated IBM data complex."

During the 1965 Christmas break the university learned that Enoch Mitchell, a popular and highly regarded historian who had headed the history department for many years before stepping down in 1963, had died. Mitchell had been on the staff since 1939. "Memphis State University and the academic community of this area have lost a fine teacher and scholar," Humphreys told *The Commercial Appeal.* "The South has lost one of its best-known historians."

In 1965–66 some 624 faculty members endured small offices and crowded classrooms in dedication to their profession. Internal pressures and stresses resulting from growth and expansion affected teachers and administrators. Clayton Braddock, an education writer, in an April 18, 1966, article, wrote: "Nearly everyone has joined the parade in search of a solution to the problem of pressures on students—pressures of rising enrollments, competition for grades, admission to college. A less publicized victim of pressures is the administrator—the principal, college president, department chairman, and superintendent."

Dr. John B. Morris, after a severe heart attack, resigned in 1966 as dean of academic affairs and returned to teaching at the University of Mississippi. Appointed to succeed him with the newly created title of "provost," a more prestigious title than "dean," was Dr. Ronald E. Carrier, who had come to Memphis State from Ole Miss as the first director of the Bureau of Business and Economic Research. At the time of his promotion he had just taken over the new Division of Research and Services where he was the overseer of $800,000 in research grants. "Dr. Carrier, only 34 years of age, had demonstrated outstanding leadership ability, tremendous energy and enthusiasm, qualities that were necessary as the role and scope of the university expanded," President Humphreys said.

Humphreys never hesitated to bring in highly qualified administrators and professors, but he always looked for potential leaders already on campus. In one of his handwritten notes he listed "finding or developing administrators who could deal with rapid growth" as a major problem. "Some adequate people when the institution was small could not handle, or resisted, new and necessary adjustments," he wrote.

"Most were good people, but some could not handle the new demands. Making necessary changes was extremely difficult because it involved old friends and dedicated people with years of service. Every effort was made to deal with this problem humanly and without loss of face."

Humphreys initiated a program of selecting younger people with leadership qualities and working them into administrative assistant positions. "We developed a 'grow our own' system which produced some able people," he said. In addition to youthful Ron Carrier, who would become academic vice president before advancing to the presidency of James Madison University in Virginia, Humphreys mentioned Walter Smith, John Richardson, John Eubank, and Grady Bogue. Victor Feisal was only a young instructor from Missouri when Humphreys became president in 1960, but his talents were detected as the decade progressed. "There were others," Humphreys said. "We didn't hit on all, but overall we were able to place good people in key positions during this time of rapid change."

The president's own schedule during this period involved many demands, a multiplicity of chores, and long hours. "When the school was much smaller," he recalled, chuckling, "President Smith put his hat on promptly at 4 o'clock and walked home." Most afternoons at 4 Humphreys was in a meeting on campus or downtown.

A strong believer in letting the public know the university's benefactors and friends, Humphreys often scheduled "thank you" luncheons or dinners. On November 9, 1965, he presented "Milestone Awards" to 26 business, civic, and governmental leaders at a luncheon in the Claridge Hotel. "I know of no other school that has the fine support that Memphis State enjoys," he told the honorees. One of the reasons was that Cecil Humphreys, who once considered himself "weak" in communications, had become a master at institutional public relations.

Those communication skills would be put to a severe test in the spring of 1966. In his notes Humphreys characterized the time as "the beginning of controversy and conflict that was to keep the campus in turmoil for the balance of the spring semester."

The first incident arose out of the adminstration's acceptance of the recommendation by the dean of the Law School that the contract of the law librarian, Edgar D. Welch, not be renewed. He was completing his three-year probationary appointment. Welch charged that he was not rehired because he had picketed a Ku Klux Klan rally in Memphis in the fall of 1965. He also filed a complaint with the House Un-American Activities Committee about Klan activities at the university. He said he hoped he would be called to testify. Welch then talked to a Memphis attorney about possible legal action against the school. Nothing came of this after the conference with the attorney.

"This was a rather ironic development," Humphreys wrote, "in that just the year before the university administration had been criticized for being 'soft' on communism for allowing one of the leaders of the Free Speech Movement to speak on campus. This incident was to be the opening round of a series of events that would bring the Memphis State campus into the company of other campuses where violent and near-violent actions had replaced discussion and debate over national political, social, and economic questions."

That same month the MSU chapter of the American Association of University Professors (AAUP) voted down a motion saying the faculty enjoyed full academic freedom. The vote was 14–2 and the results were relayed to the *Memphis Press-Scimitar*. Dr. Basil Ratiu, coordinator of graduate language and president of the chapter, told the newspaper he regretted that news of the meeting had "leaked out." He said, "Neither the chapter nor I officially have any desire for publicity on the meeting."

The meeting was called after news stories appeared about the dismissal of Welch, the law librarian. However, Jerry Welch, a professor in the language department who sponsored the resolution, said his motion had nothing to do with the situation involving Edgar O. Welch. The two were not related. "My motion concerning academic freedom at MSU concerned itself specifically with the right of professors to hold and express political opinions," Welch said. "I maintain now, as I did in the motion, that I am personally aware of no pressure from the administration on me which would have the effect of discouraging my exercise of free speech."

Ratiu said the AAUP chapter, with fewer than 90 members, did not speak for the entire faculty. Humphreys, who had urged the formation of a faculty senate early in his presidency, said he had no quarrel with the AAUP. "I think the AAUP is necessary," he told the *Memphis Press-Scimitar*, "but I do not think that a 14–2 vote is representative of the thinking of our faculty."

The newspaper said the motion "was seen as a slap" against Humphreys "who stirred up a big campus debate two years ago by discouraging teachers from getting directly involved in political campaigns." In answer to this view Humphreys said, "There has never been any political interference on my part. I have just urged caution in becoming actually involved in election campaigns of state officials and members of the state legislature. Two years ago one of the faculty members was campaigning for a candidate and made statements that were not true. I issued a statement that in the interest of historical accuracy and fairness, the statement was not correct. I thought this was not good judgment and I still think so."

That issue faded quickly, but in early March of 1966 a six-page mimeographed publication titled *Logos* appeared on campus with a denunciation of the United States' involvement in South Vietnam. The Normal Tea Room and Free Speech Movement activities would pale in comparison with events surrounding the *Logos* editors and distributors. In his personal files Humphreys has 44 pages of notes collected under this heading: "The Anatomy of a Campus Disturbance." There are also copies of documents related to the incident.

In its March 3, 1966, edition, *The Commercial Appeal* interviewed Lanny Anderson, who said he was the editor of *Logos*. He said "about six others, including professors and students" helped him, but he declined to identify them. The newspaper said a spokesman for the university said the administration had no official stand on the publication's views. A few days later the *Memphis Press-Scimitar* reported a rhubarb between students and distributors of the "ultra-liberal *Logos.*" "There was some scuffling, but apparently no one was hurt," the newspaper said.

During the next few weeks three additional issues were published and aggressively distributed on campus. It was learned that the *Logos* leadership, in addition to Anderson, included Joseph Louis Ravizza, Peter Charles Quinn, Brian Murphree, and Bruce Murphree. All but Anderson had gone to high school together in West Hartford, Connecticut. Quinn and Brian Murphree had enrolled at MSU in 1964 and Bruce Murphree in 1965. Ravizza, who had enrolled in February 1966, emerged as the leader and principal spokesman.

Student hostility to *Logos* and its distributors increased, and when President Humphreys learned that the fifth edition of the publication was to be distributed at noon on April 22 in the small Student Center extra staff personnel and security officers were sent there.

In his "Anatomy" Humphreys wrote:

> Concerned about the possibility of a physical confrontation in the crowded area of the Student Center, I remained in my office to be available if needed. Shortly after 12:30 P.M., having received no report, I walked over to the Student Center. Arriving there I found the usual crowded conditions, but no controversy.
>
> A few moments later the distributors of the publication arrived and began pushing the papers into the faces of students.
>
> In a matter of seconds a dangerous situation developed. There was pushing, shoving, and loud, angry voices raised against the four distributors, who responded by further baiting those opposed to them.
>
> University personnel fought their way through the crowd to protect the distributors. I was able to make my way through the crowd surrounding the law school librarian, who had come with the distributors. His glasses had been knocked off, but he was still haranguing the crowd that had pushed him and spat on his papers.
>
> It was no time for moral or philosophical debate. Several students held empty glass drink bottles as if ready to use as weapons.
>
> We physically pushed the crowd back and got the *Logos* distributors out of the building and across the campus. No one had been hurt, but it was an ugly and dangerous scene—one that I would not have believed could happen on the MSU campus.
>
> We truly had arrived in a new era.

In its first edition, *Logos* said, "As American citizens we are ashamed of what our government is doing in Vietnam. We protest the crime of Russians killing Hungarians." The fourth edition published a letter from Norman Thomas, the widely known socialist, who took issue with a statement by Britain's Bertram Russell which had appeared in the third edition. In concluding his remarks, Thomas said, "My own interests are peace, to be obtained by negotiations, not war and not the guaranteed complete victory of the Viet Cong, which has its own share of atrocities to account for. I do not think that is the view of the May

2 Movement, which I do not think would wholly deny its Communist sympathy. At least this is the impression a great many of us have."

From a review of many publications, including articles in *The New York Times,* and from information volunteered by students who had visited Ravizza and Quinn in an apartment they shared near the campus, Memphis State officials did not believe the *Logos* leaders were sent to Memphis as part of an organized national movement by the American Communist Party. In ideology they were closer to the Chinese Communists and the Progressive Labor Movement (PLM), which was founded in 1962 by two expelled members of the American Communist Party for following Chinese Communist beliefs. By 1965 the PLM had become the Progressive Labor Party (PLP), and its youth affiliate was the May 2 Movement (M2M), a loosely organized and poorly financed group opposing United States involvement in Vietnam.

President Humphreys' files said:

> The *Logos* group had no regular source of financial support. It depended upon small donations from a few young faculty members and a few off-campus contributors who thought they were supporting noble young intellectuals who were courageously opposing the Vietnam involvement and defending free speech.
>
> The young leaders were on a tremendous "ego trip." Within a few weeks after the arrival of Ravizza and with the assistance of four undistinguished students, they had attracted regional media attention, were manipulating some university faculty members, and succeeded in disrupting a campus.
>
> Without any direct affiliation with any organized Communist movement, they followed a basic Communist principle: There was no such thing as objective truth; truth was what served your objective.

The day after the April 22 incident in the Student Center, antiwar protestors marched from Union Avenue at East Parkway downtown to the Post Office on Front Street. *Logos* leaders claimed credit for organizing the march, and they participated, but it had a broader base. Among the marchers were three Memphis State faculty members and the Reverend James Lawson, a Memphis minister who had been an avowed pacifist for many years.

Several students reported to university officials that Ravizza had boasted that he had registered as an in-state student, although he had never been in Tennessee until he enrolled. A check of his registration card revealed that it had been altered to show Ravizza as an in-state student. He was called before the University Discipline Board, which included Dean of Students R. M. Robison, Dean of Women Flora Rawls, and three faculty members, on April 29. There were two charges: fraud against the university and social misconduct. The latter charge stemmed from a report by three fraternity men that Ravizza had offered them—for $15—the favors of a young woman who shared his apartment.

President Humphrey's "Anatomy" records said, "Ravizza appeared before the board with an advisor, which was according to the published procedures. Ravizza did not deny the first charge, and the board did not rule on the second charge even though the fraternity men testified and were believed to be telling the truth. The board ruled, apparently aware of the special nature of the case, not to expel Ravizza immediately, allowing him to finish the semester. It ruled that he could not attend Memphis State after that until June 1967, at which time his application would be taken under advisement. He was ordered to reimburse the university for the $82.50 out-of-state tuition he owed."

The hearing, under university policy, was confidential and could not be revealed without the approval of the student. There was no publicity and Ravizza was permitted to remain in school for the balance of the year. Humphreys said, "It is doubted that an 'ordinary' student would have been permitted to complete the semester."

Some students told their deans that Ravizza had boasted that he had "Humphreys in a corner," and that on May 2, the anniversary of the May 2 Movement, the *Logos* distributors planned to fake an attack on one of its members in front of the Student Center at noon while distributing the paper's sixth edition. The informants said Ravizza and his associates wanted to embarrass Memphis State by creating a riot.

Humphreys was determined to thwart the plan, and he turned to the football team for help rather than depending on his limited security forces or calling in Memphis police. He remembered that at Berkeley the situation grew much worse after the police were called to that campus.

"Several athletes were selected on the basis of their maturity of judgment and coolness under pressure," Humphreys said, "and each was assigned to protect one of the *Logos* staff or followers who would be distributing the publication. It was thought that well-known students would be more effective than the few security officers available."

The *Logos* group appeared at noon as scheduled. A large crowd gathered, some as curious spectators but many more in an angry mood. Angry exchanges broke out. "Their strategy of creating violence appeared to be working," Humphreys said, "but the one-on-one protection by the athletes prevented any physical contact, or one of them knocking another down. Even with the student guards it had become an ugly and dangerous scene."

The student guards, closely protecting the paper's distributors, moved them through the crowd and across the campus to Patterson Street. Angry, shouting students followed and when the street was reached they broke through the athlete-guards. Once the street was reached Memphis police moved in, but fistfights broke out nevertheless, and several persons were knocked down, the *Memphis Press-Scimitar* reported.

During the melee the *Logos* distributors ran through the mob, which had become more dispersed with the arrival of the police, and reached safety in the Catholic Student Center on Mynders. There were no arrests. The city's police chief said his men could not identify the assailants. The president's use of football players had proven successful, although the players evidently were not sympathetic with the aims of *Logos*. Humphreys learned that Billy Fletcher, the popular quarterback, who was one of the escorts, had knocked one of the distributors down. Humphreys called Fletcher to his office and questioned him. Fletcher said he had followed instructions to protect the *Logos* distributor on campus, but he had become so provoked by the jeers and vile language that when the group reached Patterson Street, he had taken a poke at one of them.

The next morning President Humphreys ordered this statement read in all classes: "Monday's actions on and off the Memphis State University campus destroys the atmosphere in which learning takes place. An appeal is made to all members of the university community to use your influence to maintain orderly procedures. Violence on the Memphis

As a means of protesting the Vietnam war, most campuses saw the appearance of an "underground" newspaper. At MSU the newspaper was the *Logos*, which was the subject of an Extra of *The Tiger Rag*.

State campus will not be tolerated and disciplinary action will be taken to enforce this policy."

Humphreys later said he was not certain his threat could be enforced with the limited security means available and the due process procedures required in student discipline cases. Most of all, he did not want armed law enforcement officers on campus.

After the May 2 confrontation the tension lessened. "The students began to realize that they had been deliberately provoked," Humphreys said. "Some of the younger faculty members who had encouraged the *Logos* group, but had been cautioning them to broaden their base of dissent, had become disillusioned." Other support also helped to calm matters. The faculty council issued a statement saying, "It is the feeling (of the council) that the president and the security staff have, within the confines of their ability and their jurisdiction, made a sincere and concerted effort to uphold the principles of academic freedom and responsibility. It is conceivable that some persons might quarrel with their approach or point out basic problems which remain unsolved— but we have been unable to question the integrity of the basic resolve."

Once again, *The Tiger Rag* put out a special edition. It devoted its entire May 4 issue to the *Logos* situation. It published a full account of the May 2 fracas, but it hit hard with editorials pointing out the danger of radical movements on college campuses. The editorials urged the student body to avoid violence and mass congregation, concluding that only clear thinking and mature conduct would end the confusion. The campus newspaper ran a letter from a former editor, Michael Stewart, urging students not to make martyrs out of dissidents.

"Letters to the Editor" in the Memphis newspapers were brisk following the violent skirmish at Memphis State, but the school year was winding down and not a day had been lost from the university calendar.

There was other news, too. Attorney William W. Goodman gave $10,000 to the MSU Foundation to establish a Goodman Professorship in law. He stipulated that up to $2000 a year be used to supplement the salary of a professor teaching property law. Goodman was executive vice president of Commerce Title Guaranty Company. "I feel that there is a special need for these funds during the next formative years of the School of Law," Goodman said. "It is my sincere hope that funds will be available through me or other sources to continue this program after this initial gift has been exhausted." Calling the gift "a splendid gesture," Humphreys said the future of instruction in the professions at Memphis State was assured by such confidence and support.

The school year had begun with Memphis State playing Ole Miss in the dedicatory game at Memphis Memorial Stadium, and it ended with the announcement that Dr. Eugene Lambert had resigned as athletic director and Spook Murphy would assume the dual role of football coach and athletic director.

9

The South Campus

1966–1967

THE NEWS HEADLINES

Medicare, a federal program designed to pay part of the medical expenses of citizens 65 or older, begins...Racial riots bring a "long hot summer" to Chicago, Baltimore, San Francisco, Cleveland, Omaha, Brooklyn, and Jacksonville...A white mob in Grenada, Mississippi, attacks black students attempting to integrate two neighborhood schools...Edward Brooke of Massachussetts becomes first black elected to Senate since Reconstruction...State Department announces that since January 1, 1961, 6664 Americans have been killed in Vietnam...Three astronauts die as Apollo I spacecraft burns on ground at Cape Kennedy ...Tennessee Governor Buford Ellington signs bill repealing state's "Monkey Law."

AND THE WAY WE WERE

Summer enrollment reaches record high of 6604 students from 48 states and 46 foreign countries...The cafeteria, long the subject of boycotts, picketing and editorials, is now under new management...132 new professors and instructors are being added to keep pace with 15,000 student body... Cross country team includes first black to compete in MSU varsity athletic team...The race to collect the largest number of traffic tickets continues...MSU has distinction of being first Tennessee campus with an integrated fraternity.

MEMPHIS STATE COMPLETED A DECADE of development as a university in 1967 by acquiring A $2.75 million South Campus at no cost to the school.

It was the historian in Cecil C. Humphreys that made him send the pen President Lyndon B. Johnson used to sign the bill conveying 129 acres of the old Kennedy Veterans Hospital to the university to the archives in Brister Library on October 5, 1967. It was the drive and energy of a builder of a university that led Humphreys to the South Campus two weeks later to knock down the first brick from an old hospital building to start work on a $2.2 million apartment project for married students.

The addition of a South Campus less than a mile southeast of the main campus is a study in alert patience by Humphreys and the university over a period of five years. The first public knowledge of Memphis State's interest came on December 12, 1961, when *The Commercial Appeal's* city editor, Malcolm Adams, wrote a story headlined, "MSU to Seek Hospital Land for Expansion."

But Humphreys had been at work earlier. When he learned that the Veterans Administration planned to build a new high-rise hospital on its grounds at Park and Getwell, he knew the 146-acre tract would have surplus land and a lot of old barracks-type buildings. Humphreys immediately called on Representative Clifford Davis, a former city judge and a popular figure in the old Crump organization, to seek his aid in placing the first bid.

In *The Commercial Appeal* story Representative Davis said, "Once the VA's architects and engineers determine the amount of land which will be needed, I will be able to advise Memphis State how to proceed in filing an application for the excess acreage. Memphis State's campus is just a mile away from the hospital site. The university has more than 6000 students today, and the officials tell me they anticipate an enrollment of about 10,000 in 1966. We must look ahead and take care of our boys and girls who need to go to college."

Humphreys praised Davis' support and added, "We have only 80 acres, and we are faced with a desperate situation in planning for the future. We are crowded already. This could be a tremendous help in solving our problem." Humphreys, who had talked to Senator Estes Kefauver at the same time he conferred with Davis, had a strong ally in the senator. Both had aided the university in obtaining an Air Force ROTC unit in 1951, and Senator Kefauver still remembered a radio program in 1954 when Humphreys had defended him from charges of Communist sympathies leveled by his opponent, Representative Pat Sutton, in a vicious campaign.

Humphreys told the newspaper Memphis State could use all the land in 10 years. On January 10, 1962, the *Memphis Press-Scimitar* reported that John S. Gleason, the VA administrator in Washington, had advised Senator Kefauver that some of the hospital's grounds and buildings would be declared surplus upon completion of the new hospital in about four years. If normal procedures were followed, the VA would report the land as surplus to the General Services Administration. The GSA then, if no other federal agency wanted it, would dispose of the property. Usually that took about two years.

"It was recognized that the land would not be available for a number of years," Humphreys said, "but it was important that an early and strong claim should be established for this valuable and badly needed land."

Shortly after the Veterans Administration announced its plans for a new hospital, Humphreys received a telephone call from Dr. Maston Callison, dean of the University of Tennessee Medical School. They had been fellow undergraduate students at UT in Knoxville.

"Could you use all the Kennedy property?" Callison asked.

"Yes," Humphreys replied without any hesitation.

Callison wanted the VA hospital to be built in the Medical Center where it would be a valuable asset to the medical education program of the UT Medical School, but it was opposed by Baptist Memorial Hospital, one of the nation's largest private hospitals, and other medical facilities in the area. "I told Dr. Callison that he didn't have a chance of getting a plan changed that already was in the federal pipeline," Humphreys said. "I felt that Baptist Hospital with its dynamic director,

Frank Groner, and other Baptists, including Representative Cliff Davis, who had been instrumental in getting the new hospital funded, were just too strong."

Typically, Humphreys, who knew the difference between probabilities and possibilities, hedged his bet. "With the slightest possibility of the whole tract being available," he said, "I told Callison we would do all we could to help."

Dr. Callison, a determined man, intensified his efforts, and with the assistance of Dr. Bland Cannon and others interested in the development of what is now known as the University of Tennessee Center for the Health Sciences, gained the support of the Memphis and Shelby County Medical Society. *The Commercial Appeal* on January 28, 1963, reported that the VA had decided to build its new $20 million hospital adjacent to the Medical Center.

Humphreys said little assistance came from Memphis State other than letters to federal legislators and contacts with local government officials, But the new turn of events expanded his hopes for meeting campus land needs. His goal was to fend off other challengers for the old hospital grounds by strengthening Memphis State's priority in the public mind. To help do this, in 1965 the university leased three of the 121 buildings at the hospital. It was thought important to "get your foot in the door."

President Humphreys' "greatest need" and "best possible use" campaign would continue. Meanwhile, the idea that another federal agency might lay claim to the property bothered Humphreys, and he went to work on a plan to bypass the regular Veterans Administration–to–General Services Administration procedures for disposing of surplus federal property. Congress, if it felt it was justified, could make a direct grant of the property to a state educational institution. This took some careful homework by Memphis State.

"In building our case for the acquisition I had sought information about the cost of the property to the federal government," Humphreys said. "No one in local government remembered how the federal government acquired the property in 1942. We had a title search made which revealed that the city and county governments had used eminent domain to purchase the property and had given 129 acres to the federal government as a site for the hospital."

The Kennedy Veterans Hospital (now South Campus) with Park Avenue in foreground, as it appeared when acquired by Memphis State in 1967.

The local governments paid $58,689 for 129.06 acres which were donated to the United States, and the federal government bought an additional 17.27 acres for $7294. A $10 million Army hospital was built in a complex with more than a thousand beds, with most of the work being completed in 1942. The northwest corner of the grounds were at Park and Shotwell, but everyone involved quickly concluded that Shotwell south of Park should become Getwell. The facility was transferred to the Veterans Administration on August 26, 1946, by the Secretary of War.

On January 24, 1966, Senator Albert Gore, with Senator Howard Baker as cosponsor, introduced Senate Bill 619 authorizing conveyance of the land from the United States to the State of Tennessee for use by Memphis State University. The effort to bypass the regular federal procedures had begun.

Representative Robert (Fats) Everett of the Eighth Congressional District introduced a similar bill in the House, and it won quick approval on April 3. Representative Everett steered it through the Veterans Affairs Committee, in which he was an influential member, and Representative Dan Kuykendall of Memphis played a key role in convincing H.R. Gross, an Iowa representative known as the "watch dog of the treasury," that the transfer was a good thing and not a government giveaway.

The transfer faced a tougher fight in the Senate because of the so-called Morse Formula. Senator Wayne Morse of Oregon, a member of the Committee on Labor and Public Welfare, held that the federal government should be reimbursed for its costs before disposing of U.S. property.

A hearing on April 5, 1967, before the Labor and Public Welfare's subcommittee on Veterans' Affairs would prove crucial. Its chairman was Jennings Randolph of West Virginia. Other members were Ralph Yarborough of Texas, Edward M. Kennedy of New York, Peter H. Dominick of Colorado, Paul J. Fannin of Arizona, and Robert P. Griffin of Michigan.

President Humphreys flew to Washington with Walter Armstrong, the prominent attorney and civic leader who was representing the Memphis Chamber of Commerce. With them went copies of the resolutions of the Memphis City Council and the Shelby County Commission which stated that if the federal government was not going to use the property for the purpose for which it had been given then those bodies would like to see it returned for the use of Memphis State University. Their testimony would be critical because the Bureau of the Budget and the General Services Administration had sent letters to the committee opposing any bypassing of procedures in disposing of the property.

Senator Gore spoke first in seeking to win an exception to federal rules. "An exception, as I see it, is justified, first, because of an urgent educational need," Gore said. "Memphis State now has an enrollment of more than 14,000 students. The curriculum of the university has been expanded to meet the needs of the student body, and the student body is constantly growing, as is the city of Memphis. It is anticipated that by 1970 this will be a university of more than 20,000 students. They are virtually spilling out into the street."

Senator Gore concluded by saying there was no way the founders of the institution could have envisioned that "this would become a university of truly major proportions in so short a time."

The next speaker was Senator Baker, who said the problem facing Memphis State was time. He said the university likely would get the hospital grounds under usual procedures but the school "is needful of these facilities now." Baker added: "Memphis State University was, only some 15 years ago, a small college of relatively parochial concern and influence. Today it is a full-scale state university which offers quality education to a major region of this country. Its phenomenal growth has by no means been at the expense of superior education, but it has resulted in severely overcrowded conditions. The growth of this institution has in many ways paralleled and aided the growth of the Mid-South."

The junior senator also pointed out that the land, not the buildings or improvements upon it, was the university's prime need, and that most of it had been donated by local government.

Chairman Randolph next called Walter Armstrong to speak, and he pointd out that he was representing the Memphis Area Chamber of Commerce and was not a graduate of Memphis State. But Armstrong was an eloquent spokesman.

> I have seen Memphis State, since 1960, increase from 5000 to almost 14,000 in enrollment. I have watched it participate more and more in the life of our city and I have watched the increase in the interaction between it and the City of Memphis and surrounding area which is only possible and only takes place in a great metropolitan university.
>
> Today, we have service bureaus at Memphis State in business and economic research, real estate research, educational research, and sociological research, all of which are continually turned to by the city and area for assistance. It has become such an important part of the growth of the city, the area, and the region that future growth is inconceivable without it.

Armstrong ended his remarks by reading from a recent study of the economics of metropolitan Memphis which said, "The metropolitan area must look to Memphis State University for the top-level leadership and talents that it needs. This institution has the potential of becoming a major top-ranking university if it is given vigorous and continued support. Memphis State can make an incalculable contribution to the local region and area. Indeed, without this contribution Memphis will be at a serious disadvantage with respect to other metropolitan areas throughout the county."

Turning to Chairman Randolph, Armstrong said, "Others will speak for Memphis State. I speak for Memphis and its surrounding area. The need is immediate, and we ask that it be granted. Thank you, sir."

"Mr. Armstrong," Senator Randolph replied, "we are helped by your testimony."

The chairman then called for the testimony of President Humphreys, who had come prepared with a utilization study which included charts and maps for each subcommittee member. Randolph, before he had a chance to look at Humphreys' work, said it would not be made a portion of the record, but reference would be made to it. But in a few seconds he changed his mind. "I like the way in which you presented it in charts and graphs and statistics that spell out the need and we may be able on account of the preparation to include parts of it in the record itself," the senator told Humphreys. "I had thought it was prepared in a different way."

"I might say this has been anticipated," Humphreys replied. "We have been aware of the new facility that has been completed now for the Veterans' Administration, and this is not a suddenly conceived idea nor recent plan. It is the only alternative for additional space."

One of the important points to get across to the committee was that the buildings on the old hospital site might be used temporarily, but, to get around the Morse Formula, it had to be shown they were a hindrance rather than "an improvement" of the property.

At one point when President Humphreys was showing that some of the facilities had been unused for 14 years and had "been cannibalized in order to make other facilities available for use by the Veterans Administration," Senator Randolph broke in: "Dr. Humphreys, could I inquire at this point—not to break up the continuity of your presentation, but in reference to the use of these buildings by Memphis State University—I clearly understand that you feel that they are obsolescent to a degree. That is true, is it not?

"Yes."

"But under the impact for housing requirements, you feel that they could be perhaps refurbished, reinforced, a certain amount of decorating, and the general improvement of the facilities to the extent that they could tide you over a period of housing need; is this true?"

"Yes, sir," Humphreys said. "We feel that for a number of years during this emergency period of burgeoning enrollments, considerable use could be made of present facilities but not on a permanent basis."

In the rest of his detailed testimony Humphreys traced the academic growth of the university through the addition of graduate and professional programs, including engineering and law. He also told how Memphis State had become the largest premedical training facility in the region, with 1100 students preparing for medicine, dentistry, pharmacy, and nursing.

"If Memphis State University is to meet the needs of this growing region, our land space and physical facilities must be expanded," Humphreys concluded. "We feel that the Kennedy Hospital property which will be vacated this summer will be ideal for our future development."

Senator Randolph said he was "impressed" with the testimony of Humphreys, Gore, Baker, and Armstrong and said, "There is no reluctance on my part to understand the need."

But the chairman mentioned that two other groups, the Presbyterian Church and the Southern College of Optometry, had put in bids for some of the hospital property. The church wanted to start a nursing home and the college, an outpatient clinic. This caught Humphreys a bit off guard because it was news to him, but these were relatively unimportant private requests and he did not debate their merits.

The Morse Formula remained the biggest hurdle. The university received a boost in the testimony of Howard Bernstein, assistant general counsel of the Veterans Administration, and Whitney Ashbridge, assistant administrator for construction.

Both testified the land was worth $2.75 million, but this exchange between Senator Ralph Yarborough of Texas and Ashbridge, who had just placed that value on the land, helped the Memphis State cause:

"That is the real estate?" Yarborough asked.

"That is the real estate."

"Have you included in that, Mr. Ashbridge, the value of the old buildings on it?"

"The old buildings really have no value because, as has been previously stated, they were built during the war as semipermanent construction. They really have served their purpose. And while they could be used on a temporary basis by the university, we feel that they are probably in the long run more of a liability than an asset."

The subcommittee favorably reported Senate Bill 619 to Senator Lister Hill's Committee on Labor and Public Welfare.

Senator Morse, after learning of the testimony and holding a conference with Senator Gore, relented a little in his opposition to returning, without compensation, that portion of the hospital land that had been donated by local government. However, he held to the view that the federal government should be paid for the 17.7 acres it had purchased. He also wanted a 50 percent return on the value of any improvements made.

"This is not a pleasant role for me to play," Morse told the *Memphis Press-Scimitar*. "But then I'm not known for playing pleasant roles around here." He said that his insistence that the government realize at least part of the federal investment in the disposition of federal holdings had saved the nation's taxpayers more than $1 billion during the past 20 years.

In early July Senators Gore and Baker agreed to a compromise, with the State of Tennessee to receive the 129 acres given to the United States and the federal government to retain the remaining 17.7 acres. Representative "Fats" Everett, who got the entire package through the House, went along with the plan, which was approved by the Senate without dissent. Former governor Buford Ellington, while serving as President Johnson's director of Emergency Planning, helped speed up the process of acquiring the balance of the land under the Surplus Property program. Memphis State got the remainder of the property in 1968.

President Humphreys jotted down these thoughts in his notes: "The goal set five years before, with the dedicated effort by federal legislators, local government leaders, and public support, was achieved. A tract of land of 146 acres, with a few usable buildings within a mile of

The Sports Complex on the South Campus.

the campus and valued at $2.75 million dollars, had been acquired at no cost to the university."

The addition of the South Campus would provide space for married student apartments, receiving and storage, a plant nursery, and a modern sports complex for which there was no longer space on the main campus. The hospital morgue provided a facility for research on the growing and treatment of catfish and other research projects, and some of the usable buildings were made available to the Memphis Board of Education. Acquisition of the South Campus was an enormously significant step ahead for the university, but there were many other achievements in the final year of the school's first decade as a university.

A few eyebrows went up when the 1966–1967 school year was only seven days old, and Governor Frank G. Clement came to the Claridge

Hotel in Memphis to open a bid for the Democratic nomination to the United States Senate. *The Commercial Appeal* wrote:

"The Governor opened his Shelby County campaign headquarters to the tune of praise sung by Dr. C. C. Humphreys, president of Memphis State University, who broke his school's precedent by introducing a candidate for statewide office." However, the introduction did not mention the Senate race but praised Clement's support as governor for education and his great contributions to the state mental health program.

Clement, by most standards, had been an exceedingly good friend of higher education in Tennessee and Memphis State in particular, and this obviously motivated Humphreys. Clement would not make it to the Senate, and Humphreys was not unduly criticized for his introduction.

Ten days after the Clement headquarters opened, President Humphreys was back in the news. On July 16, 1966, he announced that MSU had been awarded a five-year, $275,371 federal grant to study mental retardation; it was the largest single research grant the university had received. Humphreys said that the Department of Psychology would establish a training program for graduate psychology students in the field of retardation. Doctoral students would study the causes and kinds of mental retardation and develop ways to treat and educate mentally retarded persons. A few months later it was announced that research contracts and grants received by the university within one year had exceeded a million dollars for the first time.

There were many indications that the quality of the school was being recognized nationally. In Washington the Economic Development Administration gave MSU a $92,000 grant to help provide for a Regional Development Center to provide management counsel to businesses and industries in the 46 counties of Middle and West Tennessee.

"The university is seeking to bring its increasing talents and energies to bear on the region it serves through the education of an increasing number of students and its expanding service and research activities," Humphreys said.

New programs and activities seemed to be spawned daily during the school year. The M. L. Seidman Memorial Town Hall Lectures, with internationally known speakers, was started. The School of Business, with 31 percent of the student enrollment, began six executive development courses and seminars. The New York Pro Musica performed as a part of the newly inaugurated University Convocation Series. The Alumni Association started an Annual Fund, and, in athletics, Memphis State joined the Missouri Valley Conference.

A Distinguished Teacher Award program was initiated. Humphreys was concerned that the importance of good teaching was not being recognized and rewarded because of the greatly increased emphasis on research and publication and, to a lesser extent, on public service. One of the most common complaints of students during this period of campus unrest was that they were not being adequately taught because of the rapid growth of most schools and because of the emphasis on "publish or perish." Many educators, including MSU's president, felt that the students were at least partly correct. Humphreys believed that all three—teaching, research publication, and service—were important for the expanding university, but he did not want the outstanding classroom teacher to be forgotten.

With money from the Chapman Foundation, Greater Memphis State, Inc., and the Alumni Association, awards of $500 were given to distinguished teachers. The first three recipients were Dr. Carroll B. Bowman of the Philosophy Department, Mrs. Sophia Brotherton of the Curriculum and Instruction Department, and Dr. James R. Chumney, Jr., of the History Department.

The impact of all this did not go unnoticed. "MSU's growth can be measured in a way more important than counting students, idolizing athletes, and marveling at new buildings," *The Commercial Appeal* said in an editorial. "The list of MSU's special events scheduled during the 1966–67 term is an imposing tribute the university administration is paying to academics, high level entertainment, and that mistreated category, culture."

The editorial listed a broad variety of programs and added, "These are not simply programs for students—they are open to the public, some free and some for a nominal fee, which plainly indicates MSU's interest in serving the community at large."

MSU could have turned inward because it enrolled 14,541 for the fall term, including 3450 freshmen. The university was still growing but at a somewhat less hectic pace. Including replacements and newly created teaching positions, the faculty counted 132 new members. A new chemistry building and a new humanities classroom building on the developing mall also helped to ease the strain on facilities.

The new Highland Towers two blocks west of the campus opened and were fully occupied with 1000 students. Allen & O'Hara, the private company that owned and operated the dormitories, announced it would build two more similar ten-story structures immediately adjacent to the campus at Patterson and Central.

Governor Frank Clement scooped the first shovel of dirt as site preparation began for the new $4 million University Center on October 16. A few days later Ernest Ball, an SBE member and a member of the first Normal School class in 1912, spoke at ceremonies initiating work on the $2.5 million addition to Brister Library.

While many communitywide cultural events were being added, the annual Shakespeare Festival, which had begun in 1952, came to an end. "This cooperative effort had brought elements of town and gown closer together for the benefit of all," Humphreys said, "but the growth of the university's theater staff in size and expertise had created problems between the cooperating campus and community groups. It was probably inevitable, but a sad loss to both campus and community."

There was a cultural plus to be noted, too. The university brought Shelby Foote, outstanding writer and historian, to campus as its first "writer-in-residence."

At a luncheon on November 21 the MSU Foundation's Annual Giving Program was begun with George M. Klepper as chairman of the campaign committee. One of the speakers was Kemmons Wilson, chairman of the board of Holiday Inns, Inc., who called Memphis State a marketable product that is popular and in demand, adding that "the people of Memphis look to MSU for higher education, cultural leadership, and research."

Following in Clement's footsteps, the new governor, Buford Ellington, put great emphasis on higher education in his budget message to the General Assembly early in 1967. His budget statement said it "recognizes the unique position of Memphis State University and provides additional dollars to elevate this outstanding institution to a more prominent role in the future development of higher education." The governor advocated an increased appropriation for the coming biennium of $41.6 million more than had been provided for the state's higher education program during the preceding two years.

But it was too good to be true. "Partisan politics and a rising spirit of independence by the legislature brought about a reduction in the governor's requested budget," Humphreys said. "Even though the funding recommendations for all levels of education were reduced, improvements were made."

The appropriation to Memphis State was increased from $7,862,-400 for the 1966–67 fiscal year to $10,563,000 for 1967–68 and to $11,874,000 for 1968–69. Even with the reductions it was the largest appropriation the university had ever received. Capital outlay funds, to be financed by state bonds, gave Memphis State an additional $9,952,100, or almost double the amount that had been received the previous four years. Some of these funds would lead to a new Engineering Building on Central. The building along that street was rapidly becoming the showcase side of the university.

Another significant initiative by Ellington was the formation of the Tennessee Higher Education Commission (THEC) to serve as a coordinating board for state-supported institutions of higher learning. It was to begin operation July 1, 1967, and develop a master plan for higher education. The THEC would have final authority in approving new programs.

One of the greatest growth areas at Memphis State was in the Graduate School, and at the June 29 meeting of the State Board of Education Humphreys won approval to offer additional doctoral programs in economics, history, and chemistry. The SBE took this last opportunity and gave its approval.

In addition to acquiring a South Campus, Memphis State became affiliated with the Memphis Speech and Hearing Center in the Medical Center near the downtown. The facility had been built in 1966 by the state at a cost of $653,253, but the state provided no operating funds. The center quickly had trouble meeting operating costs and keeping a professional staff because of an increasing demand for its services. The staff also wanted affiliation with an educational institution which would expand the training and research aspects of the center and strengthen the service programs. A similar center in Nashville was associated with Vanderbilt University and Peabody College, and another in Knoxville with the University of Tennessee.

The center's board members put out feelers to both Memphis State and the University of Tennessee Medical Center regarding affiliation. Earlier, Dr. Sam Johnson, dean of the School of Education at Memphis State, had discussed the possibilities with President Humphreys. Johnson was a member of the center's board, and he felt there were many benefits to be realized by a closer relationship between the center and MSU's departments of psychology, speech and drama, and the recently expanded special education department.

Officials at the University of Tennessee said they had serious budget problems, and Dr. Freeman McConnell, director of the Nashville center and head of the Vanderbilt Department of Speech and Audiology, who was serving as a consultant for the Memphis center, recommended to the Memphis Speech and Hearing Center board that it give serious thought to merger with Memphis State. He said the university seemed receptive.

An agreement between the university and the center was reached, and a proposed contract was presented to the State Board of Education at its June meeting. "It was approved and the center became a part of the university," Humphreys said. "One of the conditions that Memphis State insisted on was that the center board continue as an advisory group. They had started to meet a community need and operated it without public fund. They were needed to maintain the private interest and local government support that had enabled the center to be a valuable factor in meeting community needs. Especially important were the chairman of the board at the time of the merger, Holton Rush, and his successor, Ed E. Jappe. Also worthy of note in the development of the center was John Irwin, who had come as its director in 1953."

It would prove to be a higher beneficial merger. Within a few years the programs and services had grown to the point that the staff was enlarged and additional space obtained.

A major news story rocked the campus in the spring semester of 1967. The *Memphis Press-Scimitar* broke the story with this headline, "MSU's President May Join Bank," on February 18. The next morning *The Commercial Appeal's* headline said, "Dr. Humphreys Moves Nearer Officer's Job with UP Bank." It quoted John E. Brown, chairman of Union Planters National Bank, as saying that the appointment of Humphreys as vice chairman "is expected to be finalized in the very near future." Humphreys confirmied that he was giving the offer serious consideration, but said, "Right now I'm concerned full time with trying to present the Memphis State case to the incoming legislature."

He told *The Commercial Appeal* his work at Memphis State had "been a tremendous challenge and would be hard to leave." He said his decision would be "based on the attractiveness of the two positions—my interest in what I'm doing and the (new) challenges that would be involved." At the time President Humphreys made $20,000 a year, plus residence at the house on Grandview. There were reports the bank would more than double his income.

Humphreys already was a member of the bank's board of directors, but student reaction was swift. Fifty students gathered on the lawn of the president's home at 4035 Grandview on the night of February 20 and held up a bed sheet with big letters painted on it saying: "MSU Needs You."

The president came out and talked to the students. "If decisions were made by the heart," he said, "you know what my decision would be."

Barry Reisenberg, student body president, said, "Dr. Humphreys, we need you, but we also stand ready to back whatever decision you make."

"It will be a real, real difficult decision," Humphreys replied, "but this means an awful lot to me—more than you will ever know."

In his March 1 "Good Evening" column in the *Memphis Press-Scimitar,* Bob Johnson told of Humphreys receiving an ovation at a meeting at the Memphis Athletic Club of the Highland 100, a booster group. As he entered Humphreys had to pass seven large signs staked at intervals. They said he was "No. 1 in Education, No. 1 in Athletics, No. 1 in his Community, No. 1 in his State, No. 1 at MSU, and No. 1 With Highland 100." When Jim Markham, the new president of the club, presented Humphreys with a plaque, he said, "We've tried in our humble way to show we don't want to lose you."

Johnson wrote further:

CECIL HUMPHREYS has received many honors, but he must have been moved to know in what high regard he was held. We are the same age, and I have known him since we were young men, watched his career with interest and admiration, know that while he was appreciative of this recognition it did not swell his ego. He has perspective, a healthy respect for his own ability, but he is a realist, not a stuffed shirt. Success is in his head, but it hasn't gone to his head.

If one were writing a success story, I don't believe you could have a better subject—high school and college athletic star, coach, FBI man, Navy combat officer, student, civic leader, family man, college head in a dramatic time, and now—recognition of his ability from a great financial institution.

He has not signified his intention. Some of us are making it difficult for him to make a change, even if he wishes. I think we are being unfair.

When I first heard some months ago that Cecil might go with Union Planters, I told him my thought that nothing he could do would be more rewarding in sense of accomplishment and more useful to society than continuing what he has been doing so well. Magnanimous me, helping Cecil do his thinking for him. He told me then he sometimes yearns for a little more time to himself and with his family, that the job was just getting where he could delegate some authority.

It has been a backbreaking job for seven years. He averages perhaps two nights a week at home. He has overseen growth of the university from 4800 to 14,000 students, with over 700 teachers. When he became president, projected enrollment of 1970 was 10,000. Now it is 20,000. Under him, 16 new buildings have gone up, over $30 million in construction, and $12 million in construction is under way or nearing completion. Five years ago it was planned to begin a law school. On July 1 they didn't have a book or a teacher, but they opened that fall, got accreditation 2½ years later, one of the fastest recognitions, and will shortly move into the new law building, one of the campus' finest.

Cecil has been the school's giver of laws, arbiter of faculty and student matters, judge, personnel director, diplomat, infighter for legislative needs, man on a tightrope, public relations man, after-dinner speaker, maker of sometimes controversial decisions with a minimum of controversy. One of his greatest achievements was the manner in which integration came to MSU. Dr. Humphreys is a well-informed man, educator, and administrator above all else.

There has been grapevine talk that the proposed new job would be a stepping stone, that a group of businessmen would like him to run for governor. He would make a good one, but I don't believe he'll go for it. He has told me he has no political ambitions. He is concerned about whether he can maintain the pace he has been keeping for 7 more years and still be as effective for the school. He admits he has to stay busy, thrives on pressure, would hate to leave.

He hasn't made up his mind. What ever he decides, I know it will be right for both him and the school.

Humphreys decided on April 27 to stay at Memphis State. He issued a one-paragraph statement: "I am staying at Memphis State University because I want to help complete the many new projects and programs we have under way. I am grateful to Union Planters National Bank for discussing another position with me, but I feel that, although the banks of our community are making great contributions to the development of this area, I can make my best contribution by staying at Memphis State. I hope to continue as a director of Union Planters Bank."

Both of the city's newspapers lauded his decision. *The Commercial Appeal* said, "That he has decided to stay at MSU is not only of public interest, but also to the benefit of Memphis, the university and students and faculty." In its editorial the *Memphis Press-Scimitar* said, "Dr. Humphreys has the confidence of the Memphis community and of the state educational authorities at Nashville. And, what is more, he has the confidence of the student body at MSU. Nowadays, that means a lot."

Humphreys worked to win the respect of students. He would put their educational progress—and welfare—above all other things. Within a year, a calm, confident university president would have to make critical judgments in the wake of the assassination of Dr. Martin Luther King, Jr., in downtown Memphis.

When the State Board of Education met in Nashville on May 5, 1967, it adopted a resolution commending Humphreys for electing "to remain as president of Memphis State University and to advance the cause of public higher education in the nation."

The resolution:

WHEREAS, President C. C. Humphreys of Memphis State University is an outstanding educator, administrator, and civic leader, and,

WHEREAS, his achievements and contributions in behalf of higher learning have brought great credit to Memphis State University, to the State Board of Education, and to the State of Tennessee, and,

WHEREAS, Dr. Humphreys' professional ability, generous spirit, and personal integrity merit acclaim and praise, and

WHEREAS, in testimony thereof, he has had numerous offers of high position bearing great prestige and reward, and,

WHEREAS, he has elected to remain as President of Memphis State University and to advance the cause of public higher education in the Nation:

NOW, THEREFORE BE IT RESOLVED, that the State Board of Education hereby commends President C. C. Humphreys and extends to him its profound appreciation and gratitude for his leadership and fidelity.

Units of One
1967–1968

Race riot in Detroit leaves 41 people dead, 2000 injured, property damage estimates reaching $400 million and up to 5000 homeless...U.S. Senate confirms Thurgood Marshall as first black justice of the Supreme Court...Police arrest 647 as 35,000 demonstrate in Washington in anti-Vietnam war protest...North Korean patrol boats seize the U.S. Navy intelligence vessel *Pueblo*...President Lyndon Johnson announces cessation of bombing north of the 21st parallel in Vietnam and tells the nation he will not seek reelection...Student protestors at Columbia University seize five buildings in protest of research connected with Vietnam war...Sirhan Sirhan assassinates Robert Kennedy.

AND THE WAY WE WERE

First Tiger victory in Ole Miss series—27–17...SGA sponsors a street naming contest to alleviate one of the major avenues of confusion on the campus...State board approves designation as "colleges" the present schools...Changing the semester and final examination schedule from January to the week before Christmas under consideration...A Black Student Association has emerged at MSU...Most massive demonstration in MSU's history parades around campus and hundreds sit-in at Student Center in support of the garbage workers' strike.

IN HIS 1967–68 *Report of the President,* Cecil Humphreys wrote, "No matter how large we may grow, we must never forget the enrollments are tabulated in units of one."

A studious, well-read man, Cecil Humphreys became an even more reflective university president in the 1967–68 school year. He worked diligently to prevent sheer numbers from blinding the administration and faculty to individual student needs. It would have been easy to drown in the figures. Memphis State's IBM 1620 computer spewed out 90,000 scores on standardized tests taken in various courses by 15,274 students. During the year the computer center moved into new quarters in a remodeled wing of the Administration Building, and an IBM 660, Model 40 computer with 131,000 positions of core storage arrived at the end of the fiscal year.

Upon the recommendation of President Humphreys, the State Board of Education acknowledged the increasing stature of the university and its undergraduate schools became colleges with impressive numbers. The College of Arts and Sciences under Dean Walter R. Smith had 5397 students; 3542 in the College of Business Administration under Dean Herbert J. Markle; 2667 in the College of Education under Dean Sam H. Johnson; and 870 in the Herff College of Engineering led by Dean Frederic H. Kellogg.

The Graduate School, directed by Dean John W. Richardson, had 1570 students seeking higher degrees in 40 different specialties, and on May 25, 1968, Grady Bogue, director of records, completed work in educational adminstration and received the university's first doctoral degree. Within a few years he would become Chancellor of Louisiana State University at Shreveport. Dean Robert Doyle Cox reported enrollment in the School of Law increased from 217 to 230, and 49 students received the new Juris Doctor degree during the year. There were 975 students who were unclassified or had not chosen a major area of concentration.

Counting heads was one thing, and the computers were excellent tools for that. But Humphreys sought much more in making a university meaningful to a student. He was pleased when he heard Dean Walter Smith say, "Personal contact between one inquiring mind and another is the sine qua non of a liberal education. In the College of Arts and Sciences we feel both obligated and privileged to provide it."

The president urged departments to emphasize small freshman classes to allow for maximum attention to the individual student. Steps were taken in the English department, which had been assailed by critics for its high failure rate, to assist students even before they enrolled. Dr. William Osborne, after serving one year in an acting capacity, became head of the English department. He set up a composition laboratory for entering freshmen during the month of August. "A report at the end of the year indicated that the program was highly successful," Humphreys said.

To further aid freshmen and sophomores, President Humphreys sought SBE approval early in 1968 to establish a University College with a dean and a staff of academic advisers. In justifying it, Humphreys said, "It should improve the advising, guidance, and counseling of students."

In a letter to J. Howard Warf, chairman of the SBE, he wrote: "We are particularly concerned about the more than 6000 freshmen and sophomores who under our present program do not get the personal attention and detailed academic advising that is needed. Under our present plan each student is assigned an academic adviser from the department in which he plans to major. Many of these advisers have up to 50 or 60 advisees, and it is not possible for them to give the personal attention to the academic program of each student and provide him with the kind of advising which he needs."

Dr. Billy M. Jones, who was head of the history department and dean of students at San Angelo State College in Texas, was a possible candidate for the new deanship. However, Jones was on leave serving an internship in college administration at the University of Colorado, and there was a hitch. The American Council on Education, which provided the internship, required that he return for at least one year to San Angelo State. The name of Billy Jones would not become a familiar one at Memphis State until 1973.

Other initiatives were taken to improve services and to free the president from the mind-boggling amount of detail work. R. M. Robison became executive dean of students, and Dr. Jess Parrish came aboard as dean of students. Parrish had been dean of student life and director of testing and counseling at San Angelo State College. Then, in December, Roy S. Nicks, former state commissioner of public welfare, became assistant to the president.

The fall session had started on a particularly pleasing note for Humphreys—the Memphis State football team defeated Ole Miss, 27–17 before 50,000 amazed fans at Memorial Stadium. There had been the epic 0–0 deadlock with the Rebels in 1973, but this was the first win by the Tigers in an old series. It was the sweetest of triumphs, for some of the older MSU supporters could recall Ole Miss winning by 91 to 0 in 1935.

Some 2000 students, after a delirious Saturday night on the town, were still marching and chanting Sunday morning. They went to hail their heroes in Robison Hall, the athletic dormitory, and their central theme was "We want a holiday Monday!" Perhaps some of them knew of President Smith's granting a holiday on the Monday following the victory over Mississippi Southern in 1959.

The Commercial Appeal reported it was flooded with calls asking, "Do we have to go to school tomorrow?"

To some student dismay, President Humphreys told the newspaper, "It was a great victory, probably the greatest in the history of Memphis State athletics. Not many have waited as long for it as I have, but the best way we can show our appreciation to the football team is to attend classes tomorrow. We have no plans for a holiday." But the excitement continued. Student euphoria on Saturday night had been such that they forgot to tear the goal posts down. But it was not too late. The Student Government Association chartered 10 buses to take students to a City Commission meeting to ask that the goal posts at Memorial Stadium be given to Memphis State so they could be put on campus. The commissioners, while in executive session, heard of the student plan and called Humphreys to say the goal posts would be given to the university. Immediately, one bus left the campus for City Hall to thank the commissioners. Everything ended happily, except for the SGA. It still had to pay for the nine unused chartered buses.

The game was played on September 23, and the victory would be a rallying point for Memphians, but the day before the contest one of

Coach Billy (Spook) Murphy was carried off the field following MSU's first win over Ole Miss.

the most significant gifts to the university had been announced. The trustees of the Edward J. Meeman Foundation gave the 623-acre Meeman Forest Farm, which adjoins the Meeman-Shelby Forest State Park, and $250,000 in cash to Memphis State. Born in Evansville, Indiana, Meeman was graduated from Central High School there, but never went to college. He became a newspaperman, working for *The Evans-*

ville Press, a Scripps Howard newspaper. Meeman started a newspaper in Knoxville for that big newspaper organization before coming to Memphis as editor of the *Memphis Press-Scimitar.* He was the newspaper's chief executive for 31 years and after retiring as editor emeritus he was conservation editor for Scripps Howard newspapers for four more years until his death in 1966.

The gift stemmed from a tip or lead that Humphreys followed with the skill of a good reporter, and Meeman had always admired the good ones. It began with a conversation between Humphreys and Dr. Herbert Lee Williams about the need for improved facilities for journalism. The department was expanding and improving rapidly but it was operating in inadequate quarters on the first floor of the Administration Building.

"It probably had the poorest teaching and office facilities on the campus," Humphreys said. There were $400,000 available for a journalism building in capital outlay funds, but the amount was insufficient for an adequate building.

Williams, who was the head of the journalism department and worked part-time on the copy desk of *The Commercial Appeal,* mentioned to Humphreys that Scripps Howard made contributions to college journalism programs. "I called on Frank Ahlgren, editor of *The Commercial Appeal,* a Scripps Howard paper," Humphreys said. "I wanted his advice and suggestions. Mr. Ahlgren had been interested in and helpful to the journalism program in a number of ways for many years. He told me that Scripps Howard's support for journalism education had been for scholarships and program improvements. He then mentioned the Meeman Foundation as a possible source of help for a building."

Humphreys grabbed this lead and ran with it. His notes said the trustees of the Meeman Foundation, associates and friends of the editor, all knowledgeable about his interests, did not show much enthusiasm about contributing to a new building, even if it were named for Meeman.

But the persistence, and the alertness, of Humphreys came into play. "In the course of the discussion the trustees mentioned their concern about the future of the Meeman Forest Farm, which Mr. Meeman had acquired parcel by parcel over many years, and their interest in keeping it in its natural state," Humphreys recalled. "They knew of Mr. Meeman's interest of many years in conservation and his role years before, when editor of a newspaper in Knoxville, in the establishment of the Smoky Mountains National Park, and later in the development of the Meeman-Shelby Forest State Park." Humphreys told the trustees that Memphis State was looking for a tract near Memphis that could be used by the biology department to locate a field station for the study of area plant and animal life. There also was a need for a conference center for meetings away from a crowded urban campus.

A master university builder was at work. "I told them the university had no funds at this time for such a project," Humphreys said, "but that I felt our board would approve our accepting the donation of the land and Mr. Meeman's home and maintaining them in a way that would perpetuate the interests of Mr. Meeman. It was also explained that we would still need some help to build a journalism building which would further another interest of Mr. Meeman, and if the $200,000 needed for the journalism building could be provided I would recommend that it be named for Mr. Meeman."

One of the trustees was Lucius Burch, Jr., the attorney whom Humphreys had debated back in 1941. Others were J. Z. Howard, Edmund Orgill, Hunter Lane, Jr., and C. R. Person. Their interest picked up.

In a letter dated September 19, 1967, the trustees advised Humphreys that formal action had been taken on his proposal and if approved by the university board and the State of Tennessee they would provide $200,000 for the proposed journalism building, $5,000 a year to strengthen the department and make an outright gift of the 623 acres and Meeman's residence to be used as a conference center and a natural area for biological studies. The proposal also stipulated that not more than 50 acres should be designated as "The Garden of the Ever Living" for the deposit of ashes resulting from the cremation of human remains. Meeman's own ashes were placed behind the house where he had lived for many years.

State officials gave quick approval, and the Meeman Building would go up on a site where some of the old Vet Village barracks stood before new apartments went up on the South Campus.

In the *Memphis Press-Scimitar*, which Meeman had edited for three decades, President Humphreys called the gift and endowment "a tremendous gesture on behalf of a man noted throughout his career for his interest in the welfare of the community. I was particularly pleased that the endowments will be for journalism and conservation, the two favorite areas of interest of Mr. Meeman."

At the November meeting of the SBE, when physical plant needs for Memphis State were discussed, Humphreys asked for permission to make a change in plans for a Physical Education and Recreation building on the South Campus. Land had become available through the land acquisition programs between Spottswood and Southern on the south side of the main campus. There were two reasons for the change, which was approved. One was that on-campus housing had increased more than 100 percent in three years, and recreation facilities were inadequate. Humphreys also pointed out that the Air Force ROTC program—the largest in the nation in 1967–68—probably would soon become voluntary. This would further crowd physical education facilities because the military training met one year of the university's two-year physical education requirement.

The new facilities would cost $2.5 million, but Memphis State had not had to build a coliseum and stadium for its intercollegiate basketball and football teams. These had been provided by the city and county. Capital outlay appropriations had been used for academic and service buildings.

The SBE also approved architects to begin planning the new engineering building on Central Avenue. A request was made for a federal grant to supplement state funds for the building, and $653,335 was awarded a few months later. Humphreys also announced that funds would be sought for the construction of a new $2-million College of Business Building, to go up on land acquired at Central and Patterson. The growth of the College of Business, both in enrollment and programs, had created a seriously over-crowded condition in a building completed in 1961.

Another plan was revealed that would provide for the construction of fraternity houses by a privately chartered corporation on land recently acquired by the university on Spottswood. Memphis State would assume responsibility for 87.5 percent of the construction costs of each house, with the fraternity making an initial payment of 12.5 percent. The fraternity would pay the balance over a 35–40 year period under a lease with the university. At the end of that period the university would continue to own the houses and continue to lease on a negotiated basis.

"Fraternity membership had levelled off or declined on most campuses during recent years," Humphreys said, "but had continued to grow at Memphis State." In the early consideration of the plan Humphreys had taken Ernest Ball, a local member of the SBE, on a tour of some of the houses near the campus that were rented and used by the fraternities. Ball was not sympathetic with college fraternities, but after the visit he stated that "those boys are living in conditions that are neither safe nor sanitary. If you are going to have fraternities it might be better to have them on state property and under better supervision."

A "Religion Row" also had developed on the west side of Patterson and its intersecting streets. Six religious centers fronted on Patterson and there were three others within a few blocks. All were financed by the sponsoring churches.

In the spring semester of 1968 Memphis State's ninth year as a racially integrated campus was drawing to a close. For a large public institution in a big southern city with a population almost equally divided between blacks and whites, the problems had been few. However, civil rights issues were very much alive.

The Tiger Rag in early March reported that a Black Student Association (BSA) had been organized and was provided an office in the University Center. It was created, the story said, "out of a feeling in black students of isolation, of having to conform to standards and values that held little meaning or enrichment for Negroes, and an awareness of losing something valuable in their own backgrounds as they attempted to fit in."

Shortly after *The Tiger Rag's* story *The Commercial Appeal* printed three articles dealing with integration at Memphis State. In the first article, headlined "Huge Negro Enrollment at MSU Has Produced Few Real Problems," the reporter said no basic hostility existed but students did segregate themselves in public areas outside the classrooms. "Even though the campus scene appeared peaceful," Humphreys said, "the feeling of dissatisfaction was developing among some black students that assimilation into the predominantly white culture was not what they wanted. They felt that pride in their heritage and their struggles should be strengthened. The theme 'Black is Beautiful' was developing."

A few days after the news articles appeared there was a peaceful demonstration by black students on the patio in front of the old student center in support of the city sanitation department strike that had been going on for several weeks. The strikers, almost all of them black, wanted better wages, better working conditions, and union recognition.

"Race relations in the city were at their lowest ebb, with the city bitterly divided," Humphreys said. A downtown march in support of the strike on March 28 was led by Dr. Martin Luther King, Jr. It broke up not long after it started with the smashing of storefront windows and looting. A black youth was shot, and National Guard troops were brought in as tension in the city increased.

Then came the shattering evening of April 4, 1968, when King was back in the city to lead another march. He was assassinated by a sniper's bullet as he stood on the balcony of the Lorraine Motel.

In Humphreys' personal papers is this account of that tragic time:

> I had been out of the city for two days, returning in the late afternoon and going directly to the campus. While working in the office I sensed an unusual quietness for a Thursday evening when the campus was normally crowded with evening students. I walked down to the security office and learned that Dr. King had been killed.
>
> News reports coming in were that buildings in black neighborhoods were being burned, snipers were firing at passing cars, buses had stopped running, a curfew had been declared, and the National Guard had been called up. Looking at the glow from the fires and listening to policemen in squad cars pinned down by snipers calling for help on their radios was almost unbelievable.
>
> Decisions affecting the university had to be made. A call was made to E. C. Stimbert, superintendent of the city schools. We agreed that classes could not be held the next day. The news media was advised. It was also decided that the city would not be calm or safe for the next several days, and that the university's spring holidays, scheduled to start a week from the coming Monday, would be advanced a week.
>
> Members of the staff were called in and arrangements were made to transport the night custodial crews as close to their homes as possible. It was realized also that there were no means of closing the several entrances to the campus. Security men were stationed there. Dormitory

students were rounded up and confined to the residence halls. Calls were being received from parents of out-of-town students asking that their children be sent home. Events of the changing times had brought new dimensions to education administrators.

Humphreys said there were many unforgettable memories of those days, but two stood out. One was the call to the chairman of the Faculty Council about the suspension of Friday's classes and the changing of the spring break. He told Humphreys he would like to call a meeting of the council and discuss the decision with the members.

"I replied," Humphreys said, "that if he could do that in 15 minutes I would be glad to hear their recommendation, but it was now 9:45 P.M. and that the announcement would have to be made on the 10 o'clock news."

The other memory involved a mission downtown. At a called meeting of the directors of the Chamber of Commerce, the next morning, Allen Morgan and Lewis McKee, both prominent bankers, and Humphreys were designated to call on Mayor Henry Loeb and tell him that the chamber had supported him in his dealings with the sanitation workers' union up until the shooting of Dr. King, but it now must be settled.

A short time after Dr. King's assassination the Memphis and Shelby County Human Relations Commission began to take shape. Both city and county government officials saw the need, and President Humphreys received calls from County Commission Jack Ramsay and others asking him to serve as chairman.

Realizing that the commission might have to deal with possible issues involving Memphis State, Humphreys declined. He agreed, however, to serve as temporary chairman and also offered the university as a site for commission sessions. Humphreys served until the commission was organized and Lester Rosen was elected its first chairman.

With news of King's assassination, racial violence broke out in more than 80 cities. Thirty people lost their lives and more than 2000 were injured, and 61,000 National Guardsmen and Army troops were sent into the troubled areas. In Washington troops encircled the White House, and machine guns were manned around the Capitol. "Mem-

phis State reopened on April 15 with no physical injury to its people,"
Humphreys wrote, "but with a noticeable tension in human relations."

Despite the turmoil, Memphis State could look back on a year of
accomplishment. It had awarded 1972 degrees: 632 in August, 545 in
January and 795 in May, an increase of nearly 400 over the previous
year. Classes began in a new Department of Nursing offering a two-
year Associate of Arts degree, and 2000 volumes were added to the
Mississippi Valley Collection. There was special music, too, with Boston's famed Arthur Fiedler directing the Yomiuri Nippon Philhar-
monic Orchestra in the campus Convocation Series.

When the 1967–68 "Report of the President" appeared, it featured
an unusual make-up. There were windows on many of the pages with
the faces of individual students and their first names: John, Joe, Mary,
Herb, Jerry, et al. The emphasis was on individuals, not large groups
of students.

In his introduction, President Humphreys wrote:

> The year just ended, with its unprecedented violent political and social
> activity and tragedy, caused most colleges and universities to pause for a
> reappraisal of student ideology. The old walls between the campus and
> the outside world, particularly on an urban campus, had fallen: students
> read about war in Vietnam, heard about hunger in America, saw riots in
> their own streets, and realized they could not expect to exist in a vacuum.
> The traditionally mature students of Memphis State University accepted
> new roles of leadership on University committees and in projects within
> the community. Although it was a year of continued rapid development
> in academic programs, service projects, and physical plant—the follow-
> ing pages will attest to this—probably more significant measures were
> taken in giving more attention to the individual student's needs than ever
> before. We realize that, no matter how large student enrollments may
> grow, they are still tabulated in units of one. We shall continue to insist
> on this through our precollege counseling programs, our proposed Uni-
> versity College for freshmen and sophomores, our recently created Uni-
> versity Counseling Center, and the all-important teacher-to-student
> contacts in and out of the classroom.

Banking would have been far more financially rewarding to Cecil
Humphreys than a university presidency in the 1960s, but it is doubt-
ful that his sense of accomplishment would have been the same.

His sense of community responsibility rubbed off on the people around him. To Humphreys and his staff, the townsmen and gownsmen were one and the same.

A few months later when James Earl Ray was apprehended and charged with the murder of Dr. King civic duty called. Sheriff Bill Morris, who was responsible for Ray's custody, was faced with dealing with representatives of the media from across the nation and many from foreign countries. He called and asked if Charles Holmes, MSU's director of community relations and a former police reporter, could handle this for him. Humphreys immediately made Holmes available full-time for as long as he was needed.

Leadership in the university did not sit and wait in a time of community need.

11

A Tumultuous Year

1968–1969

THE NEWS HEADLINES

Chicago police battle students and others outside the convention hall as Democrats choose Hubert Humphrey as their nominee...Richard Nixon wins presidency...James Earl Ray pleads guilty in Memphis to the slaying of Dr. Martin Luther King, Jr., and is given a 99-year sentence...Almost 300 students, mainly members of the SDS, take over Harvard University's administration building, evicting deans and staff; 4 persons receive injuries and police arrest 184 students...Apollo 10 splashes down in the Pacific after 18 days in space, including 31 orbits around the moon in rehearsal for a manned lunar landing.

AND THE WAY WE WERE

The Administration Building is undergoing a face lifting while Manning Hall is being remodeled...A summer work study program for black students will go into its second year with the help of Ford Foundation money...Dormitory hours for coeds have been changed with upperclassmen having unlimited overnight permission...Martin Luther King is remembered in special memorial services...Black students present demands...About 100 black students are arrested for trespassing on state property when they stage sit-in at the president's office.

CAMPUS INSURGENCIES, often coming unexpectedly, continued to grab headlines across the nation as a volatile decade began to close. Private and prestigious universities as well as the large public institutions had to face revolt by segments of the student body. Harvard and Brandeis would feel the wrath that the University of California at Berkeley had experienced.

Memphis State had witnessed its share of somewhat milder discontent with the earlier Normal Tea Room sit-in, the arrival of the Free Speech Movement, and the *Logos* episode. Adroit steps by President Humphreys had steadied the university on each occasion and quick thinking by Humphreys after the assassination of Dr. Martin Luther King, Jr., in downtown Memphis eliminated potential campus problems.

The decade's ominous shadow, however, would lengthen at Memphis State in 1960–69, a time when the university and Memphis became a microcosm of a nation troubled by dissenters, often young and usually militant.

Memphis State welcomed 16,637 students—including 1300 blacks for the fall term. They came from 79 Tennessee counties, 42 states and 36 foreign countries. John (Chip) Coscia, a 20-year-old biology major, led the student body. He was the first independent to win the Student Government Association presidency in 21 years. Greek letter candidates had won in every election since 1947, but Coscia running on the University Students for Action ticket, defeated Richard Middlecoff by 300 votes.

Under the leadership of Dr. Jerry Boone as acting dean, the University College began its first year. Boone, a professor of psychology since 1962, directed a staff of eight full-time advisers serving more than 3200 freshmen. The program would add an additional eight advisers in the 1969–70 school year and serve sophomores as well as freshmen. "The goal of the University College was to provide individualized educational advising and counseling for students who might otherwise find such a large university to be somewhat impersonal," Humphreys said. He had long since decided that a growing urban university must provide sufficient advisers to help students, the vast majority of them commuters, to find the most suitable class placement and to set the best educational goals.

It was with considerable interest that President Humphreys read an October 10, 1968, edition of the *Memphis Press-Scimitar* reporting that 120 people denouncing America's role in the Vietnam War and chanting, "Ho, Ho, Ho Chi Minh, the NLF is going to win," had participated in a Students for a Democratic Society demonstration in front of the Federal Building downtown. The article said the "demonstration was conducted yesterday by the MSU chapter of the SDS."

There was nothing to disabuse the view that some of the protestors came from Memphis State, but Humphreys knew there was no chartered SDS chapter on campus. But, within days, a request for an SDS charter would be made to the Student Government Association.

Meanwhile, the first major sit-in at a college administration building in Memphis took place at LeMoyne-Owen College, a private, predominantly black institution with an enrollment of about seven hundred. The takeover began about 4 P.M. on November 25, 1968, just hours before the college's president, Dr. Hollis Price, was to be honored as Educator of the Year by Greater Memphis State, Inc., at a banquet on Memphis State's campus. Price talked to the protestors, some of them students and some of them outsiders, before leaving about 6:30 P.M. for Memphis State. He left the ceremonies early and hastened back to LeMoyne-Owen about 9 P.M.

A list of 18 demands, most of them involving a greater student voice in the college's affairs, had surfaced before the sit-in began. The administration and the faculty were discussing the issues in the library, about 50 yards from the administration building, when a student came in and said students and strangers had occupied the building.

It would be a long night for President Price. He talked with the students for two hours. About 11 P.M., when asked how things were going, the black educator replied, "They don't have much faith in my talk."

The students demands included a cut in the tuition, which was $620 a year; lower prices in the cafeteria; improvements in the book store; more courses in black history; an end to required attendance at assemblies; and the opening of some buildings on campus for longer than the usual hours. Price said that many of the students demands had been met and others had been referred to committees for further study. He said he would withhold specifics until he had a chance to address the student body.

No force was used or threatened to get the protestors to leave. Police were called and arrived shortly after 4 P.M.; but they did not remain on the campus long, and no arrests were made. Only demonstrators, President Price, a black photographer, and the Reverend Malcolm Blackburn of Clayborn Temple AME Church were allowed to enter the administration building. One of the college's three nightwatchmen said there were about 50 people inside.

When he left in the early morning hours President Price said he did not know if the sit-in would end later that day. "I fondly hope so," he added. "It would be a major difficulty if it didn't."

About 200 students had demonstrated briefly during the afternoon meeting in the library, but few of the college's 700 students remained on campus after 5 P.M. Among the outsiders who came to the campus during the early stages of the sit-in were a small group of students from Memphis State, who said they had been invited to be observers. They left at 7:30 P.M. One of the outsiders who stayed in the administration building was Lance (Sweet Willie Wine) Watson, a leader of young black militants in Memphis.

After Hollis addressed the student body, saying some changes already had been initiated, the sit-in ended and the campus edged back to normality. But college news would remain in the public eye as it shifted from one campus to another.

The Student Senate at Memphis State held a night meeting on December 18 to decide whether or not a charter should be granted to Students for a Democratic Society. About 60 students attended the session in the University Center, but many more were downstairs watching the Louisville-MSU basketball game on television.

"We only ask that SDS be recognized, not endorsed," said James Gaylord, an SDS spokesman. "The question is not whether we are here, because we are here." Gaylord said SDS had 35,000 members in 300 chapters throughout the nation, but that the goals of the individual chapters were determined by circumstances in their own areas. He said only four or five of the chapters had been associated with violence on campuses.

But he was on alien ground at Memphis State. In a roll call vote the Student Senate voted, 14 to 9, to deny a charter to SDS.

Its members had been meeting at Westminster House at 449 Patterson early in the fall semester, but the Reverend Dick Moon, director of the house, had said in November that "they're no longer meeting with us." He said it was against the policy of the Campus Christian Life Board to allow a nonstudent organization to meet in campus religious centers. A month earlier the Memphis Presbytery of the Cumberland Presbyterian Church had voted to continue supporting Moon as a campus chaplain, but criticized him for letting SDS use Westminster House.

Early in 1969 a different national problem—drugs—had to be faced. The Shelby County sheriff's vice squad arrested a 27-year-old Memphis State philosophy instructor at his home and charged him with the illegal possession of marijuana. Authorities said they found a quarter pound of it in his kitchen cabinet.

The narcotics officer said the instructor, John Baird Callicott, married and the father of an infant son, told them he grew marijuana in his front yard at 4899 Stage Road, but the deputies said they saw no evidence of that.

President Humphreys suspended Callicott, but when his case was thrown out of General Sessions Court because of a technical error in the obtaining of a search warrant, Callicott was reinstated. Under the state's teachers tenure law, conviction of a felony was needed for dismissal. Legally the instructor had to be reinstated. However, this action brought a flood of letters and phone calls from parents of students and other concerned citizens.

Throwing the case out of court threw it into state politics. At the time the possession of marijuana carried a penalty of two to five years and a fine of up to $1000 on conviction. In Nashville Representative Bob Hawks of Memphis, upset by the release of Callicott on an error and his return to teaching, told the Tennessee House: "The State Board of Education surely has moral standards that teachers should live up to. If there are no standards we should draw them up in the Legislature."

Responding to the legislative heat, SBE Commissioner J. Howard

Warf told newsmen he had ordered President Humphreys to give him a full report on the Callicott case. Humphreys, in doing so, also notified Warf that Callicott's contract would not be renewed. Warf called the case closed.

In this same troubling period a proposed new student code on conduct and discipline drew a blast from the local chapter of the American Association of University Professors.

One of the key points in the code prohibited "unauthorized occupancy of university facilities or blocking access to or from such areas." The AAUP said the proposed code failed to provide means by which students could effect peaceful change. It also said the code was "too negative." Dr. Grant Reese, chapter president and chairman of the department of foreign languages, said, "We have voted to publicize our position within the university community. We don't necessarily want to make a public issue out of this outside the university." But actions on campuses, particularly public supported institutions, had already become public issues.

Reese was swimming against the tide. Campus news was city news and often won space on the front page. In reality this was a result of President Humphreys' decade-long campaign to tie the gown to town, to build a "communiversity." As for the conduct code, Dean of Students Jess Parrish said it was the result of 18 months of study, but contained little new in policy covering conduct and discipline.

The AAUP was not totally dissatisfied. It commended the proposed code for saying that peaceful dissent should be encouraged. The chapter also praised the code for setting forth due process procedures in academic offenses.

Humphreys obviously had an open mind on student dissent as long as it respected the rights of others. In his annual report to the SBE, he included this statement from Walter R. Smith, dean of the College of Arts and Sciences, in which 4048 students registered for classes in 16 departments, and which seemed to provide most of the protestors, both students and faculty. This was true of most arts and sciences colleges on most campuses. Dean Smith's statement was:

> During this year of discontent on campuses throughout the world, colleges of liberal arts have been singled out as the sources from which most

of the unrest has emerged. One would be more than a little foolish if he remained unconcerned over the fact that the excesses which often developed from the discontent constitute a grave danger to the very principles of a liberal education.

Liberal studies, by definition, are liberating studies; they are studies intended to free men from narrow, parochial, constrictive notions. If a college offers these studies, and if its professors and its students both do their jobs properly, then discussion, debate, and—inevitably—dissention will result.

These effects are desirable and certainly not dangerous to anything other than prejudices and other vulgar errors.

The principles of liberal education are imperiled only when professors and students fail to do their jobs properly, when teaching gives way to indoctrination, when learning is limited to those things which confirm rather than upset our cherished views. We can avoid these dangers only when, by our teaching, counseling, and examples, we encourage students to seek answers and to take stands, while at the same time—as an indispensable concomitant—we persuade them to recognize the right of their colleagues similarly to seek answers and to take different stands.

It is our expectation that the College of Arts and Sciences at Memphis State University will continue to be the focus of protestant activity; if it is not, it is moribund and without value as an educational institution. It is our determination that these movements of minds be accomplished in an atmosphere of respect for all dissent, even that which may, at the moment, be unpopular. In every sense of the word these are reasonable aims; they may not be easily achieved, but they must be earnestly pursued.

President Humphreys, building a reputation as a problem solver on campus and downtown, would be tested under fire. A spring lull in student discontent ended abruptly shortly after noon on April 23, 1969, when a group of black students began a sit-in at his office in the Administration Building.

The Commercial Appeal reported the demonstration was "spontaneous and poorly organized." The sit-in was staged without the knowledge of the 17-member board of the Black Student Association. The newspaper also said that the student doing most of the talking was James Mock, a 28-year-old freshman eduation major who had attended Marquette University in Wisconsin, and enrolled at MSU that spring.

Humphreys told newsmen the students had several grievances of a general nature, but the principal reason for the sit-in was to demand

$1500 to bring former New York Representative Adam Clayton Powell, who had been expelled from the U.S. House of Representatives, to campus to speak.

"They said they would leave if they got the demand answered to their satisfaction," Humphreys said. "There were no threats of violence. I gave everyone a chance to say what he wanted to. At 1:30 I told them they would have to leave because we had work to do. One student replied, 'We're going to stay until we get the answers we want.' "

"With this impasse, Humphreys, aware that state law and board policy prohibited taking over public facilities, called in Memphis police. When Chief Henry Lux and fifteen other officers arrived about half of the students left. At 2:10 P.M. Lux told the remaining students they would have to leave. Mock and the other students asked if they could have a discussion alone.

"I told them they could use the office for five minutes," Humphreys said, "and I went outside."

The Commercial Appeal said the students ended the sit-in at 2:13 P.M. They went to the University Center, where they and about 200 others listened to talks by Dr. H. Ralph Jackson, vice chairman of Community on the Move (COME), who said, "We are here to help you do your thing, and we'll support you financially, morally, and any other way that you request," and by Mrs. Maxine Smith, executive secretary of the Memphis chapter of the National Association for the Advancement of Colored People. She said, "We want you to know that you do have our support and if you need us call us."

At a press conference after the confrontation Humphreys said, "I did not make any concessions, nor did I suggest any solution to their problems. The atmosphere at the sit-in was not antagonistic. I did tell the group that if Powell came to Memphis they could present their request for his appearance on campus through regular channels to the Public Programs Committee. The decision to call police was because they were violating state law and SBE policy."

Under the auspices of the university's program board, Charles Evers, Mississippi field secretary for the NAACP, had spoken to 800 students on December 10, 1968. On the platform with Evers were President Humphreys and Aaron Henry, NAACP president in Mississippi. Evers told the students "soul," not violence, was the best way to obtain civil rights. He also warned against following extremists, urging students to work for change through the established framework of the university.

During the sit-in President Humphreys listened intently and spoke softly, but there was iron in his words too. At one point he said, "We are going to carry out the business of the university, regardless of what it takes to do it."

The Commercial Appeal and the *Memphis Press-Scimitar* reported that the next day representatives of the Black Student Association met with Dr. Ronald Carrier, university provost, and Dean Jess Parrish. The BSA leaders asked for a black dean of black affairs and more black faculty members. They also charged that some faculty members were racists.

Dr. Humphreys told the *Memphis Press-Scimitar*. "Memphis State University is seeking a black to serve as a dean. He will serve the needs of all students. When you segregate on campus, you are defeating the purpose of an integrated institution."

In an editorial backing the president, the morning newspaper said Humphreys "made clear that he intends to conduct the business of Memphis State—the business of education—in such a way that those who want to come there have an opportunity to do so without interference....All students at Memphis State should understand that this community stands behind Dr. Humphreys....The situation on the campus must not be permitted to degenerate, as it has in places such as Cornell University, to the extent that faculty and administrators are intimidated at gunpoint by a small group of students who impose their will regardless of the wishes of the majority."

The *Memphis Press-Scimitar* editorial said, "Some of the protests voiced by Negro students at Memphis State University—and at other universities across the country—concern the lack of Negro teachers, deans, and administrative officers. Protests serve only to highlight the problem. They do not solve it because there is a widely recognized fact that there is a shortage of qualified Negro college people at all levels of the educational structure. Where are qualified Negroes coming from? Some of them will come from the 1300 Negro students pursuing their education at Memphis State." The newspaper said the university was "always open-minded to suggestions for needed reforms; it has shown a readiness to adapt itself to the needs of its students and the Memphis public."

Meanwhile, the Memphis Police Department kept a presence on campus, and some students handed out leaflets saying, "We protest the fact the administration refuses to negotiate except in the presence of policemen armed with billy clubs, mace, and guns."

Five days after the first sit-in, students, predominantly black and with the backing of the BSA, invaded President Humphreys' office again. It may have been staged to provoke arrest as some came with toothbrushes on strings around their necks. If so, the desire was quickly met. Humphreys told police to arrest them. The students were taken downtown in buses and charged with trespassing. When the students appeared before City Judge Beverly Boushe, he bound them over to the grand jury. There were 103 blacks and six whites in the group. Five were not students at Memphis State.

James Mock, who had been the spokesman at the first sit-in, was not in the group arrested. It was known that he was on probation for a violation in Milwaukee, but this information was not used by the university. Humphreys preferred to consider the students as being sincere, but misguided.

When the buses left for the police station, David Acey, a BSA board member who had not been present at either sit-in, talked to about a hundred other students. Neither Acey nor Mock went with the group to jail.

"The show is on the road," Acey said. "Those who made the commitment must be followed. We have to stand 100 percent behind those brothers who went downtown on the buses....We have done our homework; now what we do depends on what is done to our brothers, what charges are placed and what the fines are."

In court attorneys Otis Higgs, Irving Salky, Jack Clements, and Walter Bailey made pleas for continuance, hoping Memphis State officials would withdraw the trespassing charges. "All we ask is that you give us a chance to get these students on the right path in expressing their grievances," Bailey said. The judge bound the students over under $500 bonds.

Again Humphreys received strong editorial support. *The Commercial Appeal* said, "Some hours after his office was taken over by mili-

About 100 black students were escorted to buses following their arrest for the second sit-in in President Humphreys' office.

tant black students yesterday, MSU president Cecil C. Humphreys made an unequivocal statement: 'We are going to carry on the normal functions of the university.' The stand taken by Dr. Humphreys is the same as should be taken on any campus by university administrators."

The *Memphis Press-Scimitar* said Humphreys did what he had to do—"and what he did was right." It also said the students had failed to read the signs of the times and had acted on bad advice. The editorial added: "Only last week the liberal, deeply perceptive Max Lerner, a college professor and news commentator, said in his column, 'The nation has been patient and tolerant of these (campus) disruptions. The time has come to place limits around them, to isolate those who engineer them, to take prudent but effective action to end them....The overwhelming majority of Americans, including students and faculty, have had it and don't want any more.' "

In a television appearance on April 29 President Humphreys pledged the university to "the best education possible within our changing environment." On campus Victor Smith, a white liberal supporting the black students, presented Humphreys with a petition signed by 900 students backing the Black Student Association demand that all policemen be removed from campus and urging the reinstatement of the students who had been arrested. Smith told Humphreys his were "requests" rather than demands.

Smith's petition was matched by 1200 signatures supporting President Humphreys.

"I appreciate it," Humphreys told the white student who handed him the names, "but I hope that everyone realizes that we don't need a strong polarization. I hope we all realize we are trying to present an educational opportunity for everyone."

In the wake of the sit-ins about 60 faculty members, calling themselves the Faculty Forum, met four times in ten days, and on May 6 they presented President Humphreys with a resolution calling for the establishment of a faculty senate which would have "participation in the decision-making process of the university."

Dr. Michael M. Osborn, an associate professor in the speech and drama department and temporary chairman of the Forum, said the resolution was unanimously approved at a meeting closed to students and the press. In its meetings the forum, which had no official capacity, heard from James Mock and Dr. Miriam Sugarman, a Spanish teacher and adviser to the Black Student Association. "We recommend the administration issue a directive to reduce overt racism we feel is sometimes present in some classrooms," Osborn said.

Humphreys later said that he never ceased to be amazed at how much authority some groups gave to the president when there was something they wanted done, and how little when it was something they disagreed with.

Letters to the city's newspapers heavily favored the stand taken by President Humphreys, and the *Memphis Press-Scimitar* printed a national roundup under the heading, "Classes for boycotts will now come to order." It noted that a strike was called at Stanford University to protest military research there. At the University of Rhode Island, which had fifty blacks among its 8000 students, the black students began a boycott because of low black enrollment, absence of a black studies program, and the shortage of black faculty members. The City College of New York said a 200-man police detail remained on duty because there had been a suspicious $250,000 fire in the campus auditorium.

Speaking to the Temple Israel Sisterhood in Memphis, Humphreys said he was not a college president with answers to campus unrest. But he laid the blame on "nihilists—those who would destroy our institutions, starting with universities." He said the two specific things administrators were confronting on campus were the Vietnam War and civil rights.

"The idealism of the young people who feel the Vietnam War is not one we should be participating in must be considered," he said. "It's a difficult situation for them to understand. None of the other wars we have been involved in were as far away and as unrelated to our well-being in the eyes of the students as this one. And they are the ones bearing the burden of it. In the civil rights movement, young people are more idealistic than we are. These young people have grown up in an age in which there have been great changes in society."

Humphreys said the Students for a Democratic Society was a group of young people "taking advantage of the idealism of many of the young people to try to bring about a state of chaos." Theirs, he said, is a philosophy that is anarchistic or nihilistic, one that says, "If we destroy the structure of the government, people could live together peacefully without organizations."

The college president said they were wrong. "A society as complex as ours cannot live peacefully without organization," Humphreys said. "Universities were not created to meet violence; they were created for the give and take of discussion, for thoughts and ideas. Force is foreign to universities."

Acting under a new state statute prohibiting persons from trespassing at a public school and engaging in disorderly acts, the Shelby County Grand Jury on May 13 indicted the 109 persons who had been arrested at Memphis State. The offense was a misdemeanor punishable on conviction by a jail term of eleven months and twenty-nine days and a fine of $1000.

A university spokesman said students were not forced to leave school unless convicted on a charge. He also said letters were being mailed to the students who were arrested telling them that a hearing would be held, if requested, on their suspensions.

In the student elections held on May 13, the Tiger Party, which campaigned in support of the administration, swept to victory by almost a three to one margin in a record turnout by more than 5000 students. The losing New Party was a coalition of dissenting students, many of whom were involved in the sit-ins.

On May 20, after a closed hearing set by university policy, the Social Disciplinary Committee handed out deferred suspensions to the students who were charged with trespassing.

Deferment meant that the students were on probation and would be able to take final examinations and continue their studies at MSU. Their attorney, Walter Bailey, said there would be no appeal. In essence they were being given a second chance. Their cases in court would drag on for months, but they never came to trial.

Attorney General Philip Canale was not enthusiastic about prosecuting, and Humphreys did not want the students to lose a full semester of work. He had received too many calls from parents who were making sacrifices to send their children to college to be unsympathetic. Over the next few years a young black man or woman would sometimes approach Humphreys with a big smile and say something like, "You remember me, you put me in jail." There did not seem to be any lasting animosity.

In his commencement address on May 30, 1969, Dr. Otis A. Singletary, vice chancellor of the University of Texas and president-designate of the University of Kentucky, told the 878 graduates that college was not a supermarket where a customer is always right. "College administrations should be sensitive to the needs of students, consult openly with them, and give sincere attention to their advice," he said. "But the university has no obligation to submit to intimidation and violence." Singletary said colleges must work for the common good of society.

Humphreys revealed his innermost thinking about what had happened at Memphis State when he wrote these lines at the close of the school year:

"Plaudits often are offered softly. Commendations for accomplishment given our thousands of serious students and hundreds of dedicated faculty and staff members during the past year often stir little more than a murmur in retrospect. The raucous commentary on the popular contemporary concept of confrontation, however, reverberates loudly. Memphis State University experienced progress, remarkably quiet progress, during the 1968–69 year."

Humphreys, despite the strife, had indeed gone about "the business" of education. While the 60 or so Faculty Forum professors were gaining some attention during the sit-ins, there was a full-time faculty of 625, including 100 new teachers, who quietly attended to their classroom duties.

Major facilities opened for the first time to meet needs of the university's record 16,637 students—9319 men and 7318 women. A spacious, four-level building on the mall, the University Center, offered much more than room for dissidents to meet. The $4 million structure provided many areas for study and conferences, lounges, game room, an information and scheduling center, cafeteria, and a bookstore. MSU's president had one specific request concerning the bookstore—it was to have the largest selection of new paperback books in the city.

The John Willard Brister Library added three new buildings to house the undergraduate library. A 12-story book tower provided eye appeal and space for more than one million volumes of printed material. Memphis State received a $144,000 federal grant to help stock the imposing building.

Cecil Humphreys continued to go downtown, and in October the City Council and County Commission agreed to support what the MSU president called a serious need—a two-year community college in Memphis.

The statute providing for the creation of a system of two-year community colleges specified that none would be established within 50 miles of an existing state institution of higher education. But for several years Humphreys had talked about the need for a two-year institution in Memphis that would relieve the pressure on Memphis State by providing an educational opportunity for high school graduates who were not prepared for entrance into the university, but who needed more education to compete in the job market. With better preparation some of these students might later enter Memphis State.

The location of the last three community colleges was being determined, and Humphreys wanted the city and county leaders to seek the aid of the Shelby County legislative delegation in obtaining one of these colleges for the Memphis metropolitan area. He pointed out that Shelby County had more high school graduates than all the rest of West Tennessee, in which two community colleges had already been located. The first question asked by each local legislative body and by the state legislators was, "Wouldn't it hurt Memphis State?" Humphreys replied that it would not hurt, but that it would help.

The two legislative bodies immediately started to work with the Shelby delegation, and they were able to bring about the selection of Memphis as the location for one of the last three community colleges to be created in the state. Humphreys' vision would play a significant role in the development of Shelby State Community College, and in its first years he lent space at the South Campus to the institution.

In late September there was a pleasant diversion from the books. Memphis State's football team traveled to Knoxville to play the University of Tennessee for the first time, and 61,792—the largest crowd to that time to see a sporting event in the state—watched as the Volunteers edged the Tigers, 24 to 17, in Neyland Stadium.

During homecoming in October, the university officially dedicated more than $13 million in classroom, laboratory, and residence facilities. Governor Buford Ellington joined many other dignitaries in dedicating Brister Library, J. M. Smith Chemistry Building, Patterson English Building, Ellington Biological Sciences Building, Frank L. Clement Humanities Building, Browning Hall, and the University Center. To cap the day, the Tiger football team defeated Southern Mississippi, 29 to 7, in, as one newspaper put it, "typical barroom fashion." The Tigers and the Eagles were intense rivals.

Late November brought news that the new Tennessee Higher Education Commission, which had helped to bring the private University of Chattanooga into the University of Tennessee system, was "considering" the same possibility for Memphis State. The suggestion was a lead balloon in Memphis and by December was a dead issue.

A growing Memphis State would continue on its own, and in December announced that work would begin on three engineering buildings costing $6.5 million. The units would face Central Avenue. Begun on the foundation of a $100,000 gift, the Herff College of Engineering had grown from 30 graduate students in 1964 to 830 students and 35 professors.

Another large project begun in 1969 was a physical education complex on the south edge of the main campus. A $2.4 million facility, it included indoor and outdoor Olympic-sized swimming pools, two gyms, ten handball courts, and exercise and dressing rooms. On some of the land where the old Vet Village stood, a $1.9 million psychology building was planned, and a $300,000 University Health Center would be located near the center of the campus. It would contain a ten-bed hospital for temporary treatment of students.

When the Tennessee Higher Education Commission announced on February 7, 1969, that it was recommending development of Memphis State into a comprehensive, doctoral-level institution similar to the University of Tennessee at Knoxville, it had corrected its sights. The THEC also suggested that the State Board of Education surrender its control over higher education and that two nine-member boards be set up. One would control Memphis State University and the other regional schools. The other would supervise the state's community colleges, and the University of Tennessee would remain under its separate Board of Trustees. Under the recommendations, Memphis State's student enrollment would be capped at 25,000 and UT Knoxville at 28,000.

Dr. John Folger, executive director of the commission, said SBE chairman J. Howard Warf and some other educators had proposed that all educational institutions be placed under a single roof. It was a classic case of wanting to protect the present turf, but in sending its recommendations to the Legislature, the THEC said, "None of our consultants thought this would be the best system for Tennessee."

With some refinements, and a little time, the Higher Education Commission's plan would move forward. Meanwhile, on June 19, the SBE recommended a 1969–70 operating budget of $19.3 million for Memphis State. It had been $15.7 million for the previous school year. With dormitory rent, book store proceeds, and such considered, the overall budget would be $22 million.

President Humphreys opened the ceremony which marked the dedication of 7 buildings on the campus in October 1968.

In the final weeks of the fiscal year the university announced that Dr. E. Grady Bogue, director of records for the past four years, would become director of institutional research. In addition to an increased emphasis on self-evaluation of university cost factors, human elements, and other intangible subject matter, President Humphreys said Memphis State would soon embark on the largest oral history research project ever undertaken in the South: Tracing the establishment and growth of the Tennessee Valley Authority. Humphreys said the project, to be directed by Dr. Charles W. Crawford, would take several years. The taped interviews would be stored in the University Archives and made available to authors, historians, and researchers.

Looking back on the year, President Humphreys appears to have been correct in saying that education, the business of a university, had prevailed over confrontation. Indeed, there had been remarkably quiet progress. The growing thirst for education in Memphis and the Mid-South could be seen in many areas, particularly in service to the community.

Humphreys said in his quadrennial report on academic affairs:

> A modern university in an urban setting can fulfill its responsibilities only if it reflects the educational and service needs of its constituents. Memphis State University is in the center of a growing and dynamic region, replete with the transitional problems of social and economic change characteristic of our time.
>
> During the next decade, Memphis State University will complete the transition, which began over 50 years ago, from a teachers college to a major multipurpose educational institution. Already well developed in terms of size, scope, and quality of baccalaureate programs, Memphis State University, within the foreseeable future, will extend its scope to complete its programs at the graduate and advanced graduate levels.
>
> It will enter more rapidly into research programs serving the community, the state, and the nation. It will use the knowledge gained through research for human good through service.

Humphreys did not say so, for it was not his style, but his educational leadership and sense of community had built a university of uncommonly high stature despite the distractions of a tumultuous decade. His quest for excellence in all areas of the university had become a trademark.

12

Rallying Around the Flag

1969–1970

THE NEWS HEADLINES
Divers recover body of Mary Jo Kopechne, a 28-year-old secretary, after Senator Edward M. Kennedy's car runs off a bridge into a tidal pool on Chappaquiddick Island at Martha's Vineyard, Massachusetts...American astronaut Neil A. Armstrong, commander of Apollo 11, becomes the first human to step on the moon and says, "That's one small step for man, one giant leap for mankind"..."Chicago 7" trial ends after 27 hectic weeks and Federal jury finds the defendants innocent of conspiring to incite riots during the 1968 Democratic National Convention...Americans by the millions take part in the first Earth Day with antipollution demonstrations.

AND THE WAY WE WERE
Memphis State, one of 300 colleges, readies for the Vietnam Moratorium, one of the war's largest protests; President Nixon says student opposition will have no effect on his policy...Before a sellout crowd MSU is peeled by the Big Orange, 55–16...Women attempt to have all dorm hour restrictions removed for most coeds...Men attempting to get more open hours which would allow women visitors in dorms; rules now permit women only on open house days which are few and far between...Fourteen women at MSU are organizing a women's liberation group.

WITH THE BEGINNING of the new academic and fiscal year on July 1, President Humphreys could look back over the past ten years with pride. To indulge in statistics to tell the story of President Humphreys' first ten years at the helm, the facts can be seen at a glance:

	1959–60	1969–70
Enrollment	4937	17,467
Faculty	200	715
Library volumes	80,000	600,000
Operating budget	$2,373,000	$22,185,000
Acreage	80	1000
Campus value	$17,000,000	$61,000,000

The real story of an institution, much as the soul or conscience of a leader, is not seen, and, at best, does not rest on figures printed in various reports. Qualitative results hold the truth, but are more difficult to measure. Cecil Humphreys had the courage to make decisions, even on those occasion when the wind was not at his back. He always did what he felt he had to do.

He did have some nostalgic feeling for the days when the campus was much smaller, much quieter, and the tempo much slower. There were no quiet periods now, not even in the summer.

The first day of a series of twenty-two precollege counseling and registration sessions for beginning freshmen began on July 8. They were designed to help the student become an effective member of the university and to enable university personnel to devote personal attention to the registration needs of the student. Parents were invited and encouraged to accompany the student. All were taken on a full tour of the campus, in small groups by upperclassmen. They would not feel lost or bewildered when they returned to start classes in the fall.

The university also had programs on the campus for approximately 3500 culturally deprived children that provided opportunities for physical fitness, personal development, job training and cultural enrichment during the summer. The university was provided with more than $80,000 in government and private funds to operate the program.

On July 31 at a luncheon arranged by the Memphis Area Chamber of Commerce, a representative of the Urban Institute, a nonprofit urban planning corporation, spoke to city and county officials and to a group of business executives telling them that the nation's universities should be used more to study and help solve urban problems. Both city and county officials reported that Memphis State was being used to a great extent in helping solve some of the problems of a growing urban area. A few days later the County Commission called upon the university to undertake a study of the county's personnel policies and salary schedule.

Dr. Lasley Dameron, associate professor of English, was named dean of the University College to succeed Dr. Jerry Boone, who resigned to become associate director for Academic Programs with the Tennessee Higher Education Commission.

On August 10 the Memphis State Black Student Association staged a performance at the Sheraton-Peabody Skyway titled "Happenings in Blackness" to raise money toward a scholarship fund for disadvantaged students.

The Commercial Appeal on August 13, in a new study headed "Growing MSU Meeting Demands," reported that an estimated 17,500 students would join the MSU campus next month to begin a new school year highlighted by an extensive expansion program and administrative reorganization. It noted nine separate building projects would be in progress, financed by federal, state, and private funds that would total almost $16 million. Under construction were the Herff College of Engineering Building, the Psychology Complex, the new College of Business Administration, the Meeman Communications Building, the Athletic Dressing Facility located on the old Kennedy Hospital property, the married student housing complex, at the same location, now called the South Campus, and an information center, at Central and Patterson. Of the last, Humphreys said, "I had never seen one or heard of one, but I knew we needed one."

Also reported was a change in title for three administrative officers. The State Board of Education had accepted President Humphreys' recommendation to change the titles of three deans, Dr. Ronald Carrier to Vice President for Academic Affairs, Dr. Roy S. Nicks to Vice President for Administration, and Dr. Jess H. Parrish to Vice President for Student Affairs. These were the first vice presidents to be named at any of the SBE institutions. Eugene Smith, the business manager, would become the Vice President for Business and Finance the next year.

The Commercial Appeal also reported that the fourth doctoral program, in history, would begin that fall. Ninety-six new faculty members, including 12 in the English Department, were added.

A textbook or manual on how to be a successful college president could have been a bestseller in the 1960s and early 1970s. Chief executives faced problems that simply had not occurred in the past. However, a Memphis columnist said if Hollywood casting was looking for an ideal person to play a college president it had but to look at Cecil Humphreys. He was not playing a role; he was living it.

Humphreys' hometown newspaper, the Paris *Post-Intelligencer,* on July 1, 1969—the first day of the 1969–70 school year—editorially suggested that the University of Tennessee should hire Humphreys to replace popular Andy Holt, who had announced his retirement plans. There were others who speculated along the same line, but in letters to friends Humphreys begged off. To C. C. Silberman in Chattanooga, he wrote on September 17: "Your letter makes me very proud that my old friend and teammate thinks I am qualified to be considered for the important responsibility at the University of Tennessee, but my sense of reality keeps telling me that there are so many better qualified people than this old, broken-down, ex-skinny end!"

In correspondence with Dr. Burgin E. Dossett, president emeritus of East Tennessee State University at Johnson City, Humphreys said, "I also feel very strongly that in these days, with the problems you have on campuses, they need a younger person with a different outlook about certain things than I have. Administration in higher education is extremely difficult these days, and I am not sure that I would be at all interested in taking on a new and even more demanding responsibility. I do, however, deeply appreciate the confidence you expressed in me."

The 55-year-old educator, whether he desired it or not, had become a public figure of statewide interest.

The *Memphis Press-Scimitar* announced in September that "Milady Meets the Professor," a lecture series by Memphis State faculty members, would begin its fifth season on the campus that fall. A new dimension was added—husbands, fiances, and bachelors were extended invitations to the formerly all-female program.

In September Robert Johnson devoted one of his daily columns in the *Memphis Press-Scimitar* to Memphis State. He began by asking some questions, "But what of the huge universities of today: How can they reach out and personalize themselves for the new boys and girls? How big should they be? MSU expects better than 17,000 students this fall, and a freshman can feel like a grain of sand on the beach. Among so many strangers, among the strange buildings, meeting strange new requirements of new courses leading where?"

Johnson then used an interview with Humphreys to try to provide answers. He wrote:

> MSU has not far to go before it reaches what Dr. Cecil C. Humphreys, president of Memphis State University, regards as the optimum enrollment which can provide varied degrees in both undergraduate and graduate works and cultural attractions to round out college life. The optimum, he thinks, is 20,000 and after that we should begin thinking about additional institutions. "Our enrollment estimates continue to rise, he told me, "but there is a limit. One of the best answers is the community junior colleges, such as we're going to have in Memphis."
>
> Memphis State and most large universities are becoming increasingly aware of the need for helping students maintain their identities, have a personal relationship of some sort with teachers. It is the impersonalization which has developed in the higher education population explosion which has been responsible for much of the student unrest, he believes.

The number of students coming to college campuses other than those in the traditional age group continued to increase. *The Commercial Appeal* noted that "adult women are answering school bells in large numbers in Memphis and across the country. They are returning to college to update their employment potential, to also test their enjoyment potential. Steve Castleberry, assistant to the Dean of the MSU Graduate School, said, 'It's interesting too that they are some who have gotten their youngest child in the first grade and have gone back. In other words, the adult women have children that are either just out or just in school."

On September 11, Memphis State honored 140 business and civic leaders who had contributed $100 or more at the Fourth Annual Fund for MSU toward a goal of $50,000. The fund provides special scholarships, faculty research, student leadership awards, and the alumni program. Ronald A. Terry, senior vice president of the First National Bank, was national chairman and attorney Bob T. Williams, the special gifts chairman.

The opposition to the Vietnam war was increasing on campus. The *Memphis Press-Scimitar* on October 8 reported that a group of Memphis college students was organizing a Vietnam war protest march and a boycott of classes on October 15 as a part of a national protest. It brought a comment from Humphreys. He said: "Students certainly have the right to express their opinion on any issue; it is their decision whether they should miss the day of classes which they have paid for. The position of the college will be classes as usual. We will neither support nor oppose the protest as long as it doesn't interfere with the rights of others." It was estimated that about 1200 students from Memphis State, Christian Brothers, Southwestern, Siena, Lemoyne-Owen, and the Memphis Academy of Arts would participate.

President Humphreys' leadership on campus and in the community earned him modest monetary rewards but immense public approval. In the 1960s and 1970s the most prestigious recognition went to the person selected for the annual Human Relations Award given by the Memphis Roundtable chapter of the National Conference of Christians and Jews.

It was announced on October 16, 1969, that early in the next year the award would go to Humphreys. In an editorial *The Commercial Appeal* said:

> Dr. Cecil C. Humphreys has won many honors and now is in line for one of the highest which the community can bestow.
>
> He deserves the honor if for no other reason than he has presided over the most difficult transition period Memphis State University has known, and has come through with positive, progressive results.
>
> This is not to say that the transition is complete. MSU still is involved in momentous changes. But Dr. Humphreys, as president of the institution, has had to play the roles of politician, diplomat, administrator, teacher, moderator, and monitor in addition to providing leadership ...Memphis State perforce has had to expand, which has been traumatic

to faculty, students, neighborhood, and the community at large. Dr. Humphreys has had to make tough decisions about academic standards, social demands, and national needs.

He has had to pick and choose the ways in which public funds are spent for the various divisions of a university, decisions which affect the shape of the people of the future. He has had to cope with the changing attitudes of youth, and the demands for more student participation in the decision-making. His record is enviable.

Through all this, Dr. Humphreys also has managed to find time to be concerned about many community problems beyond the campus.

More than 1000 persons were at the Holiday Inn-Rivermont on February 23, 1970, when he accepted the award. "This honor is so great when you consider what it stands for," Humphreys said. "I can only aspire to give greater efforts to the cause this group represents—the cause of brotherhood."

In the principal address Dr. William H. Masterson, chancellor of the University of Tennessee at Chattanooga, quoted the epitaph of Sir Christopher Wren, "If you would see his monument...look around you." Masterson praised Humphreys for his "calm intellect, devotion to high purposes, and the high respect in which he is held not only in his profession, but among the general citizenry of our state and region."

In his "Politics this Morning" column of December 23, 1969, William B. Street, one of the South's top political writers, said, "Dr. C. C. Humphreys, Memphis State University president, has been mentioned off and on for two years as a possible 1970 candidate for governor on the Democratic ticket. Dr. Humphreys hasn't shown any great interest in making the race, which really makes him stand out among those whose names are now being mentioned."

Seven days later in an interview with Robert Johnson of the *Memphis Press-Scimitar*, Humphreys declined to give a yes or no answer to the question, "Will you run for governor?" He explained that he had promised to talk "to some people who think it is time there was a governor from West Tennessee." But, significantly, he said there were some things he wanted to finish at Memphis State.

"He talked about engineering and research," Johnson wrote, "and one thing he was particularly happy about is the counselling service, nineteen counselors whose work is keeping up with students, helping them with their personal problems, advising them on finances, and things like that."

Johnson said he did not think Humphreys would seek political office, and he was right. The decision to turn down the offer from Union Planters National Bank had been much tougher to make than the one to stay out of politics.

Evidence of the broadening role of the university was indicated in January by a story in the *Memphis Press-Scimitar* that reported that at midyear the Office of Research Administration, under the direction of Clark Neal, had received approval for a total of $1,074,000 in grants since July 1, 1969. Forty-five proposals amounting to about $1.5 million were under consideration by various private and government agencies. The Office of Research Administration had been established in 1966 and had received $977,045 that year; $1,021,355 in 1967; $1,023,735 in 1968; and $1,393,356 in 1969; for an average of $1,103,873 or about $30,000 more than the current six-month figure.

There were few dull days on the campus in that era. The *Memphis Press-Scimitar* on October 18 reported that Memphis State's regulations relating to the dissemination of handbills had been reviewed that day by Federal Judge Bailey Brown, and that portions of the rules were unconstitutional. The university had for a number of years published a Student Handbook containing information for students on all aspects of their relations with the university. Included were traffic rules and other regulations considered necessary to a reasonably peaceful and safe coexistence of thousands of people on approximately 160 acres.

The policies had been adopted after much discussion by various committees composed of administration, faculty, and students. One of the policies adopted concerned the distribution of handbills and other material by students and nonstudents that littered the campus and blocked crowded entrances and exits. The policy required approval of material and restricted distribution to 34 racks located around the campus.

Three students or former students filed a suit in Federal Court claiming their freedom of speech was infringed when stopped in the act of passing out leaflets published by the Draft Resistance Union at the entrance to the University Center. The court ordered that the regulation be changed, deleted the approval requirement, and allowed hand-to-hand distribution of material. The judge asked attorneys in the case to draft mutually acceptable regulations that would forbid the forcing of literature on anyone and prohibit distribution indoors and around entranceways and exits.

The opposition to the Vietnam war on college campuses had led to protests against ROTC units that were preparing undergraduates for service in the military. However, the quality of the Air Force ROTC program at Memphis State, which could lead to commissions and careers in the Air Force, was popular with many students. The *Memphis Press-Scimitar* reported that there were fourteen officers teaching in the large program with an average of fourteen years experience. They included two colonels, three lieutenant colonels, three majors. The rest were captains. It was also noted that "the Arnold Air Society, a military fraternity of sorts, was voted the outstanding unit in the country for professional competence and leadership this year, and their female affiliate, The Angel Flight, was also voted the best in the land. It was the first time one school ever had both of these awards."

President Humphreys had retained a great pride and interest in the ROTC program since 1951. Since there was no ROTC unit on the campus during the Korean military action, he had persuaded President Smith to send him to Washington to try to obtain such a unit. With assistance from Senators K. D. McKellar and Estes Kefauver he had obtained an application for an Air Force unit at Memphis State. It was approved and the unit became the largest in the country. Hundreds of Memphis State students were enabled to enter into professional careers as officers in the Air Force.

Campus disturbances continued around the country. The *Memphis Press-Scimitar* in an editorial on January 17, 1970, commented that "when a group of campus dissidents stormed the entrance of the Administration building in Knoxville the University of Tennessee authorities promptly called in the city police. Sixteen students and six other individuals were arrested and face Grand Jury action on charges of violating a state law which forbids gathering on the property of a state university for the purpose of creating a disturbance."

The newspaper continued, "The disturbances at Knoxville have their parallel in what took place at Memphis State in the spring of 1969. In both instances police were called, and the trespassers were arrested. What happened in Memphis and Knoxville is in clear contrast to policies followed earlier at other universities—Cornell, Columbia, and Harvard, to name three—where adminstrators, through timidity or lack of common sense, failed to act firmly with students bent on making a shambles of orderly education."

The winter months brought a variety of activities on the campus. The annual debate tournament had teams from 70 colleges in 25 states. Greater Memphis State announced plans for a program to recruit outstanding West Tennessee students to enroll at the university. Mori E . Greiner, president of Greater Memphis State, indicated that student leaders were invited to spend a weekend in Memphis, where they would be given tours of the campus and the city. Greiner thought that the program would be an excellent way for Memphis State to attract good high school scholars from the surrounding area.

Spring, the season when campus activities usually become more lively, started early in 1970. In February, Keith Kennedy, theater director in the Speech and Drama department, came into President Humphreys office and in a very cautious manner announced that he had secured the first rights of a regional or campus theater to produce the controversial Broadway show *Hair*. He said that he had the approval of the authors that the nude scenes not be included.

Humphreys said that the first thought that came to his mind was the invitation that the Speech and Drama department had extended to the "free speech" speaker from the University of California a few years earlier, a talk that had caused such a row on the campus and in the community. He suspected that "they've done it to me again." However, Humphreys knew that in their field the theatre faculty and students had done an outstanding job and had some very talented people.

They discussed the matter, and the university president told Kennedy that he would have to have assurance that it would be done in "good taste," quite aware that his definition and the community's definition of "good taste" might not be the same as Kennedy's. Humphreys reluctantly agreed, thinking to himself, "here comes another tumultuous spring."

The Broadway play *Hair* received mixed reviews on the campus and in the community.

The announcement that *Hair* would be produced on the campus was greeted with a mixed response. Most of the students thought it was great, but many in the community were outraged and let Humphreys know with a deluge of letters and phone calls.

When the production was presented March 2–7 to sellout audiences it received mixed reviews. Edwin Howard, drama critic of the *Memphis Press-Scimitar* was exuberant in his review, Robert Jennings of *The Commercial Appeal* praised the talent and execution, but questioned its place on the campus of an educational institution. The demand for tickets from students, faculty, and community was so great that the run had to be extended for six extra performances.

The president's office received hundreds of letters, about half praising it, the other half condemning the university for allowing it. Typical of the comments were the following: "*Hair* carries a great message of love to everyone," wrote Mrs. Homer B. Branan, III. "Why can't we all take heed, understand and live with it?" Mrs. John R. Fawcette, Jr., wrote, "*Hair* is an outrageous assault on morality, an outrageous assault on patriotism, and an outrageous assault on America's youth."

If one photograph can put one college president on one campus in the middle of student unrest and bring an entire decade into focus, Barney Sellers made that picture on May 5, 1970, at Memphis State University.

It shows a tall man, his back to the campus flagpole, surrounded by a sea of faces. The picture caption in *The Commercial Appeal* said, "Students encircle MSU President C. C. Humphreys at flagpole confrontation."

Humphreys, in university crises, never sent surrogates, and shortly after noon on the tense day in May he waded into a student sea to try to quell a building confrontation. Some students wanted to lower the American flag to half staff; others were just as insistent that it remain at the top of the pole.

The incident grew out of the tragedy at Kent State University in Ohio, where four students were killed when members of the Ohio National Guard fired into a group participating in an anti-Vietnam war demonstration. Students around the nation responded with candlelight services, marches, strikes, sit-ins, and, in some cases, by throwing

Some Memphis State students wanted to lower the flag in memory of the Kent State tragedy, others opposed the action.

rocks and firebombs at National Guard armories and ROTC buildings.

Police fired tear gas into 2000 rock-throwing students at the University of Texas as they charged toward the Capital in Austin. In New York classes were suspended at Columbia and New York University; student pickets marched at Hunter College. At the University of Tennessee in Knoxville, about 4000 students massed in front of the University Center and cheered a student leader's demand for a three-day boycott of classes.

The Memphis State incident began just before noon when a small group of students who had gathered on the mall south of the Administration Building, apparently in a spur-of-the-moment decision, decided to pull the flag to half staff. Quickly, other students gathered and restored the flag to full staff.

Within minutes more than a thousand students had assembled. A potentially dangerous situation was building.

A calm President Humphreys, with the tenseness inside him revealed by a cigarette in his hand—he smoked only when he felt a need to relax—walked down the broad steps that were then on the front of the Administration Building. Students pushed in to hear him.

"We have a strong difference of opinion here which could lead to direct confrontation, which leads to bloodshed," he told the students. "I know you don't want that. If you get nothing else from education you should get the ability to discuss in a rational manner a difference of opinion. Intelligent people do try to resolve those differences."

He was not faring so well in calming the students on the steps. The pushing and shoving increased around the flagpole between those who wanted to lower the flag and those who were against doing so.

James Chisum of *The Commercial Appeal* wrote that "several times the assaulting students shouldered girls with scared eyes, who attempted to bring the flag down. The girls fumbled at the lanyard holding the flag—which had been tied eight or ten feet up the pole—before they were pulled down."

Humphreys made his way through the crowd to the flagpole, where in a loud voice he got the attention of the combatants. He told the crowd that the American flag had been a banner that stood for democracy and for which thousands of young Americans had given their lives to defeat brutal dictators and tyrants. He told them to go look at the plaque in the Administration Building and read the names of the young men who had made the supreme sacrifice in World War II, most of whom he knew and admired.

He told them the flag had not changed. "If you disagree with your country's policy makers, don't blame the flag," he said. "It's not coming down by your hands as long as I'm here." Later he said he had tried to reason with them, but "I was finally fed up." He did tell them to select six representatives from each side and come to his office, and he would discuss with them a proper way to express the sorrow all felt at the great tragedy that had happened at Kent State.

Some pushing, shoving, arguing, and fist fights continued, but the two factions selected their representatives, who came to the President's office and were seated around a conference table. After some argument, and with everyone having a chance to talk, it was decided that a memorial service would be held the next day at noon for one hour. At the beginning the flag would be lowered to half staff by representatives of the two groups. The "flag lowerers" could select the speakers. The site for the service would be on the steps of the Administration Building which faced the flagpole, where a podium with a sound system would be set up. The service would end at 1:00 P.M. and the flag would go back up.

As plans were being developed, Humphreys later said, "I kept thinking that the speakers would arouse emotions and we could have the fighting start again. I was trying to think of a way to end the service peacefully. A strange thought came to mind. I suggested that we get the chorus that closed the campus production of *Hair* with the song, 'Let the Sun Shine In,' repeat their performance as a closing for the service. The chorus, clasping hands and singing about love, not violence and hate, might defuse any anger aroused by the speakers. The negotiators thought this was a great idea."

Some minor skirmishes continued around the flagpole during the conference in the president's office. At 2:30 P.M., when the negotiators emerged from the meeting, Michael McDonald from Stamford, Connecticut, shouted from the steps of the Administration Building, "In the morning that flag will be at half mast. We are going to have a proper ceremony—all we are doing is fighting in the family."

Most of the students left, and at 5:20 P.M. two campus security men lowered the flag and carried it into the Administration Building. After sundown the remaining crowd swelled into an informal group dance, with local bands providing music far into the night. Some time before dawn someone made away with the flagpole rope, throwing a hitch into memorial plans at noon. At first it was feared that the nearest flagpole climber was in St. Louis, but university officials, after many phone calls, found a local man who got new lines installed about 10:30 A.M.

Another problem developed during the night. With students, and many nonstudents attracted by the news, gathered in groups around the campus, a crew from the County Health Department on a routine mosquito spraying mission arrived with a tank truck and began to spray the east side of the campus. Student service personnel, who had remained on duty all night, had to convince the students that the administration had nothing to do with the spraying or with pulling the flagpole rope down.

The next day the service began with President Humphreys' opening remarks that a memorial service for the Kent State students was the proper way to express sorrow. He congratulated the students for planning the service rather than using violence. The speakers did get emotional, and some were militant. Humphreys was watching the time and making sure that the chorus was prepared. At 1:00 o'clock the signal was given, the singers formed a chain, and started the song. As the flag was being raised, those in the crowd joined hands with the chorus and began to sing about love, not war.

Humphreys said he relaxed for the first time in the past twenty-four hours and thought back to all the letters he had received protesting *Hair*. "I would never have dreamed that I would someday welcome a song from the play, and that it would calm a highly emotional and dangerous scene." He added, "Police had not been called to the campus."

The Commercial Appeal said, "By words and deeds, Dr. Humphreys demonstrated, with the help of the students, that differences can be sanely resolved."

While Humphreys agreed to the memorial service and the lowering of the flag, he declined to accept a proposal by the Faculty Council for a full-day moratorium. "Some students who paid to get an education want to attend classes," he said, "and I believe they have that right. However, those who feel strong moral obligations to stay away from classes should do so but they will not be excused."

In reality the flagpole incident was not the significant story of the 1969–70 school year, but it did reflect the presence of a university president in a time of crisis.

The new $430,000, 18,000 square foot Dr. Arthur G. Hudson Center opened at the beginning of the fall semester. Named for the man who was campus physician for twenty-six years before his death in 1968, the center had new x-ray facilities and a therapy laboratory to provide day care for emergency patients. Dr. Beverley Ray was the director of a staff, which included an associate director, a part-time physician, three nurses, a technician, and a secretary. Ten years before there had been a part-time doctor and a nurse who also taught health classes located in two small rooms on the first floor of the Administration Building.

A major academic growth area was the College of Business Administration. It had 4800 undergraduate students and 350 graduate students, or about 30 percent of the total enrollment. "One of the most significant accomplishments of the college during the year," Humphreys said, "was accreditation by the American Association of Collegiate Schools of Business. The standards met are recognized as being among the highest of the nationally recognized accrediting agencies."

In the College of Education, which continued to turn out more teachers than any other state university, Dr. Sam H. Johnson returned to full-time teaching. Dr. Robert L. Saunders of Auburn University was named dean.

The School of Law enrolled a record 249 students, and the Student Bar Association was cited by the American Bar Association as the most outstanding in the nation. Humphreys treated all the schools and departments equally, but he was especially pleased with progress in the law school.

In December, President Humphreys asked the State Board of Education for permission to make the Air Force Reserve Officer Training Corps voluntary. An SBE committee studied the proposal and suggested it be retained for one year. With 2300 cadets, Memphis State maintained its position as the largest AFROTC program in the nation.

During the year a bright new trophy was placed in its case at the University Center. MSU's Panhellenic Council was selected as the best in the country when the National Panhellenic Conference met in Miami. More than 200 councils competed for the honor.

The Commercial Appeal's traditional Mile-O-Dimes program, which gives food to needy families at Christmas, got a boost from the university. Members of Lambda Chi Alpha fraternity turned in 1600 pounds of food, the result of holding for ransom the presidents of each sorority on campus. In a lilting vein Sigma Kappa sorority and Sigma Chi fraternity teamed up and threw a hootenanny with a lot of strumming and singing at a ward party for patients at Veterans Hospital.

One musical leader putting it all together was Tommy Ferguson, band director at Memphis State. In the Collegiate Jazz Festival of Notre

Dame in South Bend, Indiana, his MSU Jazz Band "A" was acclaimed one of the three outstanding jazz units in the nation. In addition to a trophy, a set of music stands, and a $150 cash prize, the band had an individual winner in Lewis Keel. A graduate student from Memphis, Keel was named outstanding tenor saxophonist. He received a $700 alto saxophone.

In the Speech and Drama Building theater, Tennessee Williams' popular "The Glass Menagerie," opened the MSU theater season.

The Commercial Appeal in its October 19 edition said, "In the next two weeks Memphis' capacity for absorbing opera will be put to a test such as usually comes only with the Metropolitan's spring visits.

"Three performances of two operas will be presented during the coming fortnight, starting with MSU's Opera Theater *Tosca* on Tuesday night at 8 and concluding with Memphis Opera Theater's *Aida* at 8 on October 30 and November 1." Famed tenor Richard Tucker of the Metropolitan was in the *Tosca* cast.

Sports did not go unnoticed in Tigerland. Coach Spook Murphy's football team won its last seven games to build an 8–2 record and set the title pace in the Missouri Valley Conference.

Called "the team that pride built" by President Humphreys, the Tigers earned a Memphis State Appreciation Luncheon at the Downtowner Motor Inn. Mayor Henry Loeb and other community leaders joined in the applause.

"This team has set a pattern for the future," Humphreys said. "We have had good teams in the past, but this team and future teams will play better schedules. The pride on which this team built its success will be carried on.

"Some people say we are aggressive. But we have to be. We didn't have some of the things other institutions had to start with. We are fair and reasonable, but you've got to fight for what you get. We are aggressive and we will keep being aggressive. If we weren't we wouldn't be where we are today."

Basketball was another picture. A struggling Coach Moe Iba was released, but there would be a dramatic turnaround under his successor, Gene Bartow, who came from Valparaiso in Indiana, where he had coached six years.

"I believe I am prepared," he said. "This has to be one of the better coaching jobs in the Missouri Valley Conference. I come to Memphis State University very happy about the prospects. I think we can win right away."

Bartow was not making an overstatement. In 1973 his Tiger team would reach the NCAA finals in St. Louis. Big Bill Walton, a seven footer, would lead Coach John Wooden's UCLA team to the title, but Larry Finch and the other Tigers won the nation's respect in the championship game.

As the school year drew to a close, Memphis State students revealed by ballot how attitudes had changed in a decade. On the question of whether students supported Humphreys in making ROTC voluntary, the vote was 3312 for and 363 against. The Vietnam vote was 1575 for staying in the country and 2067 for getting out. Bill Wheat, Student Government Association president, read the results to students at a mid-day meeting in the University Center lobby.

In the same center's ballroom on May 1 a retirement party was held for Flora Rawls, dean of women, who was leaving after forty years of distinguished service at the university. She had been dean since 1947. Dr. Jess Parrish, vice president for student affairs, sent letters of invitation to the reception and dinner saying, "We know there is no adequate way of thanking her for the years of service to MSU, her contributions to education, and her inspiring influence on the lives of hundreds of young people throughout the country."

At the appreciation dinner President Humphreys made a surprise presentation to Miss Rawls—the first Distinguished Service Award ever given by the Tennessee Education Department. The certificate, signed by State Education Commissioner J. Howard Warf, cited Dean Rawls for demonstrating merit and dedication in the advancement of education.

There had been many earlier honors for Dean Rawls. In 1964 she had been named Memphis' Outstanding Woman in Education by the Downtown Association. A newspaper poll conducted in late 1969 listed her among ten women from the Mid-South who contributed the most to the area in the 1960s. She also received a special citation for outstanding service from the National Association of Womens Deans and Counselors at its annual meeting in Los Angeles.

When commencement exercises were held on May 30, 1970, Mem-

After more than a decade of strong support by the university and by the community, the Memphis State basketball program was a national contender. Larry Finch, who became head coach in 1986, was usually surrounded by UCLA players in the NCAA Finals in 1973.

phis State awarded 1033 degrees, a record. Among the graduates was Mrs. Jean Moss Williams, the wife of a Memphis mail carrier. She was forty-two years old and the mother of six children. None of those duties prevented her from graduating magna cum laude with a bachelor's degree in education.

"I want to teach deprived elementary school children in the inner city," she said. "I worked as an assistant teacher in the Head Start program, and decided then to go to college. I felt I could contribute something to deprived school children as a teacher." Mrs. Williams attended Memphis State with three of her children.

She and her family heard Dr. Elvis J. Stahr, president of the Audubon Society, deliver the commencement address. He told his audience that if mankind "is to survive, all environmental changes must be based on the question of 'What effect will they have?' "

Stahr's comments came at a time when Memphis State was setting up an environmental studies program. Somehow the university managed to remain on the cutting edge of progress.

Meanwhile, in Nashville, a struggle over the control of higher education continued to build. The State Board of Education, under the leadership of J. Howard Warf, would resist change with considerable strength. It would take two more years to resolve the issue in the legislature, but it would have repercussions at Memphis State.

Dean of Admissions R. P. Clark also retired, completing forty-six years of service to public education in Tennessee. He had spent thirty-six years at Memphis State. Clark became director of admissions in 1946 and later, dean.

To replace these valuable leaders, President Humphreys turned to Dr. Patricia Hillman Murrell, an education professor at the University of Virginia, who became dean of women effective September 1. Her husband, an attorney with the Department of Justice in Washington, earlier had been added to the School of Law faculty. Dr. John Y. Eubank, Jr., who had been Clark's deputy, was promoted to dean of admissions.

One of Humphreys' many talents was the ability to surround himself with excellent people. The problem, of course, was that they were in high demand by other institutions and organizations. The Tennessee

Higher Education Commission hired Dr. Jerry Boone to be its deputy director. Boone had made the new University College a success.

In May it was announced that Roy Nicks, vice president for Development and Research, had been named Chancellor of the University of Tennessee's Nashville Center. And, at the time this decision was being made by UT, the State Board of Education also reached into Memphis State's administrative leadership and selected Dr. Jess Parrish to become president of the planned Shelby State Community College.

Big buildings continued to rise on the campus during the year, but President Humphreys was particularly pleased with the addition of a modern health center to the growing campus.

13

At the Pinnacle

1970–1971

THE NEWS HEADLINES

Thor Heyerdahl and a multinational crew sail into Bridge-
town Harbor, Barbados, after a two-month voyage from
Morocco in a frail papyrus boat, *Ra II*, perhaps proving that
ancient Egyptians could have crossed the Atlantic...
President Nixon signs bill creating an independent U.S.
Postal Service...Charles de Gaulle, 79, dies after a heart attack at his home in Colombey-les-Deux Eglises, France...A
California jury convicts Charles Manson and three of his
followers of first degree murder in the 1969 slaying of actress
Sharon Tate and six others...Ohio ratifies the 26th Amendment to the U.S. Constitution, making it law, and the voting
age is lowered to 18.

AND THE WAY WE WERE

Preliminary figures indicate that fall enrollment will exceed
18,000...Female residents who are over 21 or with parents'
approval will soon be able to determine own dorm hours
...1971 Gremlin—$1939...First black coed named Home-
coming Queen...The 829 students receiving their degrees in
the winter graduation exercises brings the total MSU graduates to more than 25,000...MSU, institute of higher learning, offers its students beautiful buildings, sufficient
classrooms, low-cost entertainment, and a migraine parking
problem.

AS THE NEW YEAR GOT UNDER WAY it appeared that the campus might be a little quieter. The civil rights movement had won a number of hard fought battles for equality, although the fight would continue. The student antiwar activities, which reached a climax with four deaths at Kent State, shocked the country and led to a demand for more control on campus. As Bayard Ruskin, a life-long socialist who had been jailed many times for demonstrating against war and racism, once said, the dilemma of dissent in the United States was that most middle class people believed in freedom and justice, but also believed in law and order. If it came to a choice between the two sets of values, law and order would win.

Campuses would never return to the tranquility of the 1940s or 1950s, but they would be entering a new, more peaceful era. Dr. John Eubank, the new dean of admission, reported that the university was likely to raise its minimum entrance requirements. He pointed out that the new community college could provide more remedial help for those students not ready to compete at the university level.

The Speech and Hearing Center added a number of outstanding faculty members to its staff, increasing the faculty from eight to fifteen for the new year. The additions allowed the graduate program to increase more than four times its previous number.

The SBE at its August meeting voted to make ROTC voluntary at the institutions under its supervision, with the beginning of the 1971–72 academic year. President Humphreys said a representative of the Department of Defense had visited the state institutions to discuss the change and provided statistics showing that voluntary programs generally produced as many or more military officer candidates as compulsory programs. Humphreys also said that he did not feel that the policy change was in any way connected with the antiwar sentiment. "It's just a change to meet changing education and military needs," he believed.

The new academic year brought a change in the academic calendar that had been followed for many years. The fall semester opened two

Student life and concerns in the early 1970s were far different from the tensions and agitation of the 1960s.

and a half weeks earlier than in the past. This meant that the semester would end before the Christmas holidays, and students would not have to return for final exams after the holidays. They would take the Christmas break between semesters and then return for the beginning of the spring semester. The second semester would end about the first of May, which would allow a minisemester between the end of the spring semester and the beginning of the summer sessions. Many advantages, including the fuller use of plant facilities, resulted from the new schedule.

Ronald A. Terry, national chairman of the Fourth Annual Fund Campaign, announced in August that the University had received a record $68,305.50. This was an increase of 36 percent and represented contributions by 1966 friends and alumni.

On August 21, 1970, *The Commercial Appeal* reported that after many interruptions since his graduation from South Side High School in 1954, a postal clerk with six children, Milton J. Hause of 2675 Galaxie, had received his degree. He said, "It dawned on me again in 1968 that I'd better get back to college if I hoped to be anything, and I didn't stop that time." Hause was one of 630 receiving bachelor degrees, 451 receiving masters degrees and 9 receiving doctoral degrees, who heard the commencement address by Aubrey J. Wagner, director and chairman of the Tennessee Valley Authority.

Among the graduates were Ronald England, the first police officer to receive a master's degree, and the first doctorate in chemistry, David D. Holder.

A week later *The Commercial Appeal* reported that Gail Robinson, a former Memphis State student, had been cast in her first regular season Metropolitan Opera starring role. She was to have the title role in *Lucia di Lammermoor* and also would sing Rosina, the soprano lead in *The Barber of Seville*, later in the season. Gail was the third former Memphis State student to win Metropolitan Opera tryouts and be given contracts in the previous seven years. The other two were Patsy and Ruth Welting.

Of mounting concern to the public at this time were the environmental problems created by the increasing amount of industry in the Mid-South. On September 8, 1970, Humphreys announced the creation of a committee to investigate ways in which the university could contribute to the solution of these problems. He said, "As the largest institution for higher education in the Mid-South, Memphis State University has a great responsibility to assume a leadership role in dealing with this important concern." An information center would be established to increase public awareness of the problem and to identify areas of research which should be conducted.

It was announced in the *Memphis Press-Scimitar* in early September that there was "Another MSU First." James B. Staley, who received his doctor's degree in agriculture at UT Knoxville, had been named Memphis State's first horticulturist. The appointment was in keeping with the university's building boom and with Humphreys' long interest in maintaining an attractive campus.

Other changes taking place involved the social regulation of female students living on the campus. After months of discussion between university officials and women student leaders, an announcement was made by Dr. John Jones, vice president for student affairs, and Clarence Hampton, director of housing. Twenty-one-year-old coeds and upperclass women students with parental permission would set their own dormitory curfews. Freshmen women and upperclass coeds under twenty-one who did not have special parental permission would have to check in dorms at midnight Sunday through Thursday and at 2:00 A.M. Friday and Saturday. Times had changed since Dr. Nellie Angel Smith checked each woman student into the dorms at nightfall.

The turmoil and violence on college campuses in recent years, plus the increasing importance of higher education in the minds of the public, continued to hold the attention of the community. The lecture series on the campus sponsored by P. K. Seidman in honor of his brother M. L. Seidman in the winter and spring of 1970 on the subject of the campus and society attracted overflow crowds. Dr. Clark Kerr, former president of the University of California, who had been fired on January 1, 1967, in the midst of student unrest at Berkeley, spoke on the "Future of Higher Education." Douglass L. Hallett, a Yale student and writer, spoke on the subject "The University: an Intellectual Marketplace." Dr. S. I. Hayakawa, who battled militant students at San Francisco State after taking over as president following two presidents who were fired in the preceding three years, addressed the problem of "The University Under Attack."

In September of 1970 Memphis State opened an Information Center at Patterson and Central which had a marvelously modern touch—a drive-up window. During that month more than 1100 persons drove up to the window or parked and walked inside. Usually, they asked Mrs. Frankie Hromada, the director, or one of her student assistants, for directions on a rapidly changing campus. Most of the visitors sought the way to a particular building or asked to use the telephone, but unusual requests sometimes had to be fielded. One individual wanted help in locating a Japanese businessman, who was visiting

Memphis and might be at the university. In large measure, the inquiring person had come to the right place.

Memphis State in 1970, by headcount, had 18,754 students pursuing their educational dreams. They were not, however, making that endeavor on an isolated island. Under the leadership of President Humphreys, the university openly accepted the responsibility of helping Memphis cope with the problems of city life.

"It is there, in the city, that the university's esssential contributions and its concerns are most needed," Humphreys wrote. "As an urban university it is meeting, in a much wider scope than in the past, the educational, research, and service needs of the community."

In 1960, in the first year of his presidency, Humphreys, a historian who knew of the great services land-grant colleges had rendered to the nation's rural areas, decided an urban approach must be the mission of Memphis State, and he never relented. In one decade what had begun as a lonely, one-way street downtown by an educator from a small school locked inside an 80-acre box in East Memphis turned into a splendid two-way boulevard. Memphis, a city of 624,000 and the seventeenth largest in the country, now beat a path to Central and Patterson for expertise and methodology in solving or resolving urban problems.

The leadership of Tennessee's largest city, which had changed in a dramatic way since the death of E. H. Crump in 1954, had recognized the value of the institutional goals President Humphreys had set. In the process the extraordinary talents of Humphreys did not go unnoticed in the power structure that slowly evolved after the death of Crump, whose political organization had dominated Memphis for almost a half century.

By coincidence a growing city, feeling itself unshackled, sought a new social and economic identity at precisely the same time an emerging university was expanding its programs and services.

Humphreys always credited Memphis State University and its supporting cast for his many honors; he saw himself only as the point man in the platoon. Evidence, however, suggests that his ideas and energy fashioned a community image far beyond that.

He became a key figure in the power structure of Memphis.

After six months of study and research by a reporter, Barney DuBois,

The Commercial Appeal on November 20, 1970, began a copyrighted, five-part series titled "The Power Structure."

The lead of the first article was a question: "Who runs Memphis?" It was the question DuBois had asked Angus McEachran, the newspaper's metropolitan editor, in March of 1970, and he had to admit he did not know. When DuBois got the same answer from political experts and executives of the Memphis Area Chamber of Commerce, the newspaper decided to try to pinpoint the persons responsible for major decision-making in the city.

The editors felt that readers would like to know who made up the power structure or the leadership pyramid, if there was one. Much had been said and written about a leadership void since Crump's death in 1954. It was said in newspaper articles, and perhaps with considerable validity, that E. H. Crump and his political organization decided most major issues for Memphians, down to naming the presidents of the neighborhood PTAs. Social critics said such an environment did not create leaders.

DuBois, after 180 days of research involving questionnaires, interviews, and library material, offered ten pounds of data for computerized compilation, sifting, and interpretation. David W. Cooley, chief executive officer of the Chamber of Commerce, provided technical assistance as did Dr. W. Theodore May, an associate professor of psychiatry and clinical psychology at the University of Tennessee Medical Units. Both said the study had been made with academic thoroughness. DuBois, who was assisted by others on the newspaper's staff, found that major decisions in Memphis hinged on the interaction of forty-two men and women leaders. At the pinnacle, or the slightly flattened tip of a pyramid, there were thirteen men—no women—whom the research identified as "the most influential of all in decisions which occur here."

In alphabetical order, the newspaper named them: Walter Armstrong, Jr., an attorney and cultural leader; Edgar H. Bailey, president of the Memphis Board of Education and real estate executive; E. W. (Ned) Cook, president of Cook Industries, Inc., and chairman of the Memphis-Shelby County Airport Authority; Lewis R. Donelson, attorney and city councilman; W. D. Galbreath, board chairman of the Chamber of Commerce and real estate executive; Odell Horton, president of LeMoyne-Owen College, former Criminal Court judge and the only black in the group; Dr. C. C. Humphreys, president of Memphis State University; Henry Loeb, mayor of Memphis; Lewis K. McKee, board chairman of the National Bank of Commerce; Allen B. Morgan, board chairman of First National Bank and vice president of the Chamber; Abe Plough, founder and president of Plough, Inc., a national nonprescription drug manufacturing company based in Memphis; Norfleet Turner, financier and former board chairman of First National Bank; and Kemmons Wilson, board chairman and founder of Holiday Inns, Inc.

When he picked up the morning newspaper on November 20 and began reading it, Cecil Humphreys sat back in surprise. He said he may have filled out a questionnaire, and he said he thinks there was a brief telephone conversation with someone at *The Commercial Appeal*. But the series was news to him.

The newspaper had asked 123 "judges" to make nominations. All of them were people who held positions of power or leadership in community institutions and organizations. Two other approaches in the study involved the reputational method and actual behavior method.

Humphreys' name obviously went into the computer many times as the series took shape. Accompanying the second article was this box or sidebar to the main story:

The city's most influential leaders, when asked to pick the 10 Memphis leaders most capable of solving a major problem, selected in order: Allen B. Morgan, Abe Plough, Dr. C. C. Humphreys, Lewis W. McKee, Odell Horton, Lewis R. Donelson III, Edgar H. Bailey, E. W. (Ned) Cook, Kemmons Wilson, and Norfleet Turner.

When asked which Memphis leader had the greatest amount of personal influence in the city, the leaders said they regarded Henry Loeb because of his position as mayor. Others, in order, were Dr. C. C. Humphreys, Abe Plough, Edgar H. Bailey, Allen B. Morgan, Lewis K. McKee, E. W. (Ned) Cook, Kemmons Wilson, Lewis R. Donelson III, W. D. Galbreath, and Gordon Hanna.

The leaders were asked whose opinion is most respected by other leaders in the city. The top finisher, by far, was Abe Plough. Others, in order, were Dr. C. C. Humphreys, Norfleet Turner, Lewis K. McKee, Odell Horton, W. D. Galbreath, Allen B. Morgan, Walter P. Armstrong, Jr., Frank

R. Ahlgren, Lewis R. Donelson III, Edgar H. Bailey, Lucius Burch, and Edmund Orgill.

In tying the Memphis State academic gown to the town, Humphreys had reached a personal pinnacle few educators have achieved in the power structure of a major American city.

The findings in the DuBois study help to explain why political leaders coveted him as a candidate and why a bank offered him a high executive post. He was a leader.

It was nice to see that his peers appreciated him, but he continued to shine his own shoes, and often those of his wife, Florence, and their boys, for they considered him the best shoeshine man on Grandview, maybe in all of Memphis. "It's relaxing," he said. "I probably got in the habit when I only had one pair of shoes."

He also could laugh, even at himself. In an interview in 1970 in *The Columns*, a university publication, Mrs. Humphreys recalled meeting Humphreys in a store downtown where a mutual friend introduced them. "At the time he was an FBI special agent," she said. "So a few days later he phoned me and asked me for a date. I'll never forget that first date. He gave me a history lecture!"

Humphreys laughed out loud at the memory.

In 1970, Humphreys ended a six-year wait. In 1964 he had wanted to name the new education building for Ernest Ball, the former Memphis city school superintendent and at that time a member of the State Board of Education. Ball, who had enrolled at Normal when it opened in 1912, believed that the honor was not appropriate as long as he was on the board. The other members respected his feelings, and Humphreys' recommendation was tabled. But Humphreys did not recommend another name, and his patience matched Ball's humility. When Ball retired from the SBE at seventy-five, Humphreys had his way.

On October 17, 1970, the Ernest C. Ball Education Building, which had an auditorium, seventeen classrooms, and eighty-five offices, was dedicated as a part of the Homecoming observances.

The attitudes and tensions of the preceding spring did not carry over to the fall semester. Preparations for the traditional Homecoming festivities started early in October. The activities began on Thursday night with a barbeque picnic in front of the University Center, followed by a pep rally and street dance. A golf tournament for faculty, students, and alumni was held on Friday. "The Rascals," a nationally known recording group, performed at the Mid-South Coliseum in the Homecoming Concert.

On Saturday there was an alumni brunch at 10:30 and at 12:30, a parade featuring Mayor Henry Loeb and Curtis Person, Jr., Alumni Association president. Bob Williams was presented the outstanding alumnus award for service. The parade included the University Marching Band, the Al Chymia marching band, the Millington Navy Admirals' Band, and seventeen other in-town and out-of-town high school marching bands.

The evening Homecoming football game pitted Memphis State against Florida State, with the crowning of the Homecoming Queen with her court at half-time. The queen was Maybelline Forbes of Memphis, the university's first black to be so honored. The first black candidate to enter the contest since 1966, Miss Forbes competed in a field of twelve. The senior biology major had been endorsed by several white fraternities. In a fitting climax to all the activities the football team won a great victory in the last two minutes, 16–12.

Life on a campus in those days was a series of great highs and deep lows.

Humphreys, despite a usually calm and relaxed demeanor, was not an easy study, however. Perhaps it was because he thought a lot. He might, at times, keep his hands in his pockets and count to ten to calm his emotions, but when he chose, he could speak out. He was the principal speaker at a Veterans Day observance on November 1, 1970, where American Legion Post No. 1 surprised him with the Americanism Award.

Humphreys said the nation was suffering because it had failed to punish many violators of the law, and he challenged the veterans to help solve "our society's complex problems and make our country once again a united people working toward the same goals." Humphreys said the nation had to "get away from making young people think their thoughts are more important than those of their parents and teachers. We have paid too much honor to youth. We are becoming a nation of youth worshippers and we must get away from our permissiveness toward them. We must enter a war with ourselves to restore the principles that made the country great."

Humphreys said veterans and parents need to learn "the things bothering our young people today and do something to help them overcome the decisive problems of our day."

One of the symptoms of the problem President Humphreys addressed was quite visible on Highland Street two blocks west of the campus. A score of policemen patrolled what had become known as the "Highland Strip." "That many policemen is a sometime thing in the South Highland–Normal area," *The Commercial Appeal* reported, "It eased into prominence as a hangout for kids and the long-hairs after Pop-I's was established as a place to hang around, listen to music, and play pinball machines about two years ago. Then the shops came, catering to a way of dress not exactly establishment-oriented, if establishment-priced. The Cafe was opened, offering music, beer, meals, and another in-place where long-hair, hippie-type clothing and talk of drugs were common. And, nurtured on an environment of wandering street people, the drugs were dealt."

Many of the street people crowding into the Strip were not Memphis State students. Some were. A few of them, a tiny fraction of the student body, would arrive at morning classes a bit glassy-eyed from "acid" and "pot." In time, this too would pass from the scene, and Highland would return to normality, but it got worse before it got better. *The Commercial Appeal* sent Leon Monday, a young reporter just out of Vanderbilt University, into the area to purchase drugs, and he found it as easy as buying a lollipop.

It is a testimony to Humphreys' leadership that the university, whatever the trial of fire it underwent, kept the doors to learning open.

Physical expansion to meet enrollment demands captured most of the headlines in the 1960s and early 1970s, and properly so in Memphis State's case. Humphreys said many times in his writings and speeches that the university's first responsibility was its student teaching mission, and part of that involved providing the best possible learning environment. That meant building a good faculty as well as adding brick and mortar to the campus.

As their numbers increased, students demanded a great diversity in subject matter or academic disciplines. To meet these growing needs,

President Humphreys pushed for SBE approval of new courses, departments, and schools. He won most of his justification battles with the State Board of Education and the Tennessee Higher Education Commission, and for the first decade of his presidency he had to wrestle with an acute shortage of classrooms and laboratories. Some $20 million in building projects would be completed or near completion in 1970–71.

Aware of its regional responsibilities to West Tennessee, the university extension division expanded its program in Jackson with the announcement that it would offer upper level courses in a variety of academic areas. These courses were taught by Memphis State faculty on the Lambuth College campus. Graduate students would be able to take up to nine hours of extension courses instead of the previous limit of six hours. A full-time university administrator would maintain an office on the Lambuth campus.

Memphis State was also sending some of its other talents off the campus. *The Commercial Appeal* reported in January that a truck load of students would head east with the Children's Music Theater on a tour of Tennessee schools. The cast had already presented 30 performances of Grimm's fairy tales in November.

The paper also reported a cooperative project between the DeSoto County schools in Mississippi and the university's Speech and Hearing Center to provide therapy for children with speech difficulties. Since September a team from the Speech and Hearing Center had screened 10,300 students for speech difficulties. The project was being financed through a grant of $260,000 from the Department of Health, Education and Welfare.

In November *The Commercial Appeal* reported that the university was being called upon to assist the city and county governments in their efforts to continue operating its Neighborhood Youth Corps as a a part of the War on Poverty. This program was financed by federal funds and supervised by the national Office of Economic Opportunity through its regional office in Atlanta. The federal funds had been cut off because of what they called mismanagement of the funds and program. Both local governments and a representative of the Department of Labor asked Memphis State to take over the management of the

The campus as it appeared in the early 1970s. The expansion of the university during the Humphreys' presidency was apparent from Richardson Towers (*lower right*) to the South Campus (*upper center*).

out-of-school segment of the Neighborhood Youth which involved job training and placement of young unemployed.

President Humphreys at first declined, saying that this was clearly outside the range of responsibility of the university. After calls from local officials to help prevent the loss of a program that would help young people improve their employment opportunities, and aware of the close working relationship between the university and the community, he agreed that the university would take over the operation on a temporary basis of only a few months.

Keith Kennedy's latest production, *Man of La Mancha,* which opened in the theatre of the Speech and Drama Building in early December, met with lavish praise and without protest. The troupe was nominated for the annual American College Theater Festival to be held in Washington from March 21–April 6. The local reviews called it a "brilliant production," "inspired theater," and in keeping with the "best theater."

In March the *Press Scimitar* reported that, according to the Department of Commerce, the Regional Economic Development Center at Memphis State was a major factor in the creation of 1800 new jobs in West Tennessee during the past year. The center's technical and professional assistance had proved extremely helpful to rural counties in presenting their advantages to industries seeking new locations and had furnished needed information to clients interested in the locations of new ventures.

Additional recognition for the university's academic programs was received with the accreditation of the graduate program in the College of Business by the American Association of Collegiate Schools of Business. Dr. Ralph Williams, director of graduate studies in the college, said that the University of Tennessee program was accredited at the same meeting and that the two Tennessee programs were among only 80 colleges accredited out of some 800 that offered graduate courses in business. Dean Robert L. Saunders of the College of Education also announced that all of the master's degree level programs had been accredited by the National Council for Accreditation of Teacher Education.

In 1971 there were seven service and research units in the various colleges and divisions working on city, state, and national problems.

The Bureau of Business and Economic Research, one of President Humphreys' first projects and the reason Dr. Ron Carrier had left Ole Miss for Memphis State, was in the College of Business Administration. The Center for Manpower Studies also was there.

In the College of Arts and Sciences were the Bureau of Social Research and the Bureau of Public Administration. The College of Education housed the Bureau of Educational Research, and the College of Engineering had the Institute of Engineering.

All of these areas emphasized the public service role of the university. And there were others. During the school year the Department of Conferences and Institutes in the Division of Continuing Studies reported 4121 participants.

The Commercial Appeal wrote on January 10, 1971:

> Although Memphis State University has an estimated worth of $61 million and an annual operating budget of $23 million, its contributions to the economy of the community encompass a greater spectrum. It is difficult to place a dollars and cents value on the university's impact. There are, however, specific examples of service which show the maturity attained by the institution in recent years.
>
> Bureaus, centers, and special programs usually are formed to seek solutions to problems which confront business, industry, and government....One of the service programs in which the results are most obvious is being conducted by the Regional Economic Development Center (REDC) at MSU. Since that operation began three-and-a-half years ago, it has produced projects for 165 clients in the field of business stability, business expansion, new ventures, community development, and several other areas.
>
> Reports from the REDC indicate its work has affected in some way the creation or stabilization of 5291 jobs involving $21.7 million in payrolls in Middle and West Tennessee....During the past year REDC, in its primary effort to speed economic development, conducted 59 projects that involved 1788 jobs with payrolls totaling $8.1 million.

Greater service by the university also means more work internally. To increase efficiency, President Humphreys reorganized several major administrative departments. Business manager R. Eugene Smith was named vice president for business and finance. Jerry Lee Jones was appointed director of planning and information systems, and E. Grady

Bogue became assistant vice president for academic programs and research.

Other universities, as they should, kept an eye on what was happening at Memphis State and the bright minds helping Humphreys to mold a prestigious university. It was announced on November 16, 1970, that Ron Carrier, the university's first vice president of academic affairs, had accepted the presidency of James Madison College in Harrisonburg, Virginia.

"The selection of Dr. Carrier to be president of Madison College is an honor and recognition of his abilities, and we share with him in his pride," Humphreys told reporters. "We are extremely sorry to lose a most capable administrator. Dr. Carrier has made valuable contributions not only to the university but also to the whole community."

Early in January, President Humphreys named Dr. Walter R. Smith, dean of the College of Arts and Sciences, as acting vice president for academic affairs. Dr. Smith held degrees from Lambuth College, Southern Methodist University, and the University of California at Berkeley. He taught at Southern Methodist before joining the Memphis State faculty as an English teacher in 1951. Smith also would continue to oversee the College of Arts and Sciences, which remained the university's largest college.

Humphreys also was proud when, in the late spring of 1971, the new $3 million business college complex opened at Central and Patterson. But he always managed to look beyond the brick and mortar. In his notes he commented on the college's eighty-three member faculty with fifty-two terminal degrees, but he was closest to his heart when he noted that the College of Business Administration "entered into 247 projects, including research for a variety of business and governmental units at the state and local levels. Faculty members participated in programs for local, regional, and national organizations on 169 occasions. About 2600 businessmen attended seminars and professional development programs conducted by the faculty."

Another university accomplishment was the establishment of a new Center for Housing and Urban Land Economic Research, to be directed by Paul R. Lowry, who had come to MSU with Ron Carrier in 1963 from the University of Mississippi.

In announcing his plans for the center, President Humphreys said many of the major problems of urban communities arose out of housing and land use matters. Lowery said the center would:

1. Identify the role of private enterprise in establishing housing policies for cities.
2. Develop a better understanding of the roles of public bodies in shaping housing and land development programs for cities.
3. Examine the means by which market actions and public housing policy and programs can be used to create a more promising environment.
4. provide an organized research unit competent to serve local, state and federal agencies in their needs for studies in problems of housing, real estate, recreation and real property taxation.

The game of Chinese checkers on the use of campus buildings continued in 1970–71, and, at last, Humphreys had a chance to help one of his first academic loves—history.

The old building that was vacated by the business college was refurbished and occupied by the history department, which had held memories for Humphreys since 1937 when he came to Memphis State to teach football and history. The history building was named Mitchell Hall in memory of Enoch Mitchell, first chairman of the department.

President Humphreys' master's thesis at the University of Tennessee had centered on Reelfoot Lake, and he reacted with pleasure when that subject led to a Certificate of Commendation from the American Association for State and Local History to Memphis State University Press. The certificate was presented for *Night Riders of Reelfoot Lake,* written by Paul J. Vanderwood.

In an academic step forward the State Board approved and sent to the Higher Education Commission for its concurrence President Humphreys' proposal to offer a doctoral degree in mathematics by the fall of 1972. It would be the sixth doctorate offered by the university. Others were in education, psychology, chemistry, history, and biology.

Dr. John Folger, director of the Higher Education Commission, told SBE members his agency currently was not approving new programs that cost additional money until the budgetary situation became clearer. But he noted that the initial emphasis of the proposed MSU program would be on the preparation of college-level math teachers. "That is certainly desirable," Folger said. "The essential question is whether there is going to be any money to support this type of development."

The failure of state revenue collections to meet expectations would cost Memphis State almost a million dollars. Jerry Adams, assistant to the State Commissioner of Finance and Administration, placed the loss on a statewide basis at about $9 million. He reported that income was about $20 million below estimates. Traditionally, five percent of state appropriations were impounded to create a reserve or buffer against such shortages. However, Memphis State and others had been warned ahead of time to prepare budgets with the assumption that they would not get the impounded funds in the 1970–71 fiscal year. Memphis State managed the problem and made only a few academic adjustments.

Meanwhile legislative support for higher education began to wane in Tennessee and nationwide because of a slowing of the economy and disenchantment with student dissent. "Unfortunately," President Humphreys wrote, "this came at a time when the public was demanding more services." He said the challenge that universities had to meet was convincing the public that education works for the people, that it can change patterns, and improve the quality of life. "If we don't meet that," he added, "we are indeed going to have problems."

The Tennessee Higher Education Commission, which had been created to study the programs and needs of the state-supported institutions and present recommendations for funding, came under fire by the legislature. The legislature demanded an equal voice in developing detailed spending by the institutions. The THEC and the presidents of the colleges and universities had submitted their operating budgets for the 1971–72 fiscal year. Three budget proposals were actually submitted. One budget, which envisioned program improvements, called for nearly $129.3 million; a second budget of $116.7 million would have continued programs at present levels. The third was a budget of $109.4 million which would mean program cutbacks. The 1970–71 appropriation had been $98 million. A major problem was that the state revenue for 1970–71 was falling below estimate.

John Bragg, chairman of the House Finance Committee, believed higher education had not properly responded to the legislature with information showing where the money should be spent. He said, "The legislature itself is a board of higher education—we look with suspicion at some of these budgets, tremendous suspicion."

Efforts to achieve savings in higher education in Memphis were under way. Nineteen presidents and officials of Memphis colleges and universities attended a symposium at Christian Brothers College that dealt with ways to eliminate city competition caused by duplication of courses on different campuses and to plan for education in the '80s. Concern was being felt for the future development of higher education by both public and private institutions.

The debate in the State Legislature over the funding of higher education continued. The Fiscal Review Committee was considering a recommendation that the "users and patrons of athletic contests at state colleges and universities pay the full costs of the athletic programs." It was noted that MSU and UT were the only two self-supporting athletic programs.

Asked about the possible effect of this on Memphis State University, Dr. Humphreys said, "I know local community interest and civic pride puts pressure on these colleges to have good athletic programs and these colleges certainly couldn't have the scholarships they now have under such a system, and neither could they support the nonrevenue sports." He pointed out that Memphis State and the University of Tennessee would not be affected, adding that those institutions were fortunate to be in a large city where support was easier to find. He also added, "There is a real tight squeeze on the education dollar from the state, and I can see why some people would question using education dollars to subsidize sports."

Asked what the solution might be, Dr. Humphreys said, "It seems merely a question of whether the taxpayers want part of the money to go to athletics? If the taxpayer says 'no' to state funds for athletics then schools such as Jackson State, Dyersburg State, UT-Martin, can count on drastically cutting back or eliminating sports programs."

Efforts to eliminate duplication at the state level were also being sought. *The Commercial Appeal* in an interview with Dr. John Folger, the director of the Tennessee Higher Education Commission, quoted him as saying that he thought it wise that the agency had designated Memphis State University and the University of Tennessee at Knoxville as comprehensive universities with multiple doctoral programs. Three other universities, East Tennessee State, Middle Tennessee State, and Tennessee Tech would have an incentive to excel in more limited areas rather than developing a wider range of perhaps mediocre programs.

Sports enjoyed a tremendously successful year, and it was reflected at the gate, particularly in basketball. Financially, it was an excellent school year in varsity athletics.

The title "All-Sports Champion" was awarded to Memphis State by the Missouri Valley Conference. The football team compiled a 6–4 record, its thirteenth winning season out of the last fifteen. The record kept Coach Billy Murphy among the nation's top fifteen winning coaches and brought All-Conference awards to nine players. Murphy won with tough, jaw-to-jaw defense, and some critics called for a change to a wide open offense. Murphy took his lumps from the fans, but Humphreys, who knew the game well, defended his coach.

Over in the Mid-South Coliseum the scene bordered on the joyous. Gene Bartow, the new basketball coach, led his team to an 18–8 record. The Tigers were title contenders as they compiled the school's best basketball record in eight years. All basketball attendance records were broken, with the team attracting an average attendance of more than 9300 a game. Six contests were sellouts, and Larry Finch was named the Missouri Valley's Sophomore-of-the-Year.

Winning national notice too were the new physical education facilities on the south end of the main campus. The nine-court handball complex was the scene of the 1971 United States National Handball Association finals.

In the middle of the campus the University Center, which had opened in 1968, continued to be the school's principal hub of activities and programs. It counted 192,349 students at 6635 scheduled functions, including 24 banquets and receptions.

During the 1970–71 school year, representatives from 198 corporations interviewed 2320 students, a 90 percent increase in four years. "These statistics become more meaningful when consideration is given to the fact that employment counseling is conducted individually with each student," Humphreys said. "On a nationwide comparison conducted by the College Placement Council, placement activity at Memphis State was far above the national average in both employer campus visits and interviews conducted."

In the 1950s financial aid officers were few in number at most American colleges, and Memphis State was not an exception. However, that began to change with the organization of the department of student financial aid in 1968. In fiscal 1970–71 about $1,200,000 was made available to 1792 students. The sum represented a 53.65 percent increase over the amount available only four years earlier.

More would be heard about it later, but *The Commercial Appeal* reported on November 12, 1970, that the legalization of abortion and job equality were the dominant topics at a meeting of the Women's Liberation Movement on campus.

"The meeting, attended by 10 women and a single man, was an attempt by Misses Grace Evans and Tanya Miller to form a group on campus," the newspaper said. "Both are members of the National Organization for Women (NOW)."

An era may have been starting involving "women's lib," but one ended for certain when it was announced that Dean R. M. (Bill) Robison, who had directed fifty-five commencements at Memphis State, would preside over his last one at the May ceremonies.

A great storyteller and a good humor man, Dean Robison, who was serving as assistant to the president, had completed forty-six years of service to the university when he retired on July 1, 1971. He had come to the campus in 1925, the year Normal School became West Tennessee Teachers College. Robison became bursar in 1937, when Humphreys and a football team arrived from UT-Martin.

"Then we had between 700 and 800 students," Robison recalled. "It wasn't until after the war that our enrollment began to jump."

After seven years as bursar, Robison became registrar, then dean of students and executive dean before becoming President Humphreys' assistant in 1968. For many years Dean Robison served as chairman of the school's atheltic committee. To commemorate his work with the athletic program, the athletic dormitory was named Robison Hall. Robison jokes are legendary, but he should be acknowledged as a good judge of men. It was he who said Cecil Humphreys could look out a campus building and see ten years down the road.

Four other familiar faces at the university retired in 1971, including Miss Ethel Lewis, secretary to Dean Robison for twenty-five years. R. J. Coltharp, former chairman of the Technology Department, closed out twenty-six years, and Dr. John E. Farrior, a professor of English, completed twenty-three years. Mrs. Mildred Gragg, a supervising teacher at the University's Campus School, concluded twenty-one years. Earlier she had taught in high schools and elementary schools in the Memphis area.

All of the retirees were recognized at graduation ceremonies in the Mid-South Colisesum, where Dr. David Mathews, president of the University of Alabama, delivered the convocation address. President Humphreys presented graduates with 831 bachelor's degrees, 216 masters, 46 associate degrees, and seven doctorates.

When he wrote his annual report on August 4, 1971, Humphreys sent it to a new name: E. C. Stimbert. Stimbert had been appointed by Governor Dunn to replace J. Howard Warf as commissioner of education and chairman of the State Board of Education. Stimbert had been superintendent of the Memphis city schools before the appointment.

Governor Dunn and the Tennessee General Assembly had set up an interesting situation as the state struggled to come up with a new governing structure for higher education. Decisions would be made in the spring of 1972 in Nashville, and they would touch heavily on Memphis State.

14

The Chancellorship

1971–1972

Nine hostages and 28 convicts die as New York state troopers storm the Attica State Correctional Facility to free 38 guards from 1200 inmates...Citing excess profits by U.S. firms, President Allende of Chile expropriates the Anaconda and Kennecott copper mines...Communist China gains membership in the UN on a 76–35 vote in the General Assembly...President Nixon visits Peking on a "journey for peace"...Arthur Brenner shoots Alabama Governor George Wallace in a Laurel, Maryland, shopping center.

AND THE WAY WE WERE

The MSU Summer Music Theater's production of "Fiddler on the Roof," playing to a packed house, wins a week's extension...President Nixon sends a portrait of himself as a gift to commemorate the dedication of the Edward J. Meeman Journalism Building...Marsha Alice McDonald, Miss Memphis State, wins the Miss Tennessee title...Ten coeds join the AFROTC for the first time...A modern version of a soap box for students who feel the urge to speak out comes to the campus as the administration builds a platform for just that in front of the University Center...The Student Publications Committee votes to change the name of *The Tiger Rag* to *The Helmsman* in the fall of 1972.

A CASUAL GLANCE AT THE STATISTICS suggests business as usual at Memphis State in the 1971–72 school year. It was big business too. Some 1937 people, including 918 faculty members and administrative officers, worked to meet the demands of 20,043 students with a total university budget exceeding $30 million.

Bigness, of course has a price tag. Getting to class on time remained a hassle. Commuters, at $3 a decal, registered 11,000 cars with the university, obviously overestimating their chances of parking in the 5266 spaces provided.

Bob Rutherford, director of security, said the struggle for parking space between 8 A.M. and noon was fierce. Improvisation by students on area streets led to city traffic tickets—an average of 150 a day, according to Memphis Police Inspector H. H. Leatherwood. "Some days we have given as high as 300 tickets," he said. Most citations were written for blocked private driveways and obstructed street intersections.

Some things, such as parking problems, apparently were endemic at most urban universities. But, to look at the broader university picture in 1971–72, Memphis State altered its course. Its leadership, under prodding from President Humphreys, began to assess itself, to ask questions, and to seek new approaches.

The tendency to equate progress with the growth of physical plant and student enrollment ended. Student needs were uppermost in President Humphreys' mind. In an interview with Jimmie Covington of *The Commercial Appeal*, he looked back on twelve years and ahead to the future.

"Twelve years ago we were totally involved in finding space and faculty to meet the great demand in our traditional programs," he said. "But we are finding we are taking care of numbers, but we are not meeting the needs. The old patterns are being questioned, and we have for the first time an oportunity to question what and how we've been doing. Now we are involved with the quality of the programs and finding out how to provide the programs that are most needed."

To find some of the answers, Humphreys asked the Tennessee Higher Education Commission for funds to establish a Learning Resource Center. He said institutional research in the past had dealt mainly with physical facilities and finances. He felt the new center would eliminate insufficient, unproductive, and ineffective instruction.

"I don't know any more important area that should be explored than instruction," Humphreys said. "There must be a recognition that this generation of college students is very much aware that society is changing rapidly and they are expecting from their college experiences something that will better equip them not only to live, but also contribute more to a rapidly changing society."

The winds of change touched Memphis State and all of Tennessee during the school year. Sports, as it often does in society, helped to remove some of the barriers. Memphis State on July 8, 1971, hired Aldredge (Pete) Mitchell as an assistant football coach. Mitchell, a highly successful coach at Melrose High School, became the first black coach at a predominantly white major football school in the South. Earlier, fears had been expressed outside the university that the breaking of the color line might affect scheduling with major football teams, particularly in the Southeastern Conference, but events proved them wrong.

The 1971–72 basketball team coached by Gene Bartow, who had black and white starters, tells much of the story. On March 13, 1972, Art Gilliam, Jr., a young insurance executive who wrote an editorial page column for *The Commercial Appeal*, penned an article headed, "Tigers Bring a Town Together."

Gilliam called the team "a rallying point for all Memphis." He wrote: "This city needs something like the MSU team. It is the kind of focal point which has been too long absent. It is relatively easy for less heterogenous communities to unite around political or religious leaders. But this community, complex and divided as it is, is more apt to unite around something much simpler and less controversial. And following a winner at MSU, especially a winner which itself is heterogenous but which works well as a unit, may be just the touch that is needed."

"In a broader sense," he concluded, "the MSU community, through

During halftime at the 1972 MSU-UT football game the Memphis State band
played a final tribute to President "Sonny." Humphreys had left MSU to become
Chancellor of the Regents system a few days earlier.

the many varied activities undertaken there, can become a unifying
element in this city."

Gilliam had torn a page from President Humphreys' dog-eared old
1950s playbook, and an appreciate university president clipped the
column and put it in his personal files.

The Commercial Appeal's Mid-South magazine visited the campus
to observe black students and reported its findings on April 5, 1972. It
found blacks "less militant but more aware." From eight students in
1959 the number of black students had increased to more than 2700.
The magazine found "a black corner" and "a lot of white corners" in
the cafeteria in the University Center, calling this "signs of separatism."
It also told of "evidence of togetherness"—blacks and whites in the

band, as cheerleaders, as Tigerettes, in honor societies and on various student boards and committees.

The spring semester also brought the nation's highest-ranking black military officer to the University Center, Brig. Gen. Daniel (Chappie) James, Jr. James, a heavily decorated combat flier, had become deputy assistant secretary of defense for public affairs.

General James told the students that lack of national unity was prolonging the Vietnam war. "It always angers me how many people can find so many things wrong with our country and absolutely nothing wrong with the other side," he said. Motioning toward the American flag, James said, "If someone says if you don't do it my way I'll burn it, I say, like hell you will."

Memphis State, like the city of Memphis, was not a perfect society in 1971–1972, but the university strived to be an equal opportunity educational institution. In the Homecoming Queen contest, a black coed won the crown for the second year in a row. It went to twenty-one-year-old Sandra Price.

Trees and shrubs help to make a campus. So does green grass. One of President Humphreys' goals from the beginning was to keep Memphis State a place of beauty as well as learning. He wanted the mall south of the Administration Building to remain a green front lawn. Classroom halls faced the commons, however, and 40,000 student feet in 1971 cut many paths across the lawn.

An understanding of students or human nature, rather than "Keep Off the Grass" signs, saved the lawn from shoe leather. Sidewalks, called "a miniature pedestrian expressway" by architect Gene Strong, evolved into an hourglass or figure-eight pattern with the interior built up to eight-foot high grass mounds. The plan merited an A from the psychology department. Students used the sidewalks. They had enough to worry about without walking uphill.

Memphis State saw its academic program strengthened in many ways during the year. It dedicated the $1 million Edward J. Meeman Journalism Building on November 6, 1971, and the 34,000 square foot facility with excellent equipment and a 150-seat lecture hall, pushed the entire program forward. Frank R. Ahlgren announced on April 25, 1972, that the Journalism Department had been accredited by the American Council on Education for Journalism.

Ahlgren, retired editor of *The Commercial Appeal*, was president of the ACEJ for many years. He also was the man who tipped President Humphreys to possible help from the Meeman Foundation.

During the year Memphis State became a member of the Oak Ridge Associated Universities, which conducted programs in research and information in the nuclear energy field. "Our selection to this distinguished association opens up the field for greater scientific research to the MSU faculty and our graduate students," said Dr. John W. Richardson, Jr., dean of the Graduate School.

More and more of the city's leaders recognized the university's contributions to the community, and the payback was considerable. A chair in real estate was established to honor Morris S. Fogelman, prominent Memphis real estate executive and land developer, by his sons, Robert F. Fogelman and Avron B. Fogelman. The $100,000 endowment went to the College of Business Administration's Department of Finance, Insurance, and Real Estate. In honoring their father, the Fogelman brothers said they wanted "to enrich business scholarship in this area and to enhance the understanding of real estate in the Mid-South."

In accepting the endowment, President Humphreys said the gift would "establish and perpetuate the chair in real estate, bringing about finer education in this special area as it commemorates the name of the man it honors, a man who has contributed so much to the economy and development of the city."

Born in a small town near Warsaw, Poland, Morris Fogelman came to Memphis when he was eleven years old. He quickly learned English and graduated from Central High School a year ahead of his class in 1928. Fogelman developed many subdivisions and apartment houses, including Woodmont Towers and Parkway House.

Joining in the ceremony in the University Center were the honoree's daughter, Mrs. Martin Berlanstein; Gene Smith, Vice President for Business and Finance; Dr. Peter F. Freund, Chairman of the Department of Finance, Insurance and Real Estate; and Harry Woodbury, Director of Development at Memphis State. Woodbury, who had been at Humphreys' side in the battle for university status in 1957, had returned to the campus after three-and-a-half years in a top post with Mayor Henry Loeb's administration.

In the years to come, the imprint of the Fogelman name in advances at Memphis State University would become much more visible.

The Sales and Marketing Executives of Memphis, Inc., also made a major contribution of nearly $100,000 to permanently endow the chair of sales in the College of Business Administration's Department of Marketing. Begun in the early 1960s, the chair was the first in sales in the nation. In his acceptance of the gift, President Humphreys outlined the importance of Memphis as a regional trade center and the need for the better training of sales executives.

Midway during the year, Memphis State announced that it would begin an Institute for Criminal Justice in the fall of 1972. In revealing the plans, Humphreys said the institute would emphasize human relations. "We will not be stressing the technical aspects of police work, but will be dealing with the broad picture," he said. "Ninety-five percent of the programs will be a general education program in things such as psychology. People in these fields need to know more about people and how to deal with them."

Dr. Victor Feisal, MSU's acting director of Public Service and Research, cited national concern and national interest in criminal justice. He said most professions have had an educational base, but law enforcement had not. He said students completing the four-year program would receive a liberal arts degree.

Memphis State had had a two-year law enforcement training program since 1965 in the sociology department, where 300 were enrolled at the time of the announcement. Early in 1972, Humphreys announced that the Institute for Criminal Justice would be headed by Joseph A. Canale, an assistant city attorney, and former Memphis Police Chief Henry Lux. Canale would become director and Lux assistant director.

Before retiring in 1965, Canale had been an FBI agent for 23 years. He held three degrees, including one in law, from Notre Dame University, and he had taught law enforcement at MSU since 1966.

Lux did not have a college degree, but he had attended law enforcement programs at Harvard, Michigan State, and Northwestern. He encouraged policemen to obtain more education, and he asked the Memphis City Council for extra pay for those who did. During the four years he was police chief, the number of officers attending college increased from 13 to 200.

"These two men will bring the balance of academic credentials and practical experience to the institute that will be necessary to its operation, especially in the early stages of development," Humphreys said.

The institute would be funded partly by a federal grant, but the president always had a knack for finding funds to serve the community. Memphis had helped him meet the university's needs for more than a decade, and Humphreys wanted to pay it back in kind. He also thought undergraduate enrollment at Memphis State was at or near its peak. In his own thinking, a college with 20,000 students was about as large as it should be. He said as much in his writing and in speeches.

"Projections indicated," Humphreys said, "that higher education would continue to grow, but much of the new growth would be in institutions other than traditional college and universities, such as community colleges and part–high school vocational and technical programs."

"We feel that our undergraduate enrollment will not increase substantially in the future," he told Jimmie Covington in a wide-ranging interview. "I think the growth will take place in graduate work—either full-time or those employed persons working on advanced degrees in the evening and on weekends—and in new programs such as our criminal justice program. Renovation and special facilities will be needed, but we certainly won't need to have the physical expansion that we've needed in growing from 5000 to 20,000."

Humphreys possessed an almost sixth sense about society's changing needs and priorities. He respected tradition, but he avoided its chains, and as a president he dared to be innovative.

In many ways a change in Humphreys' outlook could be detected in 1971–72. A trip to India was one of them. Acting at the State Department's request, he left Memphis in mid-September on a five-week tour of colleges in India. He traveled with five other American university presidents to arrange student and faculty exchange programs, and they visited colleges and universities throughout the country. The trip was sponsored by the American Association of State Colleges and Universities.

Normally in the fall President Humphreys worked far beyond his campus administrative duties, particularly in telling legislators of Memphis State's needs. Often he invited them to tours and to football games. This was crucial lobbying because, in large measure, each regional university had to carry its own fight for funds to the General Assembly. The State Board of Education and the Tennessee Higher Education Commission, although closely tied to the governor's office, simply did not have the clout of the University of Tennessee trustees.

President Humphreys returned on October 12 from his Asian trip, and quickly got back into his routine. There still were football games, actual and political, to be played.

Coach Billy Murphy's football team managed only a 5–6 season but the Tigers won their first invitation to a postseason bowl. They traveled to California and trounced San Jose State in the Pasadena Bowl on December 18, 1971.

The Commercial Appeal called this one of Memphis State's finest football hours:

> Memphis State, hungry for its first bowl victory, smacked its lips here Saturday afternoon and swallowed San Jose State whole. Only the San Andreas Fault would have done a more thorough job.
>
> The Tigers, once again relying on a defense that proved to be as rugged as the haze-shrouded San Gabriel Mountains that rise behind the Rose Bowl, crushed the dazed Spartans 28–9, in the fourth Pasadena Bowl, before a disappointing crowd of 15,244. It was the Tigers' first bowl appearance.

The bowl victory brought Murphy's record to 91–44–1, but it would be Murphy's last game despite one of the best 14–year coaching records in the country. He would remain as athletic director, and hire Fred Pancoast as his successor from an assistant's post at the University of Georgia.

As the 1972 session of the General Assembly neared, Humphreys decided the time had come for Memphis State to get a helping hand from the legislature on its land acquisitions. He had a good case and the timing was right. Inflation had pushed up land costs and interest rates but there were other factors.

In seeking THEC budgetary approval, Humphreys pointed out that in the entire 63-year history of Memphis State the school had never received a state appropriation to buy land. It had always acquired land by gifts, memorials, and private loans. Now, the president wanted $1 million to retire its mortgages in the area between Central and Poplar. By buying the property and renting the houses, the University had saved the state hundreds of thousands of dollars.

"We bought land for 75 cents a square foot when we started our land acquisition program," Humphreys told the officials. "It now costs $1.50 per square foot, so you see we have saved money."

His plan received support in the newspapers. "The state ought to grant the request for $1 million as an act of good faith and a vote of confidence in Dr. Humphreys' administration," the *Memphis Press-Scimitar* declared in an editorial. It was a time of retrenchment in the General Assembly, but Memphis State won its case.

Another matter of even greater implications had been building for years—a much-discussed proposal to take the six regional universities out of the State Board of Education and place them under a separate governing body. For years the SBE had controlled all aspects of public education in Tennessee except at the University of Tennessee, which had its own trustees. There was a general feeling that the SBE gave most of its attention to the elementary and secondary schools which had a powerful political constituency. In other words they had the most students, teachers, and parents; reduced further, they controlled more votes.

Higher education, while not neglected, did not have as strong an advocate as it needed. The six regional colleges and universities had friends in area legislators, but statewide support was lacking. Governors appointed lay boards to study the question from time to time, but the recommendations usually bogged down in their own cabinets or in the General Assembly. As the regional universities began to grow after World War II, it became apparent that higher education in Tennessee needed to be coordinated between the loosely knit regional system and the UT system.

President Jack Smith had put the problem into focus in a letter to Cecil Humphreys on July 24, 1956. He wrote: "The University of Tennessee Board of Trusteees presented its needs through its published Biennial Reports to the Legislature and the Governor. The state colleges under the Board of Education had no such means of publicizing their needs and requests. The procedure followed has been for the college presidents, in a conference with the Governor and the Speakers of the Senate and House, to present their requests for funds, at which time an agreement would be requested from the Legislature."

UT's slogan "The State Is Our Campus" won many adherents—and dollars.

But as the regional universities grew, especially Memphis State, the problems of budgets and duplications in disciplines increased. Governor Buford Ellington saw the need for better planning and coordination and in 1961, he appointed a Coordinating Committee on Higher Education. Its chairman was Joe Morgan, state commissioner of education and chairman of the SBE. The Board of Trustees of the University of Tennessee named three members, as did the SBE.

Memphis State ran up against the Coordinating Committee when it tried to acquire the Cumberland University Law School in 1962. The committee wanted consultants to make a study, and before it could complete its work, the law school sold its assets to Howard University in Birmingham.

In 1966 several Tennessee newspapers made editorial pleas for better coordination of higher education during the Ellington-Hooker campaign for governor. Shortly after his election Ellington asked Dr. Quill Cope, president of Middle Tennessee State University, and Dr. Edward Boling, assistant to Dr. Andy Holt of UT, to develop a plan to deal with allocations of funds and the proliferation of degrees and facilities.

Governor Ellington also asked J. Howard Warf, who had replaced Joe Morgan as State Commissioner of Education, for advice. Warf believed all public education outside of the UT system should be under the SBE. He opposed creation of a Tennessee Higher Education Commission. Two astute politicians were doing battle. Ellington had two bills drawn, one establishing a separate board for the regional universities and one creating a coordinating board, the THEC. Warf opted for the THEC plan, which charged its members with developing a master plan for higher education and a funding formula. The THEC also would have the power to approve or disapprove new programs.

Some presidents in the regional universities had their doubts, but President Humphreys was not among them. "The creation of the

THEC was absolutely necessary," he told Yvonne Wood in an interview some years later. "Before, it was a dogfight for the State Board institutions. They felt that the University of Tennessee had more influence. As long as there were two systems of higher education, someone had to study the problem and make fair recommendations."

In 1967 the Tennessee Higher Education Commission won approval in the General Assembly. A strong board included top leaders from throughout the state, and Dr. John Folger became its executive director. Folger was graduate dean of Florida State University at the time of his appointment. Earlier he had worked with the Southern Regional Educational Board in Atlanta.

Two years after its formation, the THEC recommended that the six regional universities should be taken out of the SBE and placed under a separate board. Senator Bill Bruce of Memphis introduced legislation to effect the change, and Governor Ellington once again made a deal with Howard Warf, who opposed the proposal. If Warf let up in his fight against the THEC, Ellington, who was in his final year as governor, would not make much of a fight for Bruce's bill.

Once again politics rather than higher education had been served. Warf, a competent leader, would continue to run six universities, nine community colleges, three technical institutes, twenty-five area vocational schools, and every public K-12 school in Tennessee's ninety-five counties. It would take time, but a Republican governor and the General Assembly in 1972 would decide that Commissioner Warf had more responsibilities than he could say grace over.

Humphreys had seen the need for change when the THEC had been formed. He did not, as some regional presidents feared, think he would lose autonomy. "My feeling was that I wanted help," he told Yvonne Wood, who compiled an excellent monograph "The Importance and Impact of Three Significant Political Decisions Upon Higher Education in Tennessee." "MSU had grown so much," Humphreys continued, "you didn't get much help from the State Board of Education. The UT Board of Trustees worked hard for their system. They had one goal in mind and that was the University. The State Board of Education was an arbitrator and more neutral."

A dentist from Memphis, Winfield Dunn was elected governor in 1970. He was a Republican and that meant sweeping changes. Dunn brought in E. C. Stimbert, city schools superintendent in Memphis, as the new Commissioner of Education. There would be obstacles for them. All the SBE board members had been appointed by previous Democratic governors. Governor Dunn realized that Stimbert had inherited a bulky, unwieldy governance system, and several suggestions for a change went to the General Assembly. None passed.

Governor Dunn, still seeing the need for change, appointed Nelson Andrews, a Nashville businessman, to head a special commission, which included Walter Armstrong, Jack Petree, Thornton Strang, Harold Bradley, Curtis Person, Jr., Dr. Dan M. Martin, and Dr. Lloyd Elam. They went to work in March of 1971. On December 31, 1971, the commission recommended that Memphis State and the other five regional universities be combined into a new statewide system with its own governing board and chancellor. Andrews said the universities would be strengthened, but he said he doubted the new system would evolve into as tightly knit a system as the one the University of Tennessee had.

Under the committee's recommendations, the University of Tennessee would continue to be governed by its own board of trustees. Andrews said his group had considered, and rejected, the idea of "a superboard" that would oversee all public institutions of higher learning. Andrews said his committee had found no crisis in the current system, but he said it felt the present governance was an "inadequate vehicle in view of the changes, growth, and funding pressure in the future."

President Humphreys warmly endorsed the report. "It could be very helpful," he said. "The plan calls for a chief administrative officer for the universities and a staff—a counterpart to that of Dr. Edward Boling, University of Tennessee president."

Humphreys said he did not see any radical change coming if the recommendations made it through the legislature. In making a statement to newsmen, President Humphreys pointed out that the State Board of Education had been an excellent one, but it simply had too many schools and institutions to look after.

"All this responsibility has become too broad a span," he said. "The board members, who are laymen giving their time without pay, haven't been able to cover everything they wanted to cover in the quality fashion they have wanted to do it."

In his budget message of February 21, 1972, Governor Dunn said, "I recommend that the General Assembly create a state university and community college system under which a new board of regents would manage and control the six regional universities which now are under the jurisdiction of the State Board of Education. I believe that this will...enable all institutions to maintain a more balanced growth while at the same time freeing the State Board of Education to devote its full attention to development of our kindergarten, elementary, and secondary educational programs and the community colleges as well as the state's expanding network of vocational and technical institutions."

Under Governor Dunn's original bill, the proposed board would serve only the six regional universities. It failed to receive sufficient support so the community colleges were added. The Andrews study had proposed that the community colleges be governed temporarily by the SBE, but eventually have their own board.

The General Assembly approved the restructuring, and powerful Democratic forces managed to pass an amendment to the bill stating that the former Commissioner of Education would serve on the Board of Regents for three years. That person was J. Howard Warf. Making up the new board would be seven persons appointed by Governor Dunn and four from the State Board of Education. There were four ex-officio members, which included the governor. The new measure stipulated that the new governing board would become effective July 1, 1972.

Meanwhile, back at Memphis State, President Humphreys held his usual busy pace, running a university and making program chairmen happy by accepting invitations to speak. He always had a message.

In delivering the commencement address to 132 graduates at the University of Tennessee Medical Units in Memphis, he said education must be a continual learning process to avoid obsolescence. "The rapidity of change can make today's professionally trained young man or woman obsolescent within a very short time, unless he or she systematically adds to his store of knowledge and expertise," Humphreys said.

In an editorial the *Memphis Press-Scimitar* said, "The MSU president's advice is applicable to all of us, whether in business, the trades, or the professions. Change does come these days with almost breath-taking rapidity, and it is due to man's vast increase in knowledge. As Dr. Humphreys pointed out, more books have been published in the last 25 years than were published in the previous 500 years, half the jobs open today did not exist a generation ago, and 90 percent of all scientists who ever lived are working today. In a nutshell, graduation from an institution of learning does not mean that education has ceased. Not in the world of today."

Humphreys used this theme in several speeches in West Tennessee.

During this period Humphreys had the opportunity to lend a hand to Shelby State Community College. It needed a temporary site and he arranged for the new college to use a building available at the South Campus (the old Kennedy Veterans Hospital).

There also was a key post to be filled at the university. To help Memphis State to keep increasing its drive toward academic excellence, President Humphreys called home Dr. Jerry N. Boone, associate director for academic affairs for the Tennessee Higher Education Commission, to be vice president for academic affairs.

Boone had been the first dean of the University College in 1968, and while with THEC was instrumental in developing a master plan for higher education in Tennessee.

In Nashville the new State Board of Regents, whose members were appointed by Governor Dunn on June 6, 1972, began a national search for a chancellor. One of the prime candidates, in the regents' thinking, was Cecil Humphreys. Some presidents in the state university system also pushed for Humphreys' appointment. They knew he had an excellent grasp of their problems. But, when an offer came from the regents, Humphreys said no.

The board understood his desire to remain at Memphis State and in Memphis, where he had accomplished so much. The regents, however, continued to seek advice from Humphreys, and as the weeks wore on, they realized more and more that Memphis State's president was the person the state needed to go to Nashville, build a staff, and start a new system for higher education in Tennessee.

In September 1972, Cecil C. Humphreys yielded to the regents' wishes and accepted the chancellorship. But it was not the pressure that changed his mind. There was a formidable challenge for someone

Dr. John Richardson, acting president of MSU following the resignation of Dr. Humphreys, receives advice from Humphreys *(right)* and State Commissioner of Education E. C. Stimbert *(left)*.

to make the system work and serve all Tennesseans; that, most of all, took him to Nashville.

Humphreys' acceptance meant a short retirement for Dr. John Richardson, whom the new chancellor appointed acting president of Memphis State. Dr. Richardson, whom Humphreys had selected to head the Graduate School in 1960, had retired in August. The dean would serve until the appointment of Dr. Billy M. Jones in 1973. "Someone told me it was the shortest retirement in history," quipped Richardson, whose name along with his wife's is honored in Richardson Towers at Central and Patterson.

Before leaving for his new assignment, President Humphreys wrote a fourteen-page Closing Report on his years at MSU for the Board of Regents. It recounted how Memphis State had become one of the major comprehensive, multipurpose universities in Tennessee and the

South. The report covered the tumultuous years, and the crises that seem to arrive daily, but it was optimistic and took the long view.

"The university is in good financial condition and has the basic educational programs to meet most of the needs of its primary service area," Humphreys wrote. "The various elements of the population that the institution serves have developed confidence in the educational programs available and have come to rely heavily upon the university for the research and service that can only be provided by a strong university with adequate resources and capabilities."

A city and a university, as Cecil Humphreys had sought, had become synonymous.

Humphreys served ably and well as the first chancellor of the State University and Community College System for four years before retiring. He met the challenge in Nashville. But, appropriately, he remains president emeritus of Memphis State University, now in its seventy-fifth year. Humphreys' remarkable presidency lasted from 1960 to 1972, a time and tenure unlikely to fade in the university's history.

A diamond anniversary year affords the Blue and Gray faithful, and their legion of supporters, an opportunity to toast a distinguished educator and the university he helped to shape during such exciting years.

15

The Diamond Jubilee—and Beyond

SEVENTY-FIVE CANDLES AGO Memphis State University began as a normal school to provide teachers for Tennessee's primary rural schools. Despite limited financial support, it met the challenge and achieved its goal.

In the 1960s and early 1970s Memphis State, serving the state's largest urban center, broke the shackles of a state regional school and became a comprehensive public university, one of only two in the state. With proper appreciation of its past and sturdy confidence in its future, the institution put the seventy-fifth candle on its birthday cake on September 10, 1987.

By the year 2000, little more than a dozen years distant, the university wants to be nationally recognized as a prestigious research center. That objective has been set by Dr. Thomas Carpenter, Memphis State's ninth president, and in the university's diamond anniversary year that goal cannot be viewed as an impossible dream. The institution's tenacity from 1912 to 1987 suggests that the will to shape its own destiny must never be underestimated.

"It has been a fascinating journey from 1912 to 1987, and the best is yet to come," President Carpenter contends.

Six Centers of Excellence and sixteen Chairs of Excellence, reinforced by full accreditation of each college, school or department which must meet regional and national guidelines, offer a solid foundation for continuing a bold thrust toward becoming one of the respected research centers in the nation. An imaginative administration, unperturbed by the old teaching-versus-research mission in some academic circles, has voiced determination to reach the top tier.

Carpenter wants to build the strongest possible graduate program and bring in an additional $10 million to $15 million in research grants annually. "That would put Memphis State among the top 100 research universities in the nation," he says. The president believes a strong educational program for undergraduates will remain as the university's major priority, but he adds: "That's not enough. The vacuum that you can see in Memphis, other than the valuable specialized work at the

University of Tennessee Center for Health Sciences, is in research, which is an area of prestige."

Emphasis on research may be seen as a natural progression for Memphis State.

Twenty-seven years have elapsed since January 1, 1960, when Cecil C. Humphreys became president of Memphis State University, and fifteen eventful years have gone by since he left the university to become the first chancellor chosen by the State Board of Regents.

As the record shows so dramatically, the university's building boom in the 1960s managed to keep pace with an enormous enrollment crush. For almost 13 years Humphreys prevailed despite a multitude of growth problems, but he regards the community's change in attitude toward the school as the most significant event.

"Probably the greatest achievement of the institution was the change that took place in the minds of the people of Memphis and the area we served—the change in the way they perceived or looked at Memphis State and its value to the community," he says. "The community recognition and awards I received came because of the public's recognition and interest in what Memphis State was doing and its increasing importance to the city. It was a matter of being in the right place at the right time."

The same might be said for the two presidents who have followed him. By happenstance, both excelled in college football, as did Humphreys. Dr. Billy M. Jones, who resigned as president of Southwest Texas State University at San Marcos in 1973 to succeed Humphreys, also was a historian and a capable administrator.

Under Jones' leadership Memphis State expanded the well-established community service role of the university. At that time the enrollment was stabilizing at a little more than 20,000 in degree programs and at about 12,000 in various continuing education programs.

During the first year of his presidency, Jones predicted that the university would be serving 100,000 people "within three to five years." He met the goal in a much shorter time. The *Memphis Press-Scimitar* on October 29, 1975, reported that 87,328 people were being served through a variety of programs. Added to the 22,364 students taking traditional courses, the headcount reached 109,692.

"A lot of people teased me about the prediction, but the figures are

Dr. Billy M. Jones, President of Memphis State University, 1973–1980.

there," Jones told the newspaper. "The test of our full-service concept shows it is one Memphis really wants us to have. Citizens are taking advantage of all the programs. That's a pretty good success story."

To help accomplish this, Jones established a Division of Public Service and Continuing Education directed by Dr. John A. Rhodes. Other initiatives by Jones led to the addition of two new colleges. The University College perhaps was the most innovative. The original University College had been a counseling service, but the new one broadened what the institution could do to help students, particularly mature students already at work in a profession. In essence the University College offered individual learning contracts leading to interdisciplinary degree programs: the Bachelor of Liberal Studies (BLS) or the Bachelor of Professional Studies (BPS). The program was systematic, but sufficiently flexible to permit students and their advisers to design individual studies.

The College of Communication and Fine Arts also came into being early in President Jones' administration. Some Memphis journalists debated the merits of this umbrella, but it remained.

Jones, who had been an All-American junior college football player at San Angelo State in Texas and became a star end at Vanderbilt, kept a keen eye on sports. He expanded women's athletics at MSU and led the school's entry into the Metro Conference.

After establishing a President's Council composed of business leaders, Jones successfully launched a campaign to raise $2 million to underwrite a faculty enrichment program enabling Memphis State to employ distinguished professors in business, education, and science. The Cecil C. Humphreys Presidential Scholars program was begun in 1976 through Jones' leadership.

When President Jones resigned in January of 1980 to accept a prestigious research and teaching chair at Wichita State University, Memphis State had completed 20 years of expansion, with an outstanding emphasis on community service programs.

The time appeared opportune for a change in emphasis, if not in role and direction, when the Board of Regents chose Dr. Thomas Carpenter, then president of the University of North Florida, to return to his undergraduate alma mater as president.

It was a double homecoming because Mrs. Carpenter, the former

Oneida Pruette of Memphis, also was a 1949 graduate. They had met at Baylor University, where Carpenter was a running back for a new head football coach, Bob Woodruff. Earlier, Carpenter, a navy veteran, and Woodruff had been together at Georgia Tech with Coach Bobby Dodd.

Early in his administration President Carpenter decided on a qualitative mission for the university that would be national in scope. He wanted to fine tune the excellent programs which had been developed over the years. In *Memphis State Magazine's* seventy-fifth anniversary edition, Carpenter wrote: "Memphis State has begun to achieve national recognition in select disciplines. Our goal is to make the university one of the top research centers by the year 2000, its eighty-eighth year. With the establishment of six Centers of Excellence and seven Chairs of Excellence, and with more to come, we are well on our way."

The state's Chairs of Excellence program, begun in 1984 with a $10 million legislative appropriation, has contributed significantly to Memphis State's goals. Under the program universities receive half the amount needed to set up $1.25 million endowments for chairs. Each university or private donor matches the funds, and the endowment income enables the school to hire outstanding department heads or researchers or to support work in a specific area.

Seventy-five-year-old universities are not educational graybeards in the United States, but Carpenter feels Memphis State has the maturity to become more cosmopolitan and broaden the scope of its research without sacrificing its traditional role as a teaching institution.

He is supported strongly in this by Memphis State's chief academic officer. "We need to stop debating whether we ought to be a teaching institution or a research institution," said Dr. Victor Feisal, vice president for academic affairs. "We need to be both."

Unquestionably, Memphis State has six outstanding Centers of Excellence: The Center for Applied Psychological Research, the Tennessee Earthquake Information Center, the School of Accountancy, the Center for Research and Innovative Services for the Communicatively Impaired, the Institute for Egyptian Art and Archaeology, and the College of Education's teacher preparation program.

President Carpenter, who holds a business degree from Memphis State, a master's from Baylor, and a doctorate in economics from the

Dr. Thomas G. Carpenter, President of Memphis State University, 1980-present.

University of Florida, understands dollars and their role in bettering educational programs.

But vision and determination also are of equal importance in building a great university in Carpenter's thinking. They are essential to attracting the brightest students, a prestigious faculty, and the dollars that follow, especially in graduate research programs. "The time is right," he said, "I think we are coming along."

In a quick look back at his seven years at Memphis State, President Carpenter adds a sense of humor to his dedication. "It's been the shortest twenty years of my life," he says with a big smile.

Carpenter understands the urban university that he leads. Eighty percent of its students hold full or part-time jobs, a demand on time that he felt in 1949 when he was working forty hours a week in an auto parts warehouse and meeting his classes at Memphis State.

With mandated retirement only four years away, President Carpenter says he intends to push vigorously for Memphis State's research ambitions. Meanwhile, he points out, the university's "primary mission…is to be a comprehensive university that provides an environment for intellectual, cultural, and ethical development through a wide range of programs."

The mission was much narrower at 10 A.M., September 10, 1912, when Professor Arthur Wallerstein, music director at West Tennessee Normal School, lifted his baton and a small citizens' band began to play at opening ceremonies.

The melody remains, even with all the change and growth of 75 years. So does the dedication of students, faculty, administrators, alumni, and friends; they make the Memphis State story worthy of the telling.

Appendices and Index

Headcount Enrollment

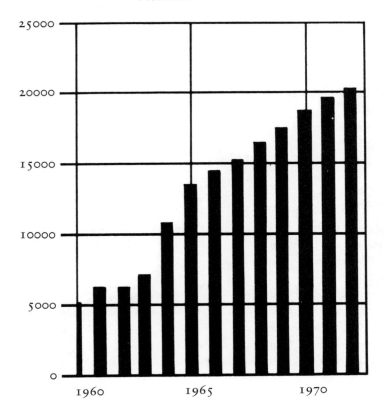

Major Sports Summary 1960–1972

FOOTBALL:
Overall Record: 81–35–1
Highlights:
  10 Winning Seasons
  1 Even Season
  1 Losing Season
  1st Win over Southeast Conference Team, Mississippi State
    (in 1962, 28–7)
  1st Win over Ole Miss (in 1967, 27–17)
  1st Appearance on Television (against Florida State in 1967)
  1st Time to Play Tennessee (1968)
  1st Major Bowl Appearance (against San Jose State in Pasadena Bowl,
    "Junior Rose Bowl," in 1971)
  1st National Coach of the Year (Billy J. Murphy in 1963)
  Move from Crump Stadium to Memphis Memorial Stadium (now Liberty
    Bowl in 1965)
  Major Win over Houston, ranked in Top Ten (in 1966)
  3 Missouri Valley Conference Championships

BASKETBALL:
Overall Record: 163–138
Highlights:
  7 Winning Seasons
  5 Losing Seasons
  6 Postseason Tournaments
  1 Missouri Valley Conference Cochampionship (in 1973)
  1 Missouri Valley Conference Championship (in 1973)
  Move from MSU Fieldhouse to Mid-South Coliseum (in 1964)

ALL-AMERICAN SELECTIONS:

Football:
  David Berrong
  Chuck Brooks
  Dave Casinelli
  Harry Schuh
  Mike Stark
  James Earl Wright

Basketball:
  Larry Finch
  Rich Jones
  George Kirk
  Ronnie Robinson
  Wayne Yates

NOTE: More than 50 athletes played in special postseason games and went into professional ranks. In addition, more than 25 went into coaching.

Memphis State University
Physical Plant Growth 1960–1972

NEW BUILDINGS

Project	Approved & Funded	Project Cost
Browning Hall (Men's Dorm)	1962	$ 514,834
Campus School	1962	597,156(1)
Mitchell Hall	1962–64	706,908
Smith Hall (Women's Dorm)	1962	550,605
Athletic Office	1963	59,904
Ball Education	1963	745,588
Ellington Biology	1963	874,302
Rawls Hall (Women's Dorm)	1963	1,249,671
Robison Hall (Men's Dorm)	1963	610,775
Old Bookstore	1963	38,372
Old Band Building	1964	49,163
Clement Hall	1965	745,412
Music	1965	1,228,070
Speech and Drama	1965	1,228,070
Athletic Dressing Facilities	1965	108,146(2)
Smith Chemistry	1965	2,370,391
Cecil C. Humphreys School of Law	1966	804,377
Patterson Hall	1966	1,297,963
Undergraduate Library	1966	2,447,243
University Center	1966	4,006,731
Power Plant (Boiler and Chiller)	1966	792,614
President's Home	1967	82,365(3)
Psychology	1967	2,085,152
Herff Engineering	1968	2,413,723
Student Health Center	1968	428,212
Power Plant	1968	363,742
Health, P.E., & Recreation	1968	2,685,714
Married Student Apartments	1968	1,814,052
Alumni House	1969	256,249
Business Administration	1969	2,349,391
Information Center	1969	71,491
Lambda Chi Alpha	1969	276,642
Dunn Hall	1969	1,325,500
Meeman Journalism	1969	946,876(4)
Newport Hall	1969	295,848

NEW BUILDINGS

Project	Approved & Funded	Project Cost
Engineering Technology	1970	1,923,471
South Hall (Men's Dorm)	1970	1,154,519
Athletic Dressing Facilities	1970	621,658
Life Sciences	1971	2,733,011
Greenhouse	1971	27,792
Meeman Biological Field Station	1972	127,653
		$43,009,356

(1) $350,000 provided by Memphis City School System
(2) Now Printing Services
(3) Purchase price $120,365; $38,000 donation by owner; net cost $82,365
(4) $250,000 provided by E. J. Meeman Foundation

ADDITIONS AND MAJOR RENOVATIONS

Project	Approved & Funded	Project Cost
Brister Library	1962	$ 308,297
Field House	1963	295,143
Panhellenic	1963	33,919
Ball Education	1963	279,811
Jones Hall	1964	240,869
Scates Hall	1965	61,089
Campus School Storage	1966	3,954
Jones Hall Cafeteria	1966	63,123
Manning Hall	1967	455,447
Field House	1967–72	161,784
Jones Hall	1970	17,796
Mitchell Hall	1971	36,937
Business Administration	1971	220,799
Administration	1972	2,510,273
Chucalissa Museum	1972	224,990
Cecil C. Humphreys School of Law	1972	1,512,282
		$6,426,513

OTHER CAMPUS IMPROVEMENTS

Project	Approved & Funded	Project Cost
Underground Electrical System	1963	$ 108,689
Walks and Paved Areas	1965–72	145,353
Telephone Lines	1965–70	17,928
Air Conditioning and Heating	1966–69	59,141
Parking Lots	1967–72	534,288
Utilities Extension—Main Campus	1969	748,448
Athletic Fields—South Campus	1969	343,043
Utilities Extension—South Campus	1970	165,392
Utilities Data Control Center	1970	156,934
Baseball & Track Stands	1971	120,682
Mall	1971	105,654
Track—South Campus	1971	162,392
Tennis Courts	1971	272,836
Swimming Pool—South Campus	1971	49,126
Utilities Improvement	1971	548,184
		3,538,090

FACILITIES ACQUIRED AND RENOVATED

Project	Approved & Funded	Project Cost
Early Childhood Education	1967	$ 147,895
Speech and Hearing Center	1967	653,253(1)
		$ 801,148
		$53,775,107

(1) Transferred from State Department of Public Health

LAND ACQUISITION ADJACENT TO CAMPUS

Year	Acreage	Cost
1969–61	.17	$ 14,076
1961–62	1.45	128,759
1962–63	1.31	87,234
1963–64	6.63	317,025
1964–65	14.12	807,433
1965–66	11.99	751,763
1966–67	17.63	1,141,962
1967–68	23.61	1,491,697
1968–69	12.28	972,697
1969–70	7.32	547,487
1970–71	6.25	505,168
1971–72	.23	29,709
1972–	1.06	52,104
	104.05	$6,847,114

OTHER LAND ACQUIRED

Year and Property	Acreage	Value
1961 Chucalissa Museum	187.50	$ 87,186(1)
1967 Meeman Farm	640.00	220,452(2)
1970 Kennedy Hospital	146.00	2,432,030(3)
	973.50	$2,739,668

(1) Transferred to MSU by State of Tennessee
(2) Gift from E. J. Meeman Foundation
(3) Gift from U.S. Government

Total Land Acquisition: $9,586,782

Memphis State University
Land Acquisition (by parcel)
Adjacent to Campus

DATE	PROPERTY ACQUIRED	ACREAGE	TOTAL COST
FY July 1960–June 1961			
12/10/60	3663 Norriswood	.17	$ 14,075.10
		17	$ 14,076.10
FY July 1961–June 1962			
8/11/61	3687 Norriswood	.17	$ 17,853.95
6/5/62	3673 Norriswood	.17	16,336.64
3/30/62	3699 Norriswood	.17	19,080.60
10/20/61	3783 Norriswood	.17	16,001.74
8/25/61	3797 Norriswood	.17	15,031.99
4/23/62	3807 Norriswood	.17	16,505.14
6/5/62	3811 Norriswood	.26	15,220.38
3/14/62	3829 Norriswood	.17	2,728.86
FY July 1962–June 1963		1.45	$128,759.30
7/27/62	583/587/591 Echles	.29	$ 32,249.65
10/29/62	582 Houston	.11	3,671.50
7/30/62	584 Houston	.11	5,148.95
1/24/63	588 Houston	.23	8,769.75
9/25/62	594 Houston	.23	11,150.45
7/27/62	3737 Norriswood	.17	13,554.18
8/28/62	3743 Norriswood	.17	12,698.16
FY July 1963–1964		1.31	$ 87,233.64
11/5/63	597 Echles	.23	$ 14,338.66
4/30/64	598 Echles and vacant lot south of 603 Echles	.23	17,688.76
1/24/64	602 Echles	.29	5,985.75
2/5/64	606 Echles	.30	10,659.75
2/17/64	613/615 Echles	.36	19,692.25
5/15/64	587 Goodman, lots 28 and 29	.37	15,442.25
6/24/64	593 Goodman	.19	8,970.14
4/1/64	604 Houston	.23	15,972.25
2/29/64	620 Houston	.36	15,972.25
2/29/64	582/588/592 Hughes	.19	31,984.75
2/29/64	597 Hughes	.28	9,597.25

DATE	PROPERTY ACQUIRED	ACREAGE	TOTAL COST
2/29/64	601 Hughes	.29	13,847.25
6/15/64	3791 Norriswood	.17	19,213.38
11/15/63	511 Patterson	.31	22,606.82
4/20/64	519 Patterson	.31	20,084.75
2/29/64	3783 Southern and vacant lot	1.74	26,634.50
3/31/64	3789 Southern	.19	13,317.25
6/15/64	3795 Southern	.19	9,625.94
6/15/64	3805 Southern	.19	13,086.30
4/15/64	3756 Spottswood	.21	12,254.75
		6.63	$317,025.00

FY July 1964—June 1965

DATE	PROPERTY ACQUIRED	ACREAGE	TOTAL COST
5/1/65	3725 Central	1.86	$ 80,644.75
8/15/64	3737 Central	.87	56,045.20
10/10/64	3751 Central	1.48	63,878.58
10/10/64	3779 Central	1.45	39,940.35
6/29/65	343 Deloach	.24	30,322.25
2/1/65	355/357 Deloach	.29	23,944.75
4/20/65	582 Echles	.23	19,159.75
3/12/65	586 Echles	.29	10,145.78
3/19/65	590/596 Echles	.23	11,192.25
1/1/65	619 Echles	.24	11,192.25
1/1/65	627 Echles	.24	12,179.75
4/15/65	631 Echles	.24	10,129.75
4/10/65	637 Echles	.24	10,943.15
7/1/64	644 Echles	.13	8,027.03
6/14/65	607 Goodman	.19	10,364.75
4/20/65	625 Goodman	.28	11,241.75
4/26/65	633 Goodman	.19	14,909.75
8/21/64	598/608 Houston and 603 Echles	.71	37,423.41
1/20/65	630 Houston	.24	16,504.75
3/12/65	634 Houston	.24	23,963.08
4/15/65	636 Houston	.23	14,909.75
3/23/65	581/583 Hughes	.28	12,254.75
6/22/65	587 Hughes	.29	16,239.75
3/23/65	591 Hughes	.29	14,379.75
4/20/65	605 Hughes	.29	10,235.75
4/15/65	608 Hughes	.19	10,235.75
5/1/65	612 Hughes	.19	11,192.25
6/5/65	644 Hughes	.19	14,956.57
3/19/65	3659 Norriswood	.18	15,972.25

DATE	PROPERTY ACQUIRED	ACREAGE	TOTAL COST
8/31/64	3667 Norriswood	.18	14,672.73
8/15/64	3677 Norriswood	.18	18,130.66
7/14/64	3683 Norriswood	.17	16,009.43
4/15/65	3693 Norriswood	.17	14,909.75
4/15/65	3709 Norriswood	.17	34,574.75
10/22/64	3710 Norriswood	.17	14,502.18
5/15/65	3714 Norriswood	.24	16,504.75
9/15/64	3774 Norriswood	.34	22,914.45
6/5/65	3697 Southern	.09	11,192.25
7/15/64	3801 Southern	.19	10,156.24
6/5/65	3734 Spottswood	.21	11,336.25
		14.12	$807,433.09

FY July 1965–June 1966

6/20/66	3817 Central	.51	$ 37,229.75
4/29/66	3823 Central	.51	29,319.75
4/10/66	3837 Central	.51	23,079.75
6/6/66	327 Deloach	.24	21,925.75
6/1/66	344 Deloach	.27	30,372.25
4/10/66	632 Echles	.28	13,772.25
8/30/65	Lots 41 and 42 Goodman	.38	7,961.51
7/15/65	617 Goodman	.28	10,890.25
6/1/66	634 Goodman	.19	12,834.75
4/20/66	637 Goodman	.19	9,967.75
11/8/65	644 Goodman	.19	10,129.75
7/14/65	626 Houston	.24	16,822.75
1/12/66	621/627 Houston	.57	14,226.92
7/15/65	593/595 Normal	.19	8,004.75
5/20/66	597 Normal	.19	10,179.75
9/20/65	603 Normal	.19	9,779.39
8/1/65	615 Normal	.19	7,938.75
9/7/65	619 Normal	.19	12,964.75
8/10/65	623 Normal	.19	8,753.25
10/19/65	643 Normal	.19	7,739.75
2/20/66	3717 Norriswood	.17	12,784.75
6/13/66	3736 Norriswood	.36	26,837.25
6/15/66	3747 Norriswood	.17	12,834.75
2/1/66	3751 Norriswood	.17	19,692.25
7/27/65	3802 Norriswood	.22	12,844.75
7/15/65	3803 Norriswood	.17	17,567.25
1/15/66	3808 Norriswood	.22	17,634.75
5/10/66	3830 Norriswood	.22	17,084.75

DATE	PROPERTY ACQUIRED	ACREAGE	TOTAL COST
8/23/65	3834 Norriswood	.22	17,832.25
7/15/65	338 Patterson	.21	19,159.75
9/27/65	3677 Southern	.12	58,488.50
6/1/66	3683 Southern	.18	21,334.75
4/2/66	3705 Southern	.27	26,599.75
6/10/66	3727/3729 Southern	.12	19,209.75
5/20/66	3733 Southern	.09	24,524.75
2/20/66	3815/3825 Southern	.55	54,239.75
6/20/66	3831 Southern	.19	13,847.25
5/25/66	3724/3726 Spottswood	.20	12,834.75
9/1/65	3746 Spottswood	.21	9,811.75
4/20/66	3816 Spottswood	.29	13,847.25
4/10/66	3824 Spottswood	1.77	9,261.25
11/8/65	3836 Spottswood	.18	9,597.25
		11.99	$751,762.82

FY July 1966–June 1967

DATE	PROPERTY ACQUIRED	ACREAGE	TOTAL COST
7/8/66	3766 Central	.50	$ 24,197.25
4/10/67	3750 Central	2.29	122,957.25
7/15/66	3770 Central	1.43	69,186.05
7/15/66	3780 Central	1.43	68,800.55
8/15/66	3793 Central	2.81	33,562.25
8/15/66	3803 Central	.51	28,777.25
10/15/66	3809 Central	.51	31,914.75
4/10/67	3820 Central	.81	41,460.25
9/1/66	3831 Central	.51	28,777.25
10/20/66	3838 Central	.81	44,617.25
12/5/66	3848 Central	.82	44,666.25
3/1/67	3854 Central	.70	37,329.85
2/21/67	628 Goodman	.28	13,374.75
11/4/66	643 Goodman	.19	9,904.75
1/21/67	608/610 Normal	.19	14,014.88
4/10/67	616 Normal	.19	10,512.25
5/5/67	624 Normal	.19	14,275.25
4/10/67	3767 Norriswood	.17	19,167.25
8/1/66	3814 Norriswood	.22	20,901.05
10/15/66	3818 Norriswood	.22	18,112.25
11/11/66	3821 Norriswood	.26	17,667.25
4/10/67	3839 Norriswood	.32	24,137.68
2/1/67	3840 Norriswood	.22	15,955.00
12/10/66	356 Patterson	.30	26,699.75
11/11/66	3687/3691 Southern	.18	24,951.25

DATE	PROPERTY ACQUIRED	ACREAGE	TOTAL COST
7/18/66	3699 Southern	.09	20,504.75
4/10/67	3721 Southern	.18	29,842.25
7/18/66	3731 Southern	.06	10,129.75
2/28/67	3735 Southern	.12	18,048.75
10/15/66	3741/3743 Southern	.12	17,672.25
11/4/66	3747/3753 Southern	.12	127,384.75
7/15/66	3757/3763/3769 Southern	.36	78,919.75
11/11/66	3827 Southern	.19	11,638.25
7/8/66	3863 Southern	.19	13,367.25
7/18/66	3792 Spottswood	.14	8,534.75
		17.63	$1,141,692.06

FY *July 1967–June 1968*

*4/9/68	First alley south of Southern between Echles and Hughes	.27	$ 7.00
*4/9/68	Portion of Norriswood between Patterson and Deloach	.81	1.00
7/10/67	Vacant lot—Central and Deloach	.22	39,551.66
5/1/68	3639 Central	.22	23,306.81
3/15/68	3655 Central	.22	19,548.59
7/1/67	3728 Central	1.42	76,572.05
6/1/68	3789 Central	2.81	45,590.50
5/21/68	335 Deloach	.24	27,755.50
10/19/67	349 Deloach	.44	26,195.50
1/25/68	618 Echles	.43	13,385.00
5/1/68	622 Echles	.28	15,753.36
12/31/67	628 Echles	.28	17,635.50
1/25/68	638 Echles	.28	10,258.00
6/1/68	643 Echles	.20	18,165.50
12/31/67	597 Goodman	.19	12,383.00
12/28/67	603 Goodman	.19	13,483.00
12/31/67	606 Goodman	.28	15,560.00
9/26/67	611 Goodman	.19	15,038.00
12/14/67	616/622 Goodman	.19	22,475.50
3/13/68	638 Goodman	.19	11,790.50
6/21/68	644 Houston	.41	30,444.01
10/13/67	602 Hughes	.19	8,013.00
7/31/67	617 Hughes	.57	17,093.00

*Conveyed to State by City

DATE	PROPERTY ACQUIRED	ACREAGE	TOTAL COST
1/25/68	622 Hughes	.19	9,198.00
12/31/67	628 Hughes	.19	12,323.00
5/1/68	631 Hughes	.28	16,100.50
1/25/68	632 Hughes	.19	10,788.00
12/8/67	637 Hughes	.28	14,978.00
12/31/67	638 Hughes	.19	13,445.50
11/3/67	584 Normal	.19	12,383.00
3/15/68	587 Normal	.19	18,915.00
11/27/67	590/592 Normal	.28	13,787.50
12/11/67	596/598 Normal	.19	14,113.37
7/20/67	604 Normal	.19	9,705.50
12/8/67	609 Normal	.19	15,600.50
7/5/67	620 Normal	.19	8,856.75
12/31/67	627 Normal	.19	13,852.50
5/15/68	628/630 Normal	.19	19,820.50
12/31/67	632/634, 638/640, 644/646 Normal	.57	40,010.50
11/27/67	633 Normal	.19	12,065.00
5/1/68	637 Normal	.19	11,320.50
6/25/68	3721 Norriswood	.17	19,700.50
6/25/68	3727 Norriswood	.17	25,603.00
6/25/68	3733 Norriswood	.16	16,040.50
5/10/68	3792 Norriswood	.22	16,640.50
5/10/68	3796 Norriswood	.22	16,640.50
2/7/68	3846 Norriswood	.26	25,133.00
11/27/67	328 Patterson	.21	19,288.00
10/15/67	334 Patterson	.21	21,945.50
4/15/68	344 Patterson	20	21,353.00
12/31/67	348 Patterson	.23	17,103.00
7/1/67	368/369/370 Patterson	.17	21,384.75
9/15/67	535/537 Patterson	.62	85,955.75
12/1/67	3771 Poplar	1.96	140,585.50
12/5/67	3851 Southern	.18	15,038.00
12/27/67	3857 Southern	.18	13,445.50
6/30/68	3696 Spottswood	.41	30,504.01
6/25/68	3706 Spottswood	.44	32,715.75
11/15/67	3730 Spottswood	.15	13,635.50
12/31/67	3740 Spottswood	.21	12,853.00
12/31/67	3750 Spottswood	.21	13,385.50
12/11/67	3760 Spottswood	.21	14,653.00
12/8/67	3766 Spottswood	.21	16,100.50

DATE	PROPERTY ACQUIRED	ACREAGE	TOTAL COST
12/31/67	3770 Spottswood	.21	16,474.00
12/31/67	3782 Spottswood	.28	16,573.00
12/31/67	3788 Spottswood	.14	10,955.50
12/31/67	3798 Spottswood	.30	17,103.00
8/10/67	3806 Spottswood	.29	20,343.00
11/3/67	3830 Spottswood	.18	11,058.50
3/20/68	3842 Spottswood and 651 Normal	.33	26,665.50
11/27/67	3862 Spottswood	.29	15,510.50
		23.61	$1,491,696.86

FY July 1968—June 1969

7/25/68	Vacant lot north side west of 3796 Central	.52	$ 39,719.00
2/10/69	598 Buck	.21	14,169.50
10/1/68	3629 Central	.27	25,689.50
4/25/69	3665 Central	.33	21,597.75
11/15/68	3904 Central	1.48	103,372.32
2/10/69	3932 Central	.68	37,322.50
3/15/69	3958 Central	.69	47,367.50
5/2/60	336 Deloach	.29	26,707.50
12/11/68	594 Goodman	.19	12,020.00
4/11/69	598 Goodman	.19	7,650.00
12/27/68	602 Goodman	.19	8,481.50
7/15/68	598/600 Hughes	.19	19,251.50
3/25/69	618 Hughes	.19	17,578.50
10/3/68	3704 Norriswood	.14	18,781.50
5/12/69	3720 Norriswood	.26	21,629.50
8/1/68	3757/3759 Norriswood	.17	23,563.50
11/8/68	3758 Norriswood	.34	27,111.50
11/1/68	3793 Norriswood	.17	19,519.50
11/1/68	329 Patterson	.30	25,159.50
10/15/68	335 Patterson	.23	29,881.50
1/15/69	339 Patterson	.34	29,146.50
12/15/68	347 Patterson	.28	23,298.50
3/15/69	369 Patterson	.31	42,655.00
6/1/69	371 Patterson	.45	38,475.50
1/15/69	3735 Poplar	.25	29,921.50
5/15/69	3839 Poplar	.98	51,164.00
9/20/68	3849 Poplar	.65	48,017.50
3/15/69	3917 Poplar	.97	58,592.50
6/25/69	3625 Southern	.32	53,413.00

DATE	PROPERTY ACQUIRED	ACREAGE	TOTAL COST
7/1/68	3688 Spottswood	.41	30,446.51
7/15/68	3854 Spottswood	.29	20,993.00
		12.28	$972,697.08
FY July 1969–June 1970			
5/6/70	3693 Central	.50	$ 40,604.00
4/15/70	3705 Central	.29	43,259.50
4/15/70	3796 Central	.80	54,963.50
4/15/70	3802 Central	.80	54,888.50
4/15/70	3830 Central	.81	55,951.50
4/8/70	235 Conlee	.17	15,472.50
1/6/70	352 Deloach	.25	34,756.50
4/10/70	3786 Norriswood	.17	21,356.25
1/20/70	3761 Poplar	.57	42,730.00
1/5/70	3825 Poplar	1.08	64,782.48
8/20/69	3899 Poplar	1.70	106,540.00
11/7/69	3843 Southern	.18	12,182.75
		7.32	$547,487.48
FY July 1970–June 1971			
8/17/70	3845 Central	.49	$ 34,681.50
10/1/70	3946 Central	.94	63,925.00
10/1/70	254 Conlee	.23	26,177.50
11/23/70	247 Deloach	.36	38,328.00
7/14/70	267 Deloach	.35	38,861.00
9/16/70	276 Deloach	.35	40,529.00
8/14/70	284 Deloach	.35	40,330.00
8/5/70	300/302 Deloach	.40	39,254.00
4/28/71	583 Normal	.19	18,807.50
7/31/70	3763 Norriswood	.17	20,254.50
7/20/70	3859 Poplar	1.60	92,323.00
10/15/70	3939 Poplar	.82	51,697.00
		6.25	$505,168.00
FY July 1971–June 1972			
5/26/72	248/250 Conlee	.23	$ 29,709.00
		.23	$ 29,709.00

DATE	PROPERTY ACQUIRED	ACREAGE	TOTAL COST
Fiscal Period July 1972–December 1972			
*7/24/72	First alley north of Spottswood between Echles and Hughes	.19	1.00
*7/18/72	North/south alley between Echles and Hughes and between first alley north of Spottswood and first alley south of Spottswood	.39	1.00
7/3/72	3728 Norriswood	.26	22,626.50
9/1/72	3824 Norriswood	.22	29,475.00
		1.06	$ 52,103.50

*Conveyed to State by City

Index